Physical Limits to Economic Growth

The debate on the physical limits and constraints to the economic growth of globalized society is now widespread. This book explores the physical and economic aspects of the conflict between humans, with their thoughtless focus on growth through material production, and environmental constraints.

In the context of the looming shortage of material resources and the latest science on climate change, *Physical Limits to Economic Growth* offers new insights which provide a broad and comprehensive picture of the conflict between humans and environmental constraints. The authors' approach goes beyond the boundaries of specialized disciplines to explore climate change, resource depletion, technical innovation and the interactions between these within the socio-economic-institutional systems we live in. This volume looks at opportunities for rethinking these systems if we moved away from fossil fuel dependence, while considering the status of current mainstream economic thinking around this subject.

Physical Limits to Economic Growth provides a genuine interdisciplinary examination of the physical limits to economic growth. It will be of interest to both students and academics in various disciplines in the areas of natural sciences, climate change and economics.

Roberto Burlando is Associate Professor in the Department of Economics and Statistics at Università degli Studi di Torino, Italy.

Angelo Tartaglia is Senior Professor in the Department of Applied Science and Technology at Politecnico di Torino, Italy.

Routledge Studies in Ecological Economics

Physical Limits to Economic Growth

Perspectives of economic, social, and complexity science

**Edited by Roberto Burlando
and Angelo Tartaglia**

 Routledge
Taylor & Francis Group

LONDON AND NEW YORK

First published 2018
by Routledge

2 Park Square, Milton Park, Abingdon, Oxfordshire OX14 4RN
52 Vanderbilt Avenue, New York, NY 10017

Routledge is an imprint of the Taylor & Francis Group, an informa business

First issued in paperback 2020

British Library Cataloguing-in-Publication Data
A catalogue record for this book is available from the British Library

Library of Congress Cataloging-in-Publication Data
A catalog record for this book has been requested

ISBN: 978-1-138-23160-3 (hbk)
ISBN: 978-0-367-59350-6 (pbk)

Typeset in Times New Roman
by Apex CoVantage, LLC

Contents

Figures

Contributors

Michelle Arnold, Utah State University, USA

Ugo Bardi, Dipartimento di Scienze della Terra – Università di Firenze, Italy

Roberto Burlando, Department of Economics and Statistics, University of Torino, Italy

Stefano Caserini, Politecnico di Milano, D.I.C.A. Sez. Ambientale

José Lobo, Arizona State University, USA

Ian Schindler, Toulouse School of Economics, France

Julia Schindler, CeReMath 21 allée de Brienne Toulouse, France

Deborah Strumsky, Arizona State University, USA

Joseph A. Tainter, Utah State University, USA

Angelo Tartaglia, Department of Applied Science and Technology, Politecnico di Torino, Italy

Temis G. Taylor, Utah State University, USA

Introduction

The debate on the physical limits and constraints to the economic growth (and to the ways of development) of our globalized society is today quite widespread. Not only scientists, experts and environmental associations are involved in it, but the media – and the general public through them – as well as politicians and rulers, continuously talk about climate change, natural resources depletion, sustainability . . . and growth.[1]

Traditionally in economics the term *growth* means a quantitative increment in production without particularly significant qualitative change (besides those implied by technological evolution), which instead characterize development, but among a large number of economists nowadays the distinction seems to have somehow faded[2] (this might partially be due also to the literature on endogenous growth, though in our view this addresses only a very limited part of the relevant issues that differentiate the two). This does not just amount to a lack of terminological accuracy; the distinction is indeed crucial for all discussions on sustainability and physical limits to growth. Whereas – as it has been argued in the past and we will also see in various points in this book – sustainable growth is just an oxymoron,[3] whether forms of sustainable development are a real possibility or not is still an open question, depending very much on what the content of development is supposed to be.

By now the existence of a real ecological sustainability problem is generally accepted – certainly in natural sciences – and the terms of the question are almost all on the table, but most often in the public perception each and every argument is mixed up in various ways and this lets emotional – when not outright ideological or interested[4] – aspects dominate or at least have an undue and unsound (scientifically) weight. Letting interests and emotions aside, a persistent peculiarity of the debate is that it tends to be split along separate and barely communicating lines: "hard" natural scientists on one side, economists on another, decision makers on their own.[5] Besides the numerous incongruous elements entering the scene, what seems a persistent dichotomy between natural sciences and economics – but sometimes also human and social disciplines in general – is a particularly disturbing feature. Despite the fact that inter-disciplinarity is a leitmotiv of the present (or expected) development of human knowledge, the scope of the cross-fertilization among different disciplines is most often confined into the separate fences of "exact" or hard sciences on one side and "soft" social sciences on the other. What qualifies an activity as being "scientific", in hard sciences, is agreed to be the method: all statements issued in a given theory should be based on facts; the data, on the one side, and the internal consistency of a theory, on the other, are treated and assessed by mathematical tools; the subject certifying the correctness of the approach is the scientific community through the peer review mechanism (which has limits due to its tendency to conservatism and to the time required for a proper evaluation). On these bases, "hard" and "soft" sciences tend to converge, though there remain differences that come from the object of each discipline in one or the other area.

A proper discussion of these aspects would imply a long tour in the debate on scientific realism,[6] which is beyond the scope of this book and even more of this introduction; so here we simply assume a very moderate (weak) form of scientific realism[7] and maintain that, in the case of "hard" sciences, very often "facts" are reasonably independent from their interpretation: the studied reality is (to various extents, depending on the philosophical stances) "objective".[8] This does not imply to deny that everybody is inevitably involved both in the interpretation and presentation of facts and in the consequences of the actions to be undertaken. Science, even hard science, is not "neutral" (even in the case of general relativity or the string theory) since the scientist needs unavoidably to put him/herself on the line in order to bind facts together in a consistent scheme, where something is subjectively induced from objective phenomena. However, it does imply to reject the conviction/assumption (sometimes explicitly stated, more often implicit, sometimes even unconscious) that the reality we live in depends entirely on us and that the behaviour of mankind also shapes the rules of the game out of the social relations and into the physical realm. Extreme philosophical formulations of this principle arrive to deny a proper independent existence of the external, even physical, world, which turns out to be moulded by the system of human relations and its historical evolution.[9]

A peculiar consequence of this tenet is that it implies that humans have no limits and can trespass any material constraint: what matters are either the minds or also social interpersonal relations, while the rest is marginal and flexible. Often this tenet is also associated with an "idealistic" attitude towards science and technology, relying more on faith and magic than on reason ("science will find the way out", "technology will save us", and so on). Unfortunately, this is not true (as will be also argued in the fifth chapter of this book); as much as the boiling temperature of water, under normal pressure, does not depend on human vicissitudes and ways of thinking; the absorption spectrum of electromagnetic waves by gasses does not depend on human conceptions and social organization and the second principle of thermodynamics is not at all affected by policies and opportunities. Unfortunately, science – unlike magic – cannot solve all problems and cannot deterministically predict future, but it can deterministically find what cannot happen: this is related to basic (non-negotiable) laws and physical constraints.

In the social sciences domain, on the other hand, facts have to do with human behaviours, attitudes, beliefs and interests, and, because of this, the disentangling of facts from interpretations and theories is not that obvious or simple.

An additional consideration concerns the use of mathematics. For hard sciences, mathematics guarantees the logical consistency of a theory and is mostly deterministic and predictive; the use of a statistical approach (not considering such fields as quantum mechanics)[10] is usually connected to the size of the data banks and the unavoidably limited knowledge of the variables at stake. In human sciences, including economics, the very nature of the variables – as well as of the reality under scrutiny – is different and requires a different mathematical treatment. As R. Nadeau[11] (already in the Introduction and later and more specifically in Chapter 6) argues:

> *the creators of neoclassical economics [. . .] developed their theories by substituting economic variables derived from classical economics for physical variables in the equations of a mid-nineteenth-century physical theory. A number of mathematicians and physicists told the economists, all of whom were trained as engineers, that the economic variables are utterly different from the physical variables and there is no way in which one can assume that they are in any sense comparable.*

> (page xi)

Moreover, the main features and characteristics of the observed reality are disputed and interpreted differently in various different (and often opposite) approaches, which move from different assumptions about human nature,[12] including psychological traits. Not surprisingly, even the role of the assumptions is disputed in economics and still a good number of economists take the instrumentalist[13] position (proposed within the discipline by M. Friedman in 1953 and now discarded by the specialists in the methodology of economics,[14] but not so much within the profession at large) that they are irrelevant as long as the predictions of the theory based on them prove reasonably correct. We simply reject this proposition and maintain that both the assumptions a theory moves from and the causal mechanisms it assumes to be in operation are crucial for the understanding of the world.

Given the weight and the uncertainties associated with the assumptions we move from in social sciences, the use of formalized approaches and even of mathematics is less straightforward, since one can easily be "perfectly mathematically coherent and as much wrong" (as a joke among economists reminds us). In human sciences, including economics, most variables do not have a deterministic nature – because of the reasons already stated – and therefore appropriate mathematical tools are fuzzy and lead to limited explanatory and predictive capacity. They are used mostly to organize empirical data (and maybe sometimes to dissuade critical eyes from peering too closely into a given statement). All the above is at the base of the mutual uneasiness and suspect between "hard" and "soft" sciences.

These considerations and the slowness with which the awareness of the impending crisis of our way of life is penetrating human understanding were the main motivation for organizing, in October 2013 at the Politecnico di Torino, Italy, the conference "Science and the future". The conference was an attempt at establishing a direct communication channel between natural disciplines on one side and economics and sociology on the other. After the end of the conference we had the idea of collecting some of the many contributions discussed at the meeting and strengthening the aim of mutual contamination among different branches of knowledge in order to provide a contribution to the public awareness of what is really going on in our globalized world, stressing the need for important and urgent changes in our lifestyles. The issue of the integration among different approaches is evidenced in the organization of the present book, with three chapters committed to natural disciplines and three more allocated to economy and sociology. This is certainly not anything like a unified treatment of the various issues across disciplines but, in our view at least, it constitutes a step forward in the direction of reciprocal listening and understanding.

There is no pretense of absolute originality and novelty for the argumentations included here, but we would like to contribute to a comprehensive view that avoids parceling understanding and action into separate and often scarcely effective interventions. The addressees are all concerned persons, with a special eye for students in their first years in university. Technicalities are not totally avoided but there is an effort to privilege global understanding with respect to formal rigor and abundance of details. All the more so, since disciplinary cultures usually adopting different languages are called in, we did try to make them complement each other rather than conflict.

Neither is this book an aseptic review of the state of the art on sustainability and related subjects. On the one side, it would not be complete for that purpose and, on the other, a work of that type would probably turn out to be rather tedious. It would also be deceptive to pretend to expound considerations in which the authors are not personally involved. We tried to invite contributions both to the Conference and to this work from economists holding a different, in relation to the issues discussed here, standing with respect to ours but we managed to get only one of them giving a talk at the Conference but not be willing to contribute any further (book chapters are less rewarding than journal papers, for economists).

In the above sense, this work is deeply concerned about the need for consistent actions to prevent the decline or even collapse of human civilization (Tainter, 1988). We want to start from the analysis of facts and the review of physical constraints limiting our actions; however, we are aware that facts always need interpretation and the latter is often not unique. Human societies, as well as the physical environment which we live in, are complex non-linear systems; furthermore, our knowledge is forcedly incomplete. Summing up, the joint evolution of mankind and the terrestrial environment is not entirely predictable and sometimes it is not predictable at all. However, the uncertainty margins must be dealt with the scientific method, which is able to define upper and lower limits for the material side of the problem and – usually – to find reliable probabilities thereupon. As to the physical constraints, there is no room for gambling or cheating and no room for will of power or magic.

There have been many attempts to deny or reduce the relevance and impact on the planet and its populations of climate change (as already pointed out this is well documented now and described in various books), but so far the scientific truth has emerged (Zwiers and Weaver, 2000), even if with too many and long delays, to which we have to add further ones due to economic and political interests in conflict (UNDP 2008 and UNFCC). Centuries ago the denial of Galileo's "inconvenient truth" caused a trial and personal prejudice to him and few others, but today these attempts at denying climate change are causing the growth of the problems and are negatively affecting millions of people.[15]

The majority of economists (and arguably a good number of people in various significant positions in the business world, though there are noteworthy exceptions) appear to be, on the one hand, still doubtful or dismissive about the results emerging from the natural science studies and evaluations on the issues – despite the conclusions of the Stern[16] Report and the fact that the leader of the project, professor N. Stern, is a well-known mainstream[17] economist and former senior vice-president of the World bank (2000–2003) – and, on the other, still adopting a peculiar "magical" view of the world, in which they see market instruments and mechanisms work perfectly by themselves (according to the myth of the invisible hand)[18] and guarantee that the best possible allocation of the available resources is always arrived at. Not surprisingly, a well-known economist,[19] W.H. Buiter, termed the mainstream view at the time (1980) as the "economics of dr. Pangloss" (after Candide's tutor, in Voltaire, who, in the face of any sort of disaster, reaffirms that they live in the best of possible worlds). He also reports (Buiter, 2009) Charles Goodhart[20] commenting that the Dynamic Stochastic General Equilibrium approach – which Buiter recall was for a while the staple of central banks' internal modelling – "excludes everything I am interested in". And Buiter adds "It excludes everything of current economic mainstream, at both macro and micro level (particularly in the form of the rational choice theory) relevant to the pursuit of financial stability".

Again R. Nadeau (as others before him)[21] pinpoint that "*market consensus is premised on metaphysical assumptions and functions as a quasi-religious belief system.*" (Introduction, page xii, and then Chapter 8). We share the evaluation about the metaphysical nature of the theories that assume the perfect working of the market and also agree that the origins of it are to be found in the religious beliefs and attitudes of economists of the past, but to us this seems more generally connected to the inclinations towards "magical" explanations, which have been used as ways of both explanation and deception cum exploitation (various recent books have highlighted the exploitative nature of part of current economics; a good example of them is Akerlof and Shiller, 2015, as both authors are Nobel Prize winners for economics).

According to the mainstream "magical" economic view, market mechanisms will start "working seriously" and redirecting all possibly useful trajectories of the relevant variables only when the problem at hand will become really serious and will start "biting" (i.e., triggering the instruments). The "blind faith" of mainstream economics (and even more of its neoliberal version, also labelled market fundamentalism), has been commented upon several times and its basis will also be discussed in the last chapter of this book. The sad truth is that such an attitude adds to the political difficulties to face the issue and is one of the causes of the current lack of results in the initiative to contrast climate change (CC). The dead weight levied by the tenets of mainstream on the development of proper scientific analysis is well illustrated by the development of ecological economics, which "was initially framed as the study of the economy grounded in the principle of ecology" while "today [. . .] has largely become the application of mainstream economics (economics as orthodox social science) to the existing agenda of ecologists and environmentalists, thus in practice facilitating a growth agenda". Therefore *"the 'unfinished journey' [of ecological economics] has much to do with reaffirming a vision of economic development that embraces ethics, affirms life, and argue for well-defined limits to human economics"* (Erickson, 2015, pages x–xi).

Consistently with the above premises and style, our first three chapters will discuss the material resources depletion and its dynamics, the global climate change and the dynamics of a growing complexity system.

This is for recalling the physical rules of the game, which constitute the basis for any further discussion but do not provide the full picture of the situation. We need to be well aware of the fact that we cannot expect our globalized society to behave as a single rational[22] person who consciously decides (possibly once and for all, unless new elements come to light) what to do. There are many further dimensions that play important roles in our world and need considering: real-life economic as well as political ones but also their interactions with the socio-psychological and cultural ones. While we are conscious of these complexities and interactions and agree that it is necessary to consider them in proper scientific ways, our purpose here is – out of necessity – much more limited. Our aim is to provide both one occasion amongst many to make some of these interactions work and some starting points for future researches along these lines. The physical, chemical and biological dimensions are more defined and constitute the foundation on which the rest can be built. In particular it seems necessary for economics to take into serious consideration the warning that H. Daly made many times: economy is a subsystem of a larger closed system, the Earth. A closed system in general exchanges only energy (we get it from the sun) but not matter . . . and this causes many troubles, including climate change. However, mainstream economists have many times refused to consider this obvious and necessary perspective[23] and have imposed their peculiarly narrow views, as T. Schelling and W. Nordhaus did in the already mentioned 1980 US National Academy of Science Report suggesting doing nothing about climate change (Oreskes and Conway, page 378).

Not all mainstream economics is to be blamed, however. Many studies on the working of specific instruments and market forms and realities deserve full respect and contribute to the advancement of our true knowledge. What needs overcoming is the "magical" vision characterizing most mainstream economics when dealing with individual choices, technological development and the working of markets in general. There is now plenty of evidence that individuals are different not just in their endowments and preferences (which can and ought to be discussed, contrary to the title of a famous paper in this ideological stream) but also in the way they see their life, face problems and choices, in their values and in the way these affect their actions and that rational choice theory followers are only a significant minority, and that perfect competition[24] is not an adequate approximation to the working of the majority of the markets in real life; rather the opposite as the role of market power appears more and more relevant and widespread. These facts in turn mean that prices are not providing the kind of useful and symmetric, not to mention all-encompassing, information required for the proper working of the incentive structures that most of economics assumes to characterize also the reality we live in. There are evidences of magical thinking also in the assumptions often made when dealing with large problems (while treated much more cautiously in specific analyses, as if in the aggregation they were surely levelled out) of almost perfect substitution rates (i.e., very high elasticity of substitution), in particular between natural and human made capital,[25] and in that that "appropriate" individual distribution of property rights will take care of the production of all goods (even those that are, by their nature, personal, democratic, public or common ones)[26] and of externalities, including all forms of pollution. Technological optimism (a variant of which, referred to as Cornucopianism, is considered in Oreskes and Conway, page 530 and following) will be dealt with, in a specific manner, in Chapter 4 of this book by Joe Tainter and his co-authors, while discussing the role of complexity in the evolution of our society. Here we only want to remember that it is associated with another – perhaps even more diffused – magical thinking approach, sometimes termed as "scientism" and defined (by Dupré, 2001, page *x*) as "*an exaggerated and often distorted conception of what science can be expected to do or explain for us*".

The other two chapters contributing to the second part of the book, discuss possible viable economic strategies to face the physical constraints preventing the persistently invoked "growth", and the limits of mainstream economics in facing sustainability and unsustainability, considered via the "building blocks" it is built on. The final conclusions will necessarily be open and debatable.

Notes

1 At least since the Report of the World Commission on Environment and Development, known also as the Bruntland Commission, 1987.
2 As much as some other very significant ones, in particular, for our topics here, the distinction between risk and uncertainty. According to the theoretical definition (due to F. Knight back in 1920s), risk refers to situations in which the various possible outcomes are clear (also because of the requirement of completeness, if one is to use utility functions) and well specified, up to the point of the definition of a reliable (even when subjective) probability distribution. In this respect, what these days goes under the name of economics of uncertainty should in reality be termed as economics of risk, as in proper uncertainty it is not possible to specify significant probabilities and often not even the full range of possible outcomes of given choices.
3 This is a point that has been argued for by a number of ecological economists, starting with Georgescu Roegen and including H. Daly, before many others. See Daly, 1992.
4 For a historical account of the struggle to deny the scientific evidence about various cases see Oreskes and Conway (2012), in particular Chapter 4, for the climate change issue, and see Washington and Cook, 2011, for a study of the ways and reasons of climate change denial.
5 The clear difference between natural scientists and mainstream economists on the topic and the actions needed has been with us at least since 1980 and the US National Academy of Sciences "Changing Climate: Report of the Carbon Dioxide Assessment Committee". See Oreskes and Conway (2012: 363–375).
6 For a brief introduction to scientific realism see the relative entry in the Stanford Encyclopaedia of Philosophy, by A. Chakravartty.

7 One that takes into account the lessons provided by Kant and by recent versions of "critical idealism".

8 Sometimes "human" scientists improperly quote Heisenberg's uncertainty principle as something manifesting the presence of subjectivity even in quantum mechanics. Actually, Heisenberg's principle is a perfectly well defined property of non-commuting abstract operators acting on state functions of a quantum system. It also has a classical analogue for wave phenomena and related parameters. Everything has a consistent and unique mathematical formulation, leaving no room for "freedom" of any sort. The uncertainty of human sciences has instead to do with free will and incomplete knowledge: an entirely different subject and no credible mathematization.

9 Far roots of this approach may be traced back to Descartes's philosophy and reach an extreme with the "ontological idealism" of Berkeley and his followers. For an updated account of idealism and of the relationship between epistemological and ontological idealism see Guyer and Horstmann, 2015.

10 Here statistics does not appear because of the incomplete knowledge of the variables at play and the impossibility to acquire all of them. It is instead an intrinsic property of the very nature of the "objects" one considers.

11 See Nadeau, 2006.

12 For an informative (and also amusing) discussion of these aspects we refer to "Human Nature and the Limits of Science", by science philosopher John Dupré, 2001. See also Hargreaves Heap et al, 1992.

13 Instrumentalism maintains "the view that theories are merely instruments for predicting observable phenomena or systematizing observation reports". The most influential advocates of instrumentalism were the logical empiricists (or logical positivists), including Carnap and Hempel, famously associated with the Vienna Circle group" (Chakravartty, 2011).

14 See Guala, 2006 Chapter 5, who points out as with respect to methodology Friedman turned economics away from its roots (and especially from JS Mill) that were realism (Mill and followers maintained economic theory to be true in abstract in that its fundamental principles describe the causal mechanisms) and introspection. Friedman substituted them with the so-called monetarist "black box", capable only of producing predictions without consideration (not to mention explanation) of the causes, as he considered theories to have only an instrumental role without any further relation with truth. The "irrelevance of the assumptions" question will be further considered in Chapter 6.

15 Again, this is now well documented in thousands of scientific papers and many books. See the various IPCC reports and Walker and King, 2008, for a brief summary of the main arguments.

16 Stern, 2007. This report defines CC as the biggest market failure in history and maintains that fighting climate change is the best pro-growth strategy in the long run, as the damages caused by it will by large overrun the costs of contrasting it (and clearly we agree on the analysis about climate change but not on the idea that material growth can go on indefinitely). See also Stern and Taylor, 2007.

17 The term *mainstream* in economics can, clearly, be declined in various different ways, but here and in the literature we refer to, it is taken to indicate the various versions of neoclassical economics that consider as their main theoretical reference, and use it for policy recommendations, the concept of general equilibrium. At the micro level this approach rests on utility functions and its most popular version is called Rational Choice Theory. For further discussion on the mainstream in economics, its evolution and some of the current alternatives, we refer to Arthur, 2013 and its references.

18 Not surprisingly, in one of the many plausible interpretations of Adam Smith's works, such an invisible hand could be a divine one, as the one he supposed to guide the planets orbits in order to avoid otherwise inevitable collisions (see Evensky, 1993, and Nadeau, 2006, Chapter 5)

19 See Buiter, 2009, where he also writes: "Indeed, the typical graduate macroeconomics and monetary economics training received at Anglo-American universities during the

past 30 years or so, may have set back by decades serious investigations of aggregate economic behaviour and economic policy-relevant understanding. It was a privately and socially costly waste of time and other resources". He in 2010 left academia to take the position of Chief Economist at Citigroup.

20 One of the better known monetary theorists in the recent past and former member of the Bank of England Monetary Committee (with Buiter).

21 To name just one (in English) Nelson and Stackhouse, 2001.

22 The concept of rationality in economics is not, and by far, uncontroversial. Mainstream economics usually takes on the notion of instrumental rationality (coming from the instrumentalist paradigm and popularized by M. Friedman), while most "heterodox" economists, starting from the contributions of H. Simon, highlight the limits of such notion and, even more, its inappropriate use (i.e., with respect to ends and not just towards means). See Hargreaves Heap SP, 1989.

23 A particularly telling story is the one H. Daly recalls in the Introduction (page 6) to his "Beyond Growth" (1996). At the presentation of "Beyond Limits" by Donella Meadows and colleagues, the (at the time) World Bank chief economist and well-known academic economist Lawrence H. Summers not only made it clear he considered that book worthless but to a specific question by Daly about "the optimal scale of the macro economy with relative to the environment" replied definitely that "That's not the right way to look at it".

24 A note for the non-economists. The textbook definition of perfect competition imposes four theoretical conditions that any market needs to satisfy to be qualified in that way, while any deviation from each of them leads to other specific market forms, which can be characterized according to this criterion. Three of the conditions are short run ones: (1) on the market there must be very many firms (sellers) and customers (buyers), each of which has to be small with respect to the size of the market (so that no one can have any degree of market power): (2) the information must be evenly distributed across market participants (again to avoid market power); (3) the goods offered on the market need to be exactly the same, without any form of differentiation (which can produce forms of market power; even small spatial differentiation could bring such effects), and one is a long run condition: freedom of entry in and exit from the market at minimal cost.

25 This even leads to one of the many definitions of sustainability within the discipline, in which "strong" sustainability is associated with the assumption of a low elasticity of substitution between the two and "weak" sustainability with that of a high rate.

26 Such a distinction among different types of "goods" used to be a classical one in economics, irrespective of the school of thought, but the drive to privatize everything has made it fading away in current market fundamentalist approach, thus reducing economics. On the differences among these goods and the "commodification" of every aspect of our lives see Anderson, 1990, 1993 and Sandel, 2010, 2013.

References

Akerlof, G., and Shiller, R. (2015). *Phishing for Phools: The Economics of Manipulation and Deception*, Princeton, NJ, Princeton UP.

Anderson, E. (1990). The ethical limitations of the market. *Economics and Philosophy*, 6.

Anderson, E. (1993). *Value in Ethics and Economics*, Cambridge, MA, Harvard UP.

Arthur, W.B. (2013). *Complexity economics: A different framework for economic thought*. Santa Fe Institute Working Paper No. 2013-04-012.

Brown, P.G., and Timmerman P. (2015), *Ecological Economics for the Anthropocene*, New York, Columbia UP.

Buiter, W.H. (1980). The macroeconomics of Dr. Pangloss: A critical survey of the new classical macroeconomics. *Economic Journal*, March, 34–50.

Buiter, W.H. (2009). The unfortunate uselessness of most 'state of the art' academic monetary economics. *VoxEU*, 6 March 2009. http://willembuiter.com/unfortunate.pdf

Burlando, R. (2001). Values, ethics and ecology in economics. *World Futures*, 56, 1.

Chakravartty, A. (2016) Scientific realism. In *The Stanford Encyclopaedia of Philosophy* (Winter 2016 edition). https://plato.stanford.edu/archives/win2016/entries/scientific-realism.

CMESPS (2008). *Report of the Commission on the Measurement of Economic Performance and Social Progress*, Paris. www.stiglitz-sen-fitoussi.fr

Daly, H.E. (1992) *Steady-State Economics* (2nd edition), London, Earthscan.

Daly, H.E. (1996). *Beyond Growth*, Boston, MA, Beacon Press.

Duprè, J. (2001). *Human Nature and the Limits of Science*, Oxford, Clarendon.

Erickson, J. (2015), Foreword, in Brown and Timmerman.

Evensky, J. (1993). Retrospectives-ethics and the invisible hand. *Journal of Economic Perspectives*, 7, 2.

Friedman, M. (1953). The methodology of positive economics. In *Essays in Positive Economics*, Chicago, Chicago UP.

Guala, F. (2006). *Filosofia dell'economia: Modelli, causalità, previsione*, Bologna, Il Mulino.

Guyer, P., and Horstmann, R.-P. (2015). Idealism. In *The Stanford Encyclopaedia of Philosophy* (Fall 2015 Edition).

Hargreaves Heap, S.P. (1989). *Rationality in economics*, Oxford, Blackwell.

Hargreaves Heap, S.P., et al. (1992). *The theory of choice*, Oxford, Blackwell.

Hausman, D. (1992). *The Inexact and Separate Science of Economics*, Cambridge, Cambridge UP.

Hawken, P., Lovins, A., and Lovins, L.H. (1999). *Natural Capitalism*, New York, Little, Brown & Co.

IPCC WG (2007). *Climate change 2007*, 3 vol. (the Physical Sciences Basis, Impacts and Adaptation, Mitigation of climate change), Cambridge, Cambridge UP.

King, D.A. (2004). The science of climate change: Adapt, mitigate or ignore? *Science*, 303.

Meadows, D.H., Meadows, D.L., and Randers, J. (2004). *Limits to Growth: The 30-Year Update*, Hartford, Chelsea Green.

Meadows, D.H., Meadows, D.L., Randers, J., and Behrens, W. (1972). *The Limits to Growth*, New York, Universe.

Nadeau, R.L. (2006). *The Environmental Endgame: Mainstream Economics, Ecological Disaster, and Human Survival*, New Brunswick, NJ, Rutgers UP.

Nelson, R.H., and Stackhouse, M.L. (2001). *Economics as Religion: From Samuelson to Chicago and Beyond*, Penn. State UP.

Nordhaus, W. (2007). Critical assumptions in the stern review on climate change. *Science*, 317.

Oreskes, N., and Conway, E.M. (2012). *Merchants of Doubts*, New York, Bloomsbury.

Ostrom, E. (2009). *A Polycentric approach for coping with climate change*. World Bank background paper to the 2010 World Development Report.

Sandel, M. (2010). *Justice*, London, Penguin.

Sandel, M. (2013). *What Money Can't Buy: The Moral Limits of Markets*, London, Penguin.

Stern, N. (2007). *The Economics of climate change: The Stern Review*, Cambridge, HM Treasury and Cambridge UP.

Stern, N., and Taylor, C. (2007). Climate change: Risk, ethics and the stern review. *Science*, 317.

Tainter, J.A. (1988). *The Collapse of Complex Societies*, Cambridge, Cambridge University Press.

UNDP (2008). *Human Development Report 2007/2008: Fighting climate change: Human Solidarity in a Divided World*, New York, UNDP.

UNFCC, United Nations Framework convention on climate change. http://unfcc.int. resource/convkp.html

Walker, G., and King, D. (2008). *The Hot Topic: What We Can Do About Global Warming*, New York, Bloomsbury Pub.

Washington, H., and Cook, J. (2011). *Climate change Denial: Heads in the Sand*, Abingdon, Earthscan.

World Commission on Environment and Development (1987). *Our Common Future*, Oxford, Oxford UP.

Zwiers, F.W., and Weaver, A.J. (2000). The causes of 20th- century warming. *Science*, 290.

1 The limits to material resources

Ugo Bardi

1 Introduction

The concept that mineral resources are finite and irreplaceable is relatively modern, probably expressed for the first time by Georg Bauer (also known as Agricola) in the sixteenth century. In a more general sense, the idea that all natural resources are finite seems to have appeared for the first time in economics with the work of Thomas Malthus, "An Essay on the Principle of Population", published from 1798 to 1826. Possibly under the influence of Malthus, economics as a scientific discipline developed during the nineteenth century as a set of concepts and ideas aimed at optimizing the use of limited resources. The result was bleak enough that Thomas Carlyle defined economics as "the dismal science". The concept of finiteness of the earth and of its resources had profound influence in various fields of science. In biology, it affected Darwin's thought and his theory of evolution by natural selection, published in 1858. Then, the idea that all living beings were part of the same global entity goes back to the 1920s, when Vladimir Vernadsky coined the term *biosphere*.[1] The concept became widely known in the 1960s, when James Lovelock developed the concept of *Gaia*,[2] borrowing the name of the ancient earth divinity to describe the planetary ecosystem. Today, the concept of Gaia remains a valid metaphor and, if life is a single, giant organism, it follows that it is tied to the limits of the whole planet.

While physical or ("hard") sciences were evolving in the direction of emphasizing the limitation of the earth system, economics gradually moved in the opposite direction. It lost the dismal veneer that it had acquires during the nineteenth century and became much more optimistic in terms of the availability of mineral resources. The process was gradual. In 1931, Harold Hotelling proposed the model that today takes the name of "Hotelling's rule".[3] The model can be seen as relatively pessimistic in the sense that it assumes that mineral resources are finite and non-replaceable. However, it also assumes that mineral resources can always be replaced by a suitable "backstop resource" when the price of the initial resource has risen enough to make the substitution convenient in economic terms. In time, the attitude of the mainstream economics thought seems to have evolved in the direction of maintaining that the physical limits to the amount of mineral deposits are either unimportant for the foreseeable future, or that they could be always circumvented by substitution or other methods. This is a position explored in particular by the group known as the "Austrian School".[4] An extreme form of this view in terms of unbounded optimism can be found in the work by Simon,[5] where we can read that mineral resources should be considered as actually "infinite".

A different approach to the issue can be defined as "physical" in the sense that it emphasizes the physical limits to resources. This approach was set on a quantitative basis starting in the 1970s with the development of "system dynamics", a method of calculation that allows one to examine the behaviour of a multi-component system where each component affects several others.[6] The first attempt to use this method in order to describe the evolution of the human industrial system was proposed by Jay Forrester in 1971 with a study titled "World Dynamics".[7] A more detailed study was performed in parallel with the study titled "The Limits to Growth" in 1972.[8] In both studies, it was found that the gradual increase of the costs of extraction of mineral resources, coupled with the growing costs of pollution abatement, would eventually lead to the world's industrial and agricultural output to peak and start an irreversible decline at some moment during the twenty-first century.

The results of the "Limits to Growth" study have been always controversial, as described for instance in Bardi in 2011.[9] However, the accusations made against the study were often unsubstantiated, such as the common one of having generated "wrong predictions". As described in detail, for instance, in Bardi in 2014,[10] the depletion process was correctly described in "The Limits to Growth" study in the assumption that the problem is not the finiteness of the amount of each element in the earth's crust. Obviously, elements cannot be destroyed and the earth is a system where the amounts of existing materials remain approximately constant in time. The depletion problem lies in the gradual dissipation of the energy potentials of the mineral deposits. These potentials were created over geological times by the energy provided mainly by geological forces but also with the contribution of biological processes and direct solar irradiations. These mineral deposits embed enormous amounts of energy, a condition that has allowed humankind to separate and collect the pure elements from their ores at a relatively low energy cost. But, with time, the high-grade ores are extracted and dispersed and the industry must move to lower grade ores. The result is that the energy cost of the production of mineral commodities increases with time. If this processes were to continue for a long time, eventually, there will not exist any exploitable mineral ores and the earth's crust may reach the condition defined as "Thanatia" in the book by the same title by Valero in 2014.[11] Such a condition corresponds to a "dead" earth from a mineral viewpoint: a planet where the energy cost needed to collect and separate elements from the undifferentiated crust in the amounts that are typical of the present industrial system is so high that it unthinkable to do so, unless it were possible for humankind to deploy flows of energy that today are unimaginable.[12] There is no need of the extreme condition called "Thanatia" to arrive to a condition in which the extraction of most minerals from their remaining ores may become so expensive in terms of the energy required that it would be beyond the means of the world's industrial system. The problem is enhanced by the fact that the concentration of many common mineral resources appears not to be linearly related to their abundance, but shows a "dead zone," also called the "mineralogical barrier",[13] a range of concentrations intermediate between exploitable deposits and the undifferentiated crust where there amount of the mineral resources is nearly zero.

The situation, however, may not be so bleak. There is nothing in thermodynamics that says that a non-isolated system must reach a state of "entropy death," that is, a stable condition of maximum entropy. Systems which have access to external energy potentials tend, rather, to reach a condition defined as "homeostasis", where the system maintains its parameters in an average static or slowly changing condition, while dissipating the available potentials. This property has been described for the first time by Ilya Prigogine[14] in terms of the formation of "dissipation structures" that maximize the flow of energy.[15, 16] In the case of the earth's surface, the system is exposed to a large flux of energy in the form of sunlight, with a minor but significant supplement in the form of geothermal energy. These two flows have kept the earth's biosphere in homeostatic conditions for billions of years. The biosphere is a material system and it needs minerals for its elements to function. These minerals can only come from the non-living parts of the earth system, from the atmosphere, the hydrosphere and the geosphere. The history of the biosphere shows that specific portions of it may suffer from "mineral depletion" of one or several elements during specific periods of time. However, on the average, we can say that the biosphere has attained the state that we define as a "circular economy" when referred to the industrial system; that is, the biosphere is able to recycle all its components at 100 percent. So, if the earth's ecosystem has remained in an average homeostatic condition for such long times, can the human industrial system achieve a similar condition? In other words, can a true circular economy be achieved? We will see that such a condition is not impossible, even though it will involve important changes in the way the industrial system works.

2 The biosphere as a homeostatic system

The earth's ecosphere is a portion of space clustered near the earth's surface, where multiple systems (the biosphere, the geosphere, the atmosphere, etc.) interact with one another. The term *biosphere* indicates the ensemble of the living creatures (or biota) and it is composed by a wide variety of organisms occupying mainly the land areas of the continents and shallow water bodies. All the systems that we define as "living" share similar characteristics in terms of overall chemical composition and structure. In thermodynamic terms, these living systems are characterized by their capability of retaining their state by repair or reproduction; with the material contents of organisms being replaced by mechanisms generated by an external flow or exergy. This property is normally called *metabolism*. The flow of energy that maintains metabolism active in the biosphere comes from sunlight, and the first step of the processing of this flow is the series of chemical reactions called photosynthesis. In this process, specialized structures in living cells use solar energy to strip hydrogen out of water molecules. In a subsequent series of reactions, the hydrogen atoms are combined with carbon dioxide to form the organic compounds that are the building blocks of organisms. Metabolic processes show multiple steps of degradation of the original exergy input carried out by different species in the ecosystem, a series of processes often called the "trophic chain". The final result of this chain of metabolic processes is the reforming the original water and carbon dioxide molecules, thereby closing the cycle of the materials involved in the process.

The amount of energy processed by metabolic processes in the biosphere is huge if compared to human standards. The average total flow of solar energy that reaches the earth's surface estimated as 89,000 TW[17] or 87,000 TW[18]. An estimate of the fraction of this energy processed by the biosphere can be obtained from the value of the gross planetary production (GPP), that is the amount of biological carbon generated by the biosphere. This amount is estimated as 105–177 Pg of carbon per year.[19] Taking into account that reducing six moles of CO_2 to one mole of hexose requires approximately 9,450 kJ,[20] we can calculate that the total energy generated by photosynthetic organism on planet Earth in the form of organic compounds is approximately 500–900 TW. According to these values, then, the average efficiency of the biosphere as an energy transduction mechanism would be around 0.8 percent. Some estimates report lower values, e.g. 0.3 percent.[21]. If we take a value of 0.5 percent as the average, we arrive to a total energy produced by photosynthesis of approximately 400 TW, some 20 times larger than the primary energy generated by human industrial processes (around 18 TW on the average[22]). Of course, in ideal conditions, photosynthesis is much more efficient and it reported that crops and vegetated areas can reach a photosynthesis efficiency in the range of 2 to 4 percent.[23]

All the metabolic processes of living creatures are based on the availability of a number of chemical elements; sometimes termed *nutrients*. As well known, the main elements that form the structure of organisms are in the form of gases in the atmosphere (C, O, H and N). Many more elements are used among those that don't have stable gaseous forms. Among these, the most important are sulfur, calcium, magnesium and phosphorous. Further elements are used in small amounts in the metabolic process, in some cases so small that can they be defined as "traces" or even "ultra-traces", perhaps as little as 0.0001 percent by weight, but still playing a role in the chemical mechanisms of metabolism.[24] All these elements must be taken from the geosphere as solid state minerals or from the hydrosphere as dissolved ions.

The processes that cycle these elements and keep them available in suitable forms for the biosphere are varied and complex, and a complete discussion would be too long for the present paper. However, some of the main features of the system will be sketched here. First of all, as a general rule, in order for any element to be 100-percent recycled for the biosphere, there must exist some kind of reservoir that can be used as source and sink of the element and that can exchange it with the biosphere. In the case of the main biological elements (C, O, N, H), the atmosphere itself acts as source and sink, even though an intermediate passage to the liquid phase may be required for water. In the case of nitrogen, we have a gas which is stable in the atmosphere for times probably longer than the expected lifetime of the ecosphere (billions of years), so that the cycling in and out of the atmosphere can continue indefinitely and the same is true for water, that is cycled in and out of its main reservoir, the oceans. Some cases are more complex. In the case of carbon (in the form of CO_2) and oxygen (in the form of O_2) we have reactive gases that would be consumed by inorganic processes in relatively short times if they were not continuously recreated by active biological processes. Oxygen, in particular, is a highly reactive gas and, as noted first by Lovelock,[2] it could not exist in a planetary atmosphere were it not for biological processes that have accumulated it over geological times. The source of molecular oxygen is the carbon dioxide present in the atmosphere in the early stages of the earth's history. A large amount of this carbon dioxide has been processed by photosynthesis and transformed into organic carbon and free molecular oxygen. Most of the carbon produced in this way was removed from contact with oxygen by segregation into the earth's crust and the formation of stable compounds, mostly kerogen,[25] but also the compounds that are called "fossil fuels". The oxygen released by the reaction has been lost in large part by reaction with inorganic elements, but a fraction is still present in the atmosphere.

In the case of carbon dioxide, we also have a reactive gas that, in an active crustal surface, would react with silicates and be slowly consumed, disappearing from the atmosphere in times of the order of a few million years, or less, according to Berner in 2003.[26] That would make photosynthesis impossible, thus ending all life on earth. However, that does not happen because the earth's mantle acts as a reservoir that continuously sources CO_2 to the atmosphere. Thus, the cycle is called the "long" or "inorganic" carbon cycle,[27,28] and it consists in the sedimentation of carbonates at the ocean floors in the forms of the shells of marine organisms. Slowly, these carbonates are pushed into the earth's mantle at the subduction regions at continental edges, with the necessary energy provided by the movement of tectonic plates. The carbonates decompose at the high temperatures of the mantle and the carbon dioxide generated in this way is re-emitted into the atmosphere by volcanic eruptions and other magmatic processes. This process continuously replaces the CO_2 lost by silicate erosion, making it available for photosynthesis and maintaining the homeostasis of the biosphere.

For the elements that are not available in gaseous form, the land organisms of the biosphere face a much more difficult problem. They rely for source and sink of these elements mostly on the entity known as "soil" or "humus", the true living skin of planet Earth.[28] The soil is a mixture of microorganisms that decompose dead organisms and make their mineral components available for plants by means of the root system. Animals, then, obtain these nutrients by consuming plants. The system is extremely efficient in recycling nutrients, but it cannot recycle at 100 percent efficiency and the soil is always at risk of being destroyed by extreme events, such as erosion or human activity. For instance, it has been calculated[29] that in a Northern hardwook ecosystem, the total amount of calcium contained in the biomass is 203 kg/ha, while 365 kg/ha are present in the soil. Of this mass, around 7.9 kg/ha are lost every year as dissolved ions and erosion, while about 3 kg/ha are restored by rain. The negative balance of 5 kg/ha is restored by weathering of the rock substrate. As another example, it is reported in Rauch and Graedel in 2007[30] that the amount of copper "extracted" by the earth's biota from the soil is about 2.5 Mt/year from soil that contains it in a concentration of about 25 ppm, not different from that of the undifferentiated crust. Over long time spans, the earth's surface is replenished with nutrients by mechanisms such as volcanic eruptions or wind erosion that bring back vital minerals to depleted areas. If left in peace, the biosphere uses these mechanisms to maintain homeostasis and has maintained it for hundreds of millions of years, at least.

3 The technosphere

The entity that we may call the *technosphere* is the ensemble of industrial structures that have been created by human beings, mostly during the past few centuries. At a cursory examination, the technosphere does not appear different in its thermodynamic properties than the other "spheres" that are part of the earth's surface region (biosphere, hydrosphere, etc.). Just as the other spheres, the technosphere is a complex dissipation structure that does its work at dissipating energy potentials by a hierarchy of dissipating structures, an industrial trophic chain which we may see as equivalent to the trophic chains of the biosphere. In analogy with the concept of "biota" for the biosphere (the total collection of organisms in a given region at a given time) we could define the concept of *technota* as the ensemble of technological artefacts existing in a given area, at a given time.

The fundamental difference between the biosphere and the technosphere is that the latter interacts only marginally with the solar energy potentials, which are instead the main exergy source of the biosphere. The technosphere can be described as a "detritivore" organism in the sense that it uses mainly detritus created in the past by the biosphere and the geosphere in the form of the carbon compounds normally defined as "fossil fuels"; petroleum, natural gas and coal. The same definition can be applied to the various mineral ores exploited by the technosphere, the result of geological and biological processes that have created them over time spans typically of the order of millions of years and more. The accumulation of energy created by these ancient processes makes their extraction possible at low energy costs for the technosphere. These ores have been termed "Gaia's Gift",[10] noting that it was given only once in the history of humankind.

The primary energy available as thermal energy at the input of the industrial system of the technosphere corresponds to an average power of approximately 18 TW.[22] Of these, about 81 percent (or ca. 14.5 TW) were produced by the combustion of fossil carbon, the rest is a mix of other technologies, including renewables and nuclear fission. This primary energy must be transformed into exergy (energy able to do work) in order to maintain the transduction structures of the technosphere. This is done by means of a variety of processes; mostly thermal engines, whose efficiency can be taken as around 30 percent on the average. The world's agricultural system processes an additional output in terms of food energy which can be estimated as ca. 1 TW. Overall, the technosphere may be seen as more efficient than the biosphere in processing the available potentials, but it is much more limited in terms of the total amount of energy processed since, as discussed earlier on, the biosphere produces some 500 TW at the output of the photosynthesis process.

The other main difference between the biosphere and the technosphere lies in the use of different chemical elements. Whereas the biosphere uses just a few elements, the technosphere utilizes practically all the elements of the periodical table, also in chemical forms not available to the biosphere. For instance, the technosphere uses a variety of elements in their reduced (metallic) form, despite the strongly unfavourable potential needed to reduce them from their oxidized ores. Some examples are aluminum, silicon, magnesium and titanium, which are never used in metallic form by the biosphere. This is possible because the technota can manage to control much higher temperatures than the biosphere and can process molten metals.

The problem with the supply of mineral nutrients to the technosphere is that at present there exists no sink that can return the nutrients to the technosphere in the same form in which they were supplied. In other words, the nutrient cycle of the technosphere is not closed. As an example, the technosphere extracts fossil fuels from the crust and releases the carbon contained in these fuels to the atmosphere in the form of CO_2 but is unable, at present, to reprocess this CO_2 to reform the original hydrocarbon compounds, as instead the biosphere can do. The same is true for most mineral nutrients originating from the crust. They are returned to the crust but not in forms that the technosphere can exploit again. This is the essence of the "Thanatia" model.[11]

To estimate the size of the nutrient cycle, we may note that, according to Haas and colleagues[31] in 2005, the global economy processed 62 Gt of materials. Of this large amount, a fraction of 4.5 Gt/yr (ca. 8 percent) were metal ores, of which 0.8 Gt was the actual amount of metals mined, the rest being tailings and other waste. Of this approximate gigaton of metallic materials, most common minerals (say, copper, zinc, etc.) are recycled at about 50 percent. Only two are recycled at higher rates (iron and lead) while many rare metals (e.g. indium, gallium, tantalum, etc.) are recycled only below 1 percent or not recycled at all.[10] There are no geological mechanisms that can reform the original ores of these minerals at the speed at which they are consumed, therefore we may conclude that we are traveling toward the planet Thanatia at a speed of the order of half a gigaton per year. Once we arrive there, we may discover that the human industrial system may have been a strictly "one shot" adventure. That may, at best, leave to humankind a long sunset based on wood and stone tools.

Yet, it is not unthinkable that the technosphere could learn how to close the cycle of most, if not all, mineral it uses in such a way to maintain at least part of its current characteristics. The thermodynamics of dissipative systems doesn't say anything that would make 100 percent recycling impossible, only that recycling becomes progressively more expensive as the fraction cycled increases. Even in a completely "Thanatized" world, the chemical elements that were once present in mines would still be around, although in very small concentration, and in many cases just in traces. That would make their extraction expensive, but not impossible. This is a concept that was termed the "universal mining machine" by the present author.[12] Such a hypothetical machine would process the undifferentiated crust to separate it in the various elements it contains. The technical details of the machine can vary; in the most brutal approach, it would crush rock, gasify it, ionize the products to a plasma, and then separate it in the different chemical components by means of a magnetic field. A more sophisticated, and less energy-hungry, version of the same concept is used by the biosphere that uses the process called "weathering" in order to extract elements from the rock of the earth's crust, mainly by means of chemical leaching.[29]

The problem for the technosphere with extracting minerals from the undifferentiated crust is that it is hardly compatible with the amount and the kind of mineral nutrients that are presently supplied. As an example, taken from Bardi in 2014[10], we can consider copper, present at very small concentrations in the upper crust, ca. 25 ppm. That is, 40 tons of crust contain about one kg of copper. To extract this copper, we would need to provide sufficient energy in order to pulverize rock at the atomic level, an amount that can be calculated as some 10 MJ/ kg. As a consequence, we would need at least 400 GJ/kg to extract copper from this source. In order to maintain the present rate of copper production from mines, ca. 16 Mt/year, the total amount of energy needed by this process can be calculated as 6×10^9 TJ, which is about one order of magnitude larger than the present global primary energy production (ca. 10^8 TJ).[32] This is, obviously, impossible in any conceivable scenario for the short- and medium-term future. The situation is even worse if these calculations are performed for the rarest materials utilized by the technosphere (e. g. indium, gallium, gold, platinum, etc.), which are present in concentrations of the order of parts per billion in the crust.

Nevertheless, the strategy of mining from the crust is not impossible for the technosphere if its limitations and needs are taken into account: after all; the biosphere can use it, and has been using it for billions of years. So, the technosphere could use the same strategies of the biosphere in order to avoid the Thanatia trap. That is:

1 Use solar energy to power the metabolic process driving the trophic chain.
2 Use only mineral elements that are relatively common in the earth's crust.
3 Recycle and reuse as much as possible.
4 Use the crust as a reservoir to close the cycle.

I will now examine these four points in order.

3.1 Using solar energy to power the technosphere's metabolic process

The first question to be considered is how to provide the technosphere with relatively large energy flows. Evidently, the question makes sense for the future only if it will be possible to switch from its present detrital resources, fossil fuels and uranium, to renewable ones; i.e., to solar energy (other forms of energy potentials are available in the form of geothermal energy[33] and tidal energy,[34] but they are several orders of magnitude smaller than sunlight). As mentioned earlier on, the flow of solar energy that arrives to the earth's surface is very large, of the order of 90,000 TW. A variety of transduction systems are known; these systems are able to transform solar light it into forms of energy that the technota can process. They are the equivalent to the *chloroplasts* (green formers) that the biosphere utilizes to transform sunlight into chemical energy and hence could be called *cyanoplasts,* from the Greek term κυανός, meaning dark blue, intended as the colour of solar cells.

In the technosphere, sunlight can be exploited directly (solar energy) and indirectly (biomass, wind, hydro). The subject is complex and has been discussed elsewhere (e.g.,[35,36,37]). Basically, it seems that the most promising energy transduction technologies are, at present, wind and solar, the latter mainly in the form of photovoltaic (PV) plants. In principle, the potential of solar plants is very large: in the US alone it is estimated as more than 150 TWp.[38] According to the data reported by Liu and colleagues,[39] about 1/5 of the area of the Sahara Desert (2 million square km) could generate around 50 TW at an overall PV panel area conversion efficiency of 10 percent. Note also that photovoltaic devices do not need liquid water and can operate in a temperature range both higher and lower than the range optimal for photosynthesis. Summing up the various possibilities, PV plants could generate an average power of the order of 100 TW while appropriating a fraction of the earth's surface that would not impede the functioning of the biosphere. A similar potential of energy generation, although somewhat lower, could result from wind systems.[37,35] Overall, it appears that it would be possible to exceed the present technosphere energy generation capability by at least one order of magnitude. Of course, the installation of such a large energy infrastructure has a cost in energy terms and it is conceivable only if this cost doesn't exceed the energy that the infrastructure can produce. This concept can be described by the parameter known as EROI or EROEI (energy return for energy invested), defined as the ratio of the energy generated by the system (more correctly, exergy) divided by the exergy needed to maintain and then replace the system at the end of its useful life.[40] Applying the EROEI concept to solar energy, all the recent studies on photovoltaic systems report EROEIs larger than one for the production of electric power[41,42,43,44,45,46,47] The EROEI of wind systems is reported to be even higher.[48]

3.2 Limiting the number of the chemical species used by the technosphere's metabolism

The second question is how to provide the necessary flow of mineral resources to the technota and, in particular, to the technota's cyanoplasts. As mentioned before, one of the basic strategies for this purpose is to use only elements that are abundant in the earth crust. This appears to be possible. Some solar cells technologies use rare elements, such as CdTe or CIGS (copper indium gallium selenide) whose long-term potential is limited. However, the current technology uses mainly silicon and aluminum for the cells, both very abundant in the crust. Some silver is used for the back contacts,[49] but it is not crucial.[50,51,35]. That doesn't mean that the presently exploited resources for these two elements, bauxite for aluminum and silica sands for silicon, are infinite. It means, however, that the "universal mining machine" concept could be practical if applied to these two elements and it would be possible reach and maintain installation capable of operating in the multi-terawatt range.[52] As a proof of concept of this idea, it may be worth mentioning that the biosphere does cycle silicon from the crust and that the silica content in some plants may be as high as 4 percent in weight.[53] Also, aluminum can be extracted by plants from crustal sources, although it is not used in the metabolic process.[54] Other promising materials for PV cells are sulphides, also abundant elements in the earth's crust.[55,56] Regarding wind power, the main structural element of wind towers is steel which, in turn, is mainly based on an abundant element, iron. However, steel used as a structural element contains also rare elements whose long-term supply could be problematic and that would probably lead to lower performance turbines. Wind turbines also use rare earth magnets to transform the kinetic energy produced by the rotor into electric power. Rare earths can be recycled, but in the long run their supply could become problematic. They can be replaced by iron based magnets, at the price of a reduced efficiency. On the whole, some compromise would have to be attained between performance and material availability, but no insurmountable obstacles appear to create and maintain the technosphere's "chloroplasts" in order to provide the system with energy resources for a long time to come.

With a supply of energy coming from the sun powered cyanoplasts, it is possible to conceive an industrial trophic chain that would use only elements that are common in the earth's crust, although it would not be limited to the same small set used by the biosphere. As structural materials, it could use metallic aluminum, magnesium and titanium. Among these metals, titanium could replace stainless steel, removing the need of the rare element chromium. Fiberglass, formed of inorganic silica and an organic glue, could also be used as a structural element replacing plastic in many applications. The technosphere could also use carbon based compounds that could either be obtained from the biosphere as traditional wood and fibres, or created by activating the atmospheric CO_2 by inorganic processes that would lead to precursors for the Fischer-Tropsch reaction.[57] For non-structural applications, aluminum can be used to replace copper as an electricity conductor for most applications. In terms of magnetic materials, at present there is no equivalent to rare earth magnets in terms of field strength,[58] although traditional, iron-based, magnets could be used in many applications. For some applications, such as, for instance, the catalytic converters at the output of thermal engines based on the Otto cycle, there is no known replacement for the presently used noble metals, Pt, Pd and Rh[59] – thermal engines would have to be replaced by electric motors, but that's a perfectly possible strategy that provides also higher efficiency. Many applications in electronics use a variety of rare metals and semiconductors; tantalum for condensers, gallium for microchips and other applications, indium for video screens, and more; these applications would have to be abandoned in the future, given the impossibility of closing the cycle for these elements. Electronic devices fully based on silicon only would not be impossible, but would entice a considerable loss of performance in comparison to the current generation of electronic devices. In a different field, high-temperature materials, such as superalloys and high-performance ceramics based on zirconium, also have no obvious replacement. High temperature turbine engines would have to be abandoned and replaced with completely different technologies.

This is just a sketch of the possible developments of an industrial system that would use only common elements in the earth's crust. On the whole, it is clear that some of the presently used technologies would have to be abandoned, but it appears that there doesn't exist an application that is both critical for the survival of an industrial civilization and is at the same time critically dependent on some rare and non-replaceable mineral.

3.3 Recycling and reusing

The subject of recycling and reusing the materials used by the technosphere is currently discussed in the context of the concept of "circular economy". [31,60,61,62,63] Overall, it is clear that the industrial system is moving towards higher and higher levels of recycling by means of a series of mechanisms that involve unproved citizen awareness, better industrial procedures and standards, national and international protocols and regulations. The diffusion of these concepts is creating a sophisticated trophic chain dedicated to the processing of what once was called "waste" and that today is more and more often referred to as "secondary resources" or, sometimes, "urban mines". [64,65] This industrial trophic chain is the equivalent of the soil for the biosphere and its final reservoir exists in the form of landfills. At present, landfills are almost never used as sources of mineral commodities, even though their role as "secondary mines" has been discussed and proposed. [66] Still, things could change in the future and landfills could play a fundamental role in the idea of "circular economy". Obviously, no matter how sophisticated a recycling system can be, it can never reach a 100-percent level. However, it is possible to get to much higher values than the present ones. For instance, Fthenakis reports having reaching values over 99 percent for the recycling of CdTe solar cells. [67] A high efficient recycling system is not sufficient, alone, to ensure the survival of the technosphere, but can be highly effective if used in combination with the other strategies described here.

3.4 Mining the earth's crust

Using the undifferentiated earth crust as a source of minerals for the technosphere is simply unthinkable for the present rates of extraction. However, the task becomes much less unthinkable if seen in view of a transformation of the technosphere that would mimic the strategies of the biosphere; which does mine the undifferentiated crust. Taking the example of copper, as discussed before, the amount of energy needed to maintain the present copper production rate from the undifferentiated the crust would be at least an order of magnitude larger than the present global primary energy supply. However, if we apply the strategies discussed before, we see that we could replace most of the current uses of copper with aluminum, while recycling could be raised higher levels than the present ones. If each of these strategies reduces to 10 percent the need of copper for industry, then the technosphere doesn't need any more tens of millions of tons of copper per year, but can have a sufficient supply with amounts of the order of 100,000 tons per year. If nothing else, it lengthens the present supply from ca. 40 years[68] at current rates of production to thousands of years at the projected lower future rates. But lower-grade resources could be accessed, and, as a last resort, leaching minerals from the earth's crust is expensive, but possible. [69] If sufficient amounts of energy are available, the cycle can be closed and the supply of resources maintained for a long time.

4 Conclusion

At present, it is not possible to prove that a completely "circular" economy is possible over the long term. However, it is not possible to prove the opposite, that is that the industrial system would necessarily wind-down and disappear in a fully "thanatized" world,[11] while human beings would return to a technologically primitive existence based on agriculture or hunting and gathering. What we can say is that the planetary ecosphere is facing a bifurcation: either the return to an earlier pre-Anthropocene state, or the evolution to something completely different, where the human industrial system, the technosphere, would continue to operate.[36] If a large supply of renewable energy can be maintained to the technosphere, it is not impossible to close the cycle and create a long-term industrial system that will not exceed the limits of the planetary resources. The spaceship directed to planet Thanatia can still make a u-turn and come back to the earth.

Acknowledgement

This work is part of the MEDEAS project, funded by the European Union's Horizon 2020 research and innovation programme under grant agreement No 691287.

Notes

1 Weart, S.R. *The Discovery of Global Warming*. Cambridge MA: Harvard University Press; 2003.
2 Lovelock, J. A physical basis for life detection experiments. *Nature*. 1965; 207 (August 7): 568–570.
3 Hotelling, H. The economics of exhaustible resources. *J Polit Econ*. 1931; 39(2): 137–175.
4 Bradley, R.L. Resourceship: An Austrian theory of mineral resources. *Rev Austrian Econ*. 2007; 20(1): 63–90. doi:10.1007/s11138-006-0008-7.
5 Simon, J. *The Ultimate Resource*. Princeton, NJ: Princeton University Press; 1981.
6 Richardson, G. System dynamics. In: *Encyclopedia of Operations Research and Management. . . .* New York: Springer; 2013: 1519–1522. doi:10.1007/978-1-4419-1153-7_1030.
7 Forrester, J. *World Dynamics*. Cambridge, MA: Wright-Allen Press; 1971. http://documents.irevues.inist.fr/handle/2042/29441. Accessed June 3, 2013.
8 Meadows, D.H., Meadows, D.L., Randers, J., and Bherens, III W. *The Limits to Growth*. New York: Universe Books; 1972.
9 Bardi, U. *The Limits to Growth Revisited*. New York: Springer; 2011.
10 Bardi, U. *Extracted: How the Quest for Mineral Resources Is Plundering the Planet*. New York: Chelsea Green; 2014.
11 Valero, A., and Valero, A. *Thanatia: The Destiny of the Earth's Mineral Resources*. Singapore: World Scientific Publishing Company; 2014.
12 Bardi, U. The oil drum: Europe | The universal mining machine. *The Oil Drum*. www.theoildrum.com/node/3451. Published 2008. Accessed August 24, 2013.
13 Skinner, B.J. Earth resources. *Proc Natl Acad Sci U S A*. 1979; 76(9): 4212–4217. www.jstor.org/stable/70053. Accessed August 16, 2013.

14 Prigogine, I. On symmetry-breaking instabilities in dissipative systems. *J Chem Phys.* 1967; 46(9): 3542. doi:10.1063/1.1841255.

15 Sharma, V., and Annila, A. Natural process – natural selection. *Biophys Chem.* 2007; 127(1–2): 123–128. doi:10.1016/j.bpc.2007.01.005.

16 Kaila, V.R., and Annila, A. Natural selection for least action. *Proc R Soc A Math Phys Eng Sci.* 2008; 464(2099): 3055–3070. doi:10.1098/rspa.2008.0178.

17 Tsao, J., Lewis, N., and Crabtree, G. *Solar FAQs.* US Department of Energy. http://rogachev.dyndns-at-home.com:8080/Copy/Engineering/Solar FAQs.pdf. Published 2006. Accessed January 5, 2015.

18 Szargut, J.T. Anthropogenic and natural exergy losses (exergy balance of the Earth's surface and atmosphere). *Energy.* 2003; 28(11): 1047–1054. doi:10.1016/S0360-5442(03)00089-6.

19 Xia, J., Niu, S., Ciais, P., et al. Joint control of terrestrial gross primary productivity by plant phenology and physiology. *Proc Natl Acad Sci.* 2015 (February): 201413090. doi:10.1073/pnas.1413090112.

20 Taiz, L., and Zeiger, E. Plant physiology online: Energy demands for photosynthesis in land plants. *Plant Physiology.* http://5e.plantphys.net/article.php?ch=t&id=419. Accessed February 20, 2015.

21 Kheshgi, H.S., Prince, R.C., Marland, G. *The Potential of Biomass Fuels in the Context of Global climate change: Focus on Transportation Fuels.* Annu Rev Energy Environ. 2000; 25(1): 199–244. doi:10.1146/annurev.energy.25.1.199.

22 *International Energy Statistics – EIA.* www.eia.gov/cfapps/ipdbproject/iedindex3.cfm?tid=2&pid=37&aid=12&cid=regions&syid=2008&eyid=2012&unit=BKWH. Published 2014. Accessed January 6, 2015.

23 Zhu, X-G., Long, S.P., and Ort, D.R. What is the maximum efficiency with which photosynthesis can convert solar energy into biomass? *Curr Opin Biotechnol.* 2008; 19(2): 153–159. doi:10.1016/j.copbio.2008.02.004.

24 Mann, J., and Truswell, A.S. *Essentials of Human Nutrition* (3rd edition). Oxford: Oxford University Press; 2007.

25 Vandenbroucke, M., and Largeau, C. Kerogen origin, evolution and structure. *Org Geochem.* 2007; 38(5): 719–833. doi:10.1016/j.orggeochem.2007.01.001.

26 Berner, R.A. The long-term carbon cycle, fossil fuels and atmospheric composition. *Nature.* 2003; 426(6964): 323–326. doi:10.1038/nature02131.

27 Falkowski, P., Scholes, R.J., Boyle, E., et al. The global carbon cycle: A test of our knowledge of Earth as a system. *Science (80-).* 2000; 290(5490): 291–296. doi:10.1126/science.290.5490.291.

28 Frissel, M.J. (ed.). *Cycling of Mineral Nutrients in Agricultural Ecosystems.* Amsterdam: Elsevier; 1978.

29 Bormann, F.H., and Likens, G.E. Nutrient cycling. *Science (80-).* 1967; 155(January 27): 424–429.

30 Rauch, J.N., and Graedel, T.E. Earth's anthrobiogeochemical copper cycle. *Global Biogeochem Cycles.* 2007; 21(2): n/a–n/a. doi:10.1029/2006GB002850.

31 Haas, W., Krausmann, F., Wiedenhofer, D., and Heinz, M. How Circular is the global economy? An assessment of material flows, waste production, and recycling in the European Union and the world in 2005. *J Ind Ecol.* 2015; 19(5): n/a–n/a. doi:10.1111/jiec.12244.

32 Cleveland, C.J., and Morris, C. *Handbook of Energy.* Elsevier; 2014. doi:10.1016/B978-0-12-417013-1.00015-7.

33 Davies, J.H., and Davies, D.R. Earth's surface heat flux. *Solid Earth.* 2010; 1(1): 5–24. doi:10.5194/se-1-5-2010.

34 Munk, W., and Wunsch, C. Abyssal recipes II: energetics of tidal and wind mixing. *Deep Sea Res Part I Oceanogr Res Pap.* 1998; 45(12): 1977–2010. doi:10.1016/S0967-0637(98)00070-3.

35 Garcia-Olivares, A. Energy for a sustainable post-carbon society. *Sci Mar.* 2016; In Press.

36 Bardi, U. What future for the anthropocene? A biophysical interpretation. *Biophys Econ Resour Qual.* 2016; 1(1): 2. doi:10.1007/s41247-016-0002-z.
37 Jacobson, M.Z., and Delucchi, M.A. Providing all global energy with wind, water, and solar power, Part I: Technologies, energy resources, quantities and areas of infrastructure, and materials. *Energy Policy.* 2011; 39(3): 1154–1169. doi:10.1016/j. enpol.2010.11.040.
38 Lopez, A., Roberts, B., Heimiller, D., Blair, N., and Porro, G. *U.S. Renewable Energy Technical Potentials: A GIS -Based Analysis*; 2012. www.nrel.gov/docs/fy12osti/ 51946.pdf.
39 Liu, Q., Yu, G., and Liu, J.J. Solar radiation as large-scale resource for energy-short world – Volume 20, Number 3/July 2009 – Multi Science Publishing. *Energy Environ.* 2009; 20(3): 319–329. http://multi-science.metapress.com/content/qt143r2n20326731/. Accessed January 15, 2015.
40 Hall, C., and Gupta, A. A review of the past and current state of EROI data. *Sustainability.* 2011; 3: 1796–1809. doi:10.3390/su3101796.
41 Rydh, C.J., and Sandén, B.A. Energy analysis of batteries in photovoltaic systems. Part II: Energy return factors and overall battery efficiencies. *Energy Convers Manag.* 2005; 46(11–12): 1980–2000. doi:10.1016/j.enconman.2004.10.004.
42 Richards, B.S., and Watt, M.E. Permanently dispelling a myth of photovoltaics via the adoption of a new net energy indicator. *Renew Sustain Energy Rev.* 2007; 11(1): 162–172. doi:10.1016/j.rser.2004.09.015.
43 Weißbach, D., Ruprecht, G., Huke, A., Czerski, K., Gottlieb, S., and Hussein, A. Energy intensities, EROIs (energy returned on invested), and energy payback times of electricity generating power plants. *Energy.* 2013; 52: 210–221. doi:10.1016/j. energy.2013.01.029.
44 Blankenship, R.E., Tiede, D.M., Barber, J., et al. Comparing photosynthetic and photovoltaic efficiencies and recognizing the potential for improvement. *Science.* 2011; 332(6031): 805–809. doi:10.1126/science.1200165.
45 Chu, Y. *Review and Comparison of Different Solar Energy Technologies*; 2011. www.geni.org/globalenergy/research/review-and-comparison-of-solar-technologies/ Review-and-Comparison-of-Different-Solar-Technologies.pdf.
46 Bekkelund, K. *A Comparative Life Cycle Assessment of PV Solar Systems*; 2013. http:// smartgreenscans.nl/publications/SmartGreenScans-2014-Life-Cycle-Assessment-of-Photovoltaics-Status-2011-Part-1-Data-Collection – Sample-Pages.pdf.
47 Bhandari, K.P., Collier, J.M., Ellingson, R.J., and Apul, D.S. Energy Payback Time (EPBT) and Energy Return on Energy Invested (EROI) of solar photovoltaic systems: A systematic review and meta-analysis. *Renew Sustain Energy Rev.* 2015; 47: 133–141. doi:10.1016/j.rser.2015.02.057.
48 Kubiszewski, I., Cleveland, C., and Endres, P. Meta-analysis of net energy return for wind power systems. *Renew Energy.* 2010; 35(1): 218–225. www.sciencedirect.com/ science/article/pii/S096014810900055X. Accessed January 11, 2015.
49 Grandell, L., and Thorenz, A. Silver supply risk analysis for the solar sector. *Renew Energy.* 2014; 69: 157–165. doi:10.1016/j.renene.2014.03.032.
50 Rudolph, D., Olibet, S., Hoornstra, J., et al. Replacement of silver in silicon solar cell metallization pastes containing a highly reactive glass frit: Is it possible? *Energy Procedia.* 2013; 43: 44–53. doi:10.1016/j.egypro.2013.11.087.
51 Hamann, L., Haas, M., Wille, W., Mattheis, J., and Zapf-Gottwick, R. 30% Silver reduction in rear bus bar metal paste. *Energy Procedia.* 2013; 43: 72–79. doi:10.1016/j. egypro.2013.11.090.
52 Feltrin, A., and Freundlich, A. Material considerations for terawatt level deployment of photovoltaics. *Renew Energy.* 2008; 33(2): 180–185. doi:10.1016/j.renene.2007. 05.024.
53 Bauer, P., Elbaum, R., and Weiss, I.M. Calcium and silicon mineralization in land plants: Transport, structure and function. *Plant Sci.* 2011; 180(6): 746–756. doi:10.1016/j. plantsci.2011.01.019.

54 Imadi, S.R., Waseem, S., Kazi, A.G., and Azooz, M.M. *Plant Metal Interaction*. Elsevier; 2016. doi:10.1016/B978-0-12-803158-2.00001-1.

55 Wadia, C., Alivisatos, A.P., Kammen, D.M. Materials Availability Expands the Opportunity for Large-Scale Photovoltaics Deployment. *Environ Sci Technol*. 2009; 43(6): 2072–2077. doi:10.1021/es8019534.

56 Todorov, T.K., Reuter, K.B., Mitzi, D.B. *High-efficiency solar cell with Earth-abundant liquid-processed absorber*. Adv Mater. 2010; 22(20): E156–E159. doi:10.1002/adma.200904155.

57 Schulz, H. Short history and present trends of Fischer – Tropsch synthesis. *Appl Catal A Gen*. 1999; 186(1–2): 3–12. doi:10.1016/S0926-860X(99)00160-X.

58 Massari, S., and Ruberti, M. Rare earth elements as critical raw materials: Focus on international markets and future strategies. *Resour Policy*. 2013; 38(1): 36–43. doi:10.1016/j.resourpol.2012.07.001.

59 Bardi, U., and Caporali, S. Precious metals in automotive technology: An unsolvable depletion problem? *Minerals*. 2014; 4(2): 388–398. doi:10.3390/min4020388.

60 Sauvé, S., Bernard, S., and Sloan, P. Environmental sciences, sustainable development and circular economy: Alternative concepts for trans-disciplinary research. *Environ Dev*. 2015; 17: 48–56. doi:10.1016/j.envdev.2015.09.002.

61 Ghisellini, P., Cialani, C., and Ulgiati, S. A review on circular economy: The expected transition to a balanced interplay of environmental and economic systems. *J Clean Prod*. 2015; 114: 11–32. doi:10.1016/j.jclepro.2015.09.007.

62 Lieder, M., and Rashid, A. Towards circular economy implementation: A comprehensive review in context of manufacturing industry. *J Clean Prod*. 2015; 115: 36–51. doi:10.1016/j.jclepro.2015.12.042.

63 Ashby, M.F. *Materials and Sustainable Development*. Elsevier; 2016. doi:10.1016/B978-0-08-100176-9.00014-1.

64 Ongondo, F.O., Williams, I.D., and Whitlock, G. Distinct urban mines: Exploiting secondary resources in unique anthropogenic spaces. *Waste Manag*. 2015; 45: 4–9. doi:10.1016/j.wasman.2015.05.026.

65 Sun, Z., Xiao, Y., Agterhuis, H., Sietsma, J., and Yang, Y. Recycling of metals from urban mines – a strategic evaluation. *J Clean Prod*. 2016; 112: 2977–2987. doi:10.1016/j.jclepro.2015.10.116.

66 Krook, J., Baas, L., Jones, P.T., et al. Enhanced landfill mining in view of multiple resource recovery: A critical review. *J Clean Prod*. 2013; 55: 45–55. www.sciencedirect.com/science/article/pii/S0959652612002442. Accessed September 25, 2013.

67 Fthenakis, V. Sustainability of photovoltaics: The case for thin-film solar cells. *Renew Sustain Energy Rev*. 2009; 13(9): 2746–2750. doi:10.1016/j.rser.2009.05.001.

68 *Long term availability of copper*. International Copper Study Group. www.icsg.org/index.php/the-world-of-copper/71-uncategorised/114-long-term-availability-of-copper. Published 2013. Accessed May 29, 2016.

69 Norgate, T., and Jahanshahi, S. Low grade ores – Smelt, leach or concentrate? *Miner Eng*. 2010. www.sciencedirect.com/science/article/pii/S0892687509002568. Accessed August 16, 2013.

2   Global climate change

Stefano Caserini

2.1 Introduction

Global climate change is happening and an overwhelming majority of the scientific community consider the risk of climate change real and severe. The knowledge summary in Fifth Assessment Report (AR5) of the Intergovernmental Panel on climate change (IPCC, 2014a),[1] provided new evidence of the reality of climate change, on the basis of many independent analyses from observations of the climate system, paleoclimate archives, theoretical studies of climate processes and simulations using climate models.

There is now a widespread and increasing consensus about the fact that temperature increase should be kept as low as possible in order to limit damages. The IPCC's AR5 produced a consistent framework for possible future scenarios about the expected impacts on human activities and ecosystems, and about possible strategies for reducing emissions in the next decades.

Global warming has been for long a scientific and environmental problem, and only recently it has been recognized as one of the most important issues of this century, along with poverty eradication, terrorism and loss of biodiversity. To tackle this global threat, it is fundamental to point out the connection between causes and effects, the necessary actions and all interests involved.

This chapter begins with an overview on causes and consequences of global warming; since still nowadays many "alternative" theses find room in the debate on climate change, the main argument proposed by climate denial will be analyzed.

Then, the main solutions proposed to manage and minimize the problem will be briefly presented. The chapter ends with the discussion of three aspects of global climate change issue, more and more important in the outstanding increase of scientific knowledge of the climate systems characterizing the last two decades.

2.2 Causes of global warming

The attribution of most present global warming to anthropogenic greenhouse gases comes from a robust phenomenological explanation, as well as from the correspondence between the trend of key measured climatologic indexes (temperatures, sea level, ice melting) and the values simulated by models based on the knowledge about physical and chemical phenomena ruling the global climate in computer codes. If these models consider greenhouse gases and the consequent greenhouse effect, a phenomenon that humans started studying back in the nineteenth century, model results substantially match observation. Without considering the man-made input of greenhouse gases, one could not explain such rate of warming in the last 50 years, its global average value and its spatial distribution. According to the Fifth IPCC Assessment Report, it is "extremely likely [probability over 95%, ndr] that human influence has been the dominant cause of the observed warming since the mid-20th century" (IPCC, 2013)." Such warming of atmosphere and oceans has also caused changes in global water cycle, in snow and ice coverage, in the average global sea level and in changes in the frequency of extreme meteorological events.

Climate science also evaluates the "radiative forcing" of each cause, i.e., the contribution to variation of Earth energy balance, and this allows to identify natural causes as a minor player in the climate change of the last 50 years. Theories presented by media for too many years, such as the important role of solar spots and cosmic rays in recent climate change, or the cyclic nature of terrestrial temperatures changes, have been now largely dismissed.

Due to the inherent complexities of the terrestrial climatic system, there are areas that need to be better understood, for example the interaction between aerosols and clouds. Model results have margins of error and the reliability of climatic projections must be improved, but the results of the many disciplines contributing to climatology are undeniably consistent: the energy unbalance caused by greenhouse gases accumulation increases atmosphere and ocean temperature and this growth leads to ice melting and sea level rise.

The extent of future warming depends on the quantity of greenhouse gases emitted in the next decades; this requires the use of climate "scenarios", to evaluate the possible response of the climate system related to such greenhouse gases emissions.

The Fifth IPCC Assessment Report, summarizing the results of hundreds of simulations on temperature projections in the next centuries developed by several research groups all over the world, clarified the extent of the possible climate change in the future: according to scenarios without significant emission decrease, by the end of this century global average temperatures are expected to increase by 3–5°C (Scenarios RCP8.5, RCP6.0 and RCP4.5 in Figure 2.1) compared to the pre-industrial period, with further increase in the following centuries.

These variations are not only incomparable with temperature variations occurred during the whole Holocene, rather they are unprecedented in Homo sapiens' history: the 1°C warming experimented in the last 150 years is just the first and smallest part of a future and more substantial warming.

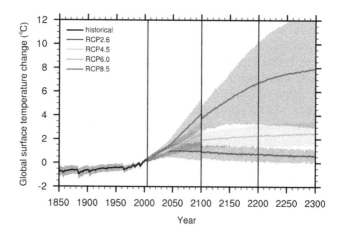

Figure 2.1 Projections of global temperature increase (compared to the average 1986–2005), in a scenario with high emission reduction (RCP2.6), in two scenarios with intermediate reductions (RCP4.6 and 6.0.) and in a scenario without reductions (RCP8.5).

Source: IPCC, AR5-WG1, Chapter 12, Figure 12.5 (Collins et al., 2013).

2.3 Consequences of global warming

In the last decades, climate change has had impacts on natural and human systems all around the world. Several scientific works provide detailed analysis of the different impacts, already observed or expected in different geographical areas; these analyses are periodically summarized in the second of the three volumes included in IPCC reports (IPCC, 2014b).

Even if many effects are difficult to identify, because of the natural variability and the adaptation capability of the same systems, today we already have clear evidence of global warming effects in several regions of the world: for instance, many terrestrial, aquatic and oceanic species moved their geographical limits and their migration habits in response to present climate change. The speed of present changes makes the natural adaptation of species more difficult; few examples of species extinction have been directly ascribed to climate change up to now, nevertheless natural climate change occurred in the last millions of years, even if they have been much slower than the present anthropogenic changes, caused in significant changes in ecosystems and an increase of extinction rate.

In many regions of the planet, changes in rainfall and snow patterns, or in the extension of glaciers, are causing modification in hydrological systems, affecting the quality and quantity of water resources. Glaciers have shrunk almost on the whole planet and the seasonal coverage of the arctic sea ice is decreasing. The minimum extension of marine arctic ice is reached in September, at the end of summer of

Northern Hemisphere; in September 2012, the minimum extension was 3,4 million km², with a loss of nearly 4 million km², 13-fold the surface of Italy (NSIDC, 2012)..

For human societies, impacts of climate change worsen other stress factors, with many more negative effects on poorest and more vulnerable people. In particular, extreme events such as heat waves, droughts, floods and forest fires have already showed both direct impacts on living conditions, reduction of crop production, destruction of houses and infrastructures, and also indirect impacts in terms of increase of food prices and food insecurity. Even if CO_2 concentrations and temperatures increase can theoretically foster crop production at high latitude, negative impacts on crops on global scale have been more common than the predicted positive impacts.

A greater warming increases the probability of severe, diffused and irreversible effects. With an increase of global average temperature of 4°C or more, in the case of business as usual, available studies show severe and diffused impacts on the most precious ecosystems, a substantial increase of extinction rates, relevant risks for global and regional food security, as well as damages on several human activities, as food production or outdoor work in some areas and periods of the year, due to the combined effect of high temperature and humidity.

Future impacts of climate change will considerably vary depending on the regions, and they will not be uniformly spread. It is not only a geographical issue: the richest countries will be more able to adapt and they will be less vulnerable to damages, because they are less densely populated and they have many more resources. Vice versa, poorest countries will be heavily affected, because they rely more on crops for their livelihood, and this makes them more exposed and sensitive to temperatures and hydrological variations.

The Mediterranean region has been identified as the most endangered region in Europe for climate change, due to the negative impacts of rising temperature on several sectors as tourism, agriculture (for example, decrease of grains production), forestry activities, infrastructures, energy production and population health. Climate projections show a possible temperature increase in all European regions, while an increase in Northern Europe and a decrease in Southern Europe are foreseen for rainfalls; the latter is identified as the European area most vulnerable to climate change.

At present, there is a large consensus on the fact that net costs due to climate change are and will be significant, and they will increase, especially if we wait to act in contrasting global warming.

2.4 The never-ending arguments of climate denial

Although global warming is widely recognized by now as one of the main environmental issues of the twenty-first century, it is still possible to hear alternative voices, even if widely marginal among scientists, which question the existence of the problem or its severity. To define this kind of attitude, the term *climate denial* is used, to identify the stubborn and unreasonable denial of very robust scientific facts, on which the scientific community has reached a consensus.

The term *denial*, originally used to identify who denies the terrible tragedy of the Shoah, is used in other contexts too, and it is more precise than the term *skeptic*, which identifies an only initially suspicious attitude, willing to accept new evidences emerging from the improvement of the scientific knowledge.

The use of wrong and outdated arguments, even after the scientific community has been showing their insubstantiality for years, is typical of climate denial. Examples of these arguments, the Greenland-was-a-green-land, many-vine-yards-in-Medieval-England, sunspots-and-cosmic-rays-are the-causes of-global-warming, are outright slogans often repeated in obsessive way. Even if today many easily available resources (journals, books, websites, apps) show the errors in these theses, denialist voices are still sometimes repeated on corporate press and television, though to a lesser extent than in the past, when these voices were taken into account in climate policies decisions.

Emissions and concentrations

Some climate denial arguments aim to convince the population that "nothing has changed", and greenhouse gas emissions due to human activities are not able to alter carbon dioxide (CO_2) level.

According to this theory, CO_2 emissions by human activities would be insignificant if compared with the emissions generated by living species. Even if emissions by living organisms could be really relevant, this is about carbon of photosynthetic origin, a close cycle, which doesn't contribute to a net change of CO_2 content in the atmosphere.

It is true that CO_2 emissions by combustion of fossil fuels are not the main source of CO_2 for the atmosphere, because other sources, originating from photosynthesis and breathing of terrestrial and oceanic living organisms, are definitely larger; but the fact is that other carbon fluxes are in balance, and remained rather unvaried in the last 10,000 years. A small contribution can alter an equilibrium involving far greater forces; known natural factors could not explain the fast increase of CO_2 concentrations during the last two centuries, shown in Figure 2.2 together with the increase of two other greenhouse gases, methane (CH_4) and nitrous oxide (N_2O).

Human perturbation occurs not only with emissions from fossil fuel combustions and industrial process as cement, steel or glass production, but also because of the reduction of natural "CO_2 sinks", that is by means of deforestation, as forest ecosystems absorb carbon dioxide, the main greenhouse gas, during photosynthesis.

The role of volcanoes is sometimes mentioned as one of natural causes. Actually, explosive volcanic eruptions, which can release huge amounts of dusts and sulphates in the atmosphere, create occasional, discontinuous emissions, which perturb the atmosphere for few weeks, months or years, depending on the intensity of the eruption. But with regard to CO_2, volcanoes contribution is on average less than 1 percent of anthropogenic emissions.

Even if it is true that in the past CO_2 levels have been greater than the current ones, this happened in a very remote past. When the earth formed, CO_2

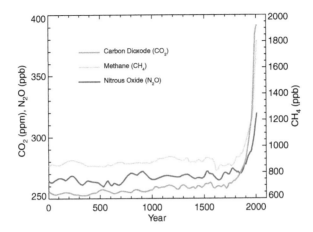

Figure 2.2 Atmospheric concentrations of carbon dioxide, methane and nitrous oxide in the last 2,000 years. 2016 concentrations reached respectively 403 ppm, 1853 ppb and 329 ppb.

Source: IPCC, AR4-WG1, Chapter 2, Figure FAQ2.1-1 (Forster et al., 2007).

concentrations in the atmosphere were thousand times greater than the current ones, and 4–5 million years ago there was more CO_2 in the air than today. However, it is demonstrated that during the last 1–2 million years, that is since largely before the Homo sapiens' appearance, levels have always been lower, and changing at slow rate at best.

The inevitable conclusion is that human contribution to CO_2 level increase is clear and unprecedented in human history.

The warming of the planet

The reality of global warming at this point is evident and, today, it is less and less called into question: most denialists have now abandoned this topic, but for several years, the debate has been heated. The doubts still today are related to the qualities of measures of temperatures, to their representativeness, to potential mistakes in the measurement or calculation of global variables, to the interference of disturbance factors in measurement points, as the urban heat islands, which could lead to consider local heating phenomena as if they were global level variations.

A first argument is that some measuring stations don't show any atmospheric warming, or they show a minor warming. Actually, this is plausible and compatible with the theory of greenhouse effect: it is exactly the global nature of planet warming to cause a change in atmospheric circulation, which leads to a stabilization or light decrease of temperature in some areas, for limited periods.

Regarding the "heat island" effect, in-depth studies show how it is a real effect, but at the local scale, not significant on larger areas. Average temperature calculated at global level, for both the northern and southern hemispheres, are not affected by the influence of "heat islands". The most detailed researches, which have closely analyzed the possible sources of errors in measurements and in statistical elaborations, assert peremptorily that potential uncertainties are largely lesser than the registered temperature increase.

Another argument used to deny planet global warming, for instance, is the fact that in some periods temperature did not increase. This can be disproved by showing how temperatures increased or decreased in some periods in the past, too. Analysing data not in an isolated way, but as long-term series, the temperature increase emerges, as global average temperatures in the twenty-first century have been nearly always the highest since when instrumental measurements exist.

One of the reason of misunderstanding of the global warming problem is often the confusion between weather and climate, which is the global atmospheric situation, and must be evaluated over long periods – decades or more. Thus, many people, between 2000 and 2014, claimed the existence of a supposed pause of global warming. This was due to the normal variability of climatic system, as some fluctuations of the climatic system, due for example to the oceanic flows El Niño-La Niña, in addition to the trend of temperature increase due to greenhouse gases. Global temperatures record of 2014 and the even higher one of 2015 (see Figure 2.3) have invalidated the thesis of a possible warming hiatus.

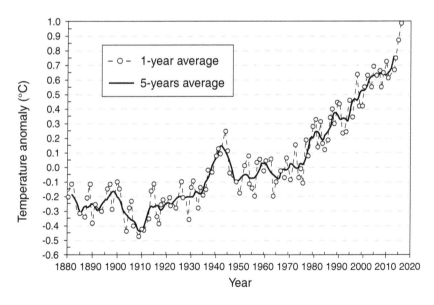

Figure 2.3 Global temperature changes between 1880 and 2015. Temperature anomalies are referred to 1951–1980 average.

Data source: GISS GLOBAL Land-Ocean Temperature Index (http://data.giss.nasa.gov/gistemp/tabledata_v3/GLB.Ts+dSST.txt).

Comparison with past temperatures

Another way to weaken the importance of global warming is to claim that "climate has always changed". If in the past climate was much colder or hotter, present variations would not be important.

Myths of a past when climate was hotter or colder describe a Greenland "green land", thriving vineyards in England, shepherds on Alpine glaciers, frozen Thames and Venetian Lagoon. These stories are somehow based on real events, but they are improperly used to weaken the importance of present climatic changes.

Average planet temperatures registered in the last decades are unusually high, if compared to the last millennium. It is a clear information coming from many studies reconstructing past temperatures, particularly in the last 2,000 years, using "proxy" data, indirect indicators as tree ring width, pollen analysis, coral analysis, analysis of oceanic sediments, analysis of air micro-bubbles trapped in ice cores. They are huge and complex studies, with hundreds of quotations, presenting some uncertainties, because past climate reconstruction is not easy. Scientists who worked on the Fourth IPCC Assessment Report stated the conclusions of their examination of these works in terms of probability degrees, but with a clear indication: "it is very likely that average Northern Hemisphere temperatures during the second half of the 20th century were higher than for any other 50-year period in the last 500 years. It is also likely that this 50-year period was the warmest Northern Hemisphere period in the last 1.300 years" (Jansen et al , 2007).

The role of sun

One of the main thesis of climatic denial states that the variability of sun activity is the most influential factor affecting climate variations registered in the recent past and accountable for most of future changes. The ones claiming that sun influence is crucial often show some diagrams where we can notice stunning similarities between trends of past temperatures and some indexes linked to sunlight (as sunspots) or to its consequences (cosmic radiation reaching the earth, which depends by sun magnetic field force). Other scientists refuted the validity of these studies, demonstrating that many of these diagrams have been created manipulating available data in a sophisticated way.

All the different theories that tried to ascribe a crucial role to sunlight in temperature trends of the last century, particularly on the last 50 years (through sun spots variability or cosmic rays influence), have not gone through the scientific scrutiny. The Fifth IPCC Assessment Report, reviewing all the studies appeared in literature and supported by simulations through mathematic models, has demonstrated that sun "force" in global warming in the last 250 years has been less than 2 percent of the "force" of anthropogenic greenhouse gases.

Even if the contribution of solar variation to recent climate change would allow to avoid, or at least diminish, human responsibility on climate change, solar parameters variations have been a minor factor in temperature changes in the last decades.

2.5 The influence of vested interests

The consensus among scientists on the issue of global change is demonstrated by the analysis of articles published by the scientific literature and by surveys on scientists' opinions. One of these surveys (Doran and Zimmerman, 2009) asked scientists some questions, like *"Is the planet warming?"* and *"Is human activity a significant factor in planet global temperature change?"* Registered "yes" answers have been respectively 90 percent and 82 percent of the interviewees, with an increase of "yes" when you move from scientists without publications, to scientists with publications in other sectors (for example geology, meteorology), to experts identified for having published more than 50 percent of their works in the climate change sector. Amongst the latter, the percentage of "yes" increased respectively to 96.2 and 97.4 percent. This is the conclusion of the research: "it seems that the debate on the authenticity of global warming and the role played by human activity is largely nonexistent among those who understand the nuances and scientific basis of long-term climate processes (Doran and Zimmerman, 2009)".

Today, climate denial is de facto only important in the United States, where it achieves a success proved by still very high percentages of people who don't believe in human responsibility on climate change, definitely higher than the ones in European countries. According to different opinion polls realized over the years, almost the half of US population doesn't believe to human responsibility on climate change. It could seem strange, since it is the same country contributing in a fundamental way to climate science, with some of the main research centres and the main percentage of authors of IPCC reports. However, scientists are a small part of the population; they are too few to influence percentages referred to the whole population of a country. Moreover, and it is less intuitive, education or scientific culture in the United States do not affect the concern for climate risk: social and political ideas are a very important factor. Different studies[2] have shown that an individualistic vision, adverse to political disturbance in personal or corporate decision-making processes and favourable to less structured and hierarchical forms of social order, makes the denial of climate problem more probable. On the contrary, results of climate sciences tend to be accepted by individuals with a more egalitarian vision preferring less strict and more communitarian social organization forms.

The ones with an ideological attitude leading to deny the evidences on global warming, and even more if they have a higher education or scientific preparation, will tend to find more sophisticated arguments to support the denial, with the help from plenty of websites or from pseudoscientific reports made by *think tanks* more or less directly financed by the fossil fuel industry.

Another factor which explains the situation in US is, in fact, the influence of coal and oil lobbies on climate debate and on politics. The obligation to publicize the accounts of listed corporations revealed the huge funding given by large corporations to research centres with a conservative approach, obstructing environmental policies.[3] Denial in United States is important because it affects federal climate policy and the policies of many states. The Senate is still today the stumbling block to federal policy proposals on reduction of greenhouse gases emissions, after being the obstacle to the US ratification of the Kyoto Protocol. Obscurantist proposals, which have caused clamour and worry, have found room in some conservative states: in North Carolina, a 2012 law imposed to ignore more recent data in the projections on sea level rise in coastal area defence planning; in Louisiana and Tennessee the teaching of climate science (and of evolution theory) has been forbidden; in Florida in March 2015, it was forbidden for public officials to say or to write about "climate change" and "global warming" during the discussions on sea level rise.

However, we must say that precisely in the United States a huge work to obstruct denial is underway, in order to understand its deep motivations, its dynamics and to identify its financiers. Some books, as *Merchants of Doubt* by Naomi Oreskes and Erik Conway, or the blogs Realclimate, Skeptical Science and Demosblog, are a treasure trove of information about denial origins and techniques, about links and funding among corporations, research centres and political groups. They have shown the similarities with actions of other lobbies which, in the past, worked in order to prevent and to slow down environmental policies limiting the use of substances destroying stratospheric ozone or to prevent research on damages caused by smoking. There are even online university classes analyzing the conceptual and rhetorical stratagems used by climatic denial (University of Queensland, 2015): exalting doubts and the impossibility for scientist to guarantee the total reliability of their conclusions, using false experts, creating false dichotomies, leaps of logic and fake conspiracies.

We must say, however, that denialist positions often do not have economic and financial reasons, i.e., corporative profits, as main explanation. Denial is often based on psychological and sociological reasons, exhibitionism, narcissism, research of visibility by standing out of the crowd. Alternatively, it could be one of the fronts of an ideological battle, aimed to defending at all costs the present concept of development and production, or a religious vision on man and nature. For some other people, denial is a way to conquer political space, to defend personal profits.

Popular success of denialist positions also has to be searched in the fact they are comfortable, reassuring, supporting the refusal of the sense of limit typical of our society. Even if it is presented as rational and moral, the exaltation of doubt and of the impossibility of scientific community to guarantee the total reliability of its conclusions, the continuous recall to the too many uncertainties or to the need of more sounded proofs can be a precise strategy, an excuse, a mask for partisan interests.

One of the fundamental requirements for policies entailing strong efforts and a wide economic and social relevance is, however, the widespread awareness about the seriousness of climate crisis at different levels of society. The danger of climatic denial is the weakening of this awareness.

2.6 What needs to be done

Adaptation to climate change

Adaptation measures assume a fundamental importance, since an additional warming of at least 0.5°C is "in the pipeline", inevitable due to past, current and near future emissions. These are measures at different levels to minimize damages due to climate change, through actions of prevention, monitoring and warning systems, rescue and civil protection actions; there are further prevention actions regarding the different organization of territory and communities, the change in building techniques of buildings and infrastructures, farming and irrigation techniques.

Each country is vulnerable to climate change, a vulnerability originated by population density, lack of basic resources, geo-morphological features of the territory, political and social structures managing the adaptation to changes.

There are several ongoing adaptation experiences, both in rural and urban communities, in the public and private sector. Governments and authorities at different levels are beginning to develop adaptation strategies and policies, trying to integrate the issues set by climate change in wider development plans. Adaptation measures give benefit also in the short term, but they can be developed only integrating them in existing decision-making processes.

Adaptation to climate change implies costs, but it can prevent most of the potential damages to the socio-economic system. It has to be said that evaluation of economic impacts of climate change on a global scale is extremely difficult, both methodologically and practically. First, a part of damage due to climate change is not quantifiable or it is with a very high uncertainty. This happens because many countries still don't have statistically reliable survey systems for damages, and because several consequences on human life, environment or landscape are not monetizable or they are in a very controversial way. Furthermore, damages regard the next generations too, for decades and centuries, and we need to decide how to compare these costs with the present ones, what "interest rate" must be adopted; it is a moot choice, both ethical and political, as it implies an assessment of the value of future costs compared to present costs.

Mitigation of climate change

If the increase of greenhouse gases in the atmosphere is the problem, the reduction of emissions of these gases is the main solution to reduce them drastically, as soon as possible. Many studies showed that it is possible to reduce greenhouse gases emissions in the next decades, in a very significant way, by at least 50 to 80 percent within the half of the century and reset them to zero in the following decades.

The main cause of greenhouse gases emissions in the atmosphere is the combustion of coal, oil and gas for energy production in the main three forms: electrical, thermal, kinetic. The first one is produced in thermal power plants, using the heat produced by combustion to heat water until vaporization, and twirl around a turbine that produces electricity. The second one is the use of boilers bringing heat to houses using hot water. The third one is the energy used to move people and goods, through gasoline or diesel engines in transportation. Then other emissions come from cement production, agriculture, livestock, changes in land use which release in the atmosphere the carbon accumulated in fertile soils and in the vegetation in past decades or centuries.

The reduction of emissions means first of all to burn fewer fossil fuels, and this can be done in several ways. One way is to develop alternative energy sources: sun, wind, geothermal, tidal, hydroelectric energy, etc. Another way is to produce less energy, supporting energy conservation which reduces energy demand. Another one is to use more efficient technologies, which burn less fuels to produce the same amount of energy.

Moreover, a part of the carbon in the atmosphere can be stocked in the biomass, by diverting the trend of deforestation. Other mitigation measures deal with CH_4 and N_2O emissions from agriculture and livestock, as well as with action "from the bottom"; for example, restricting meat consumption, which is linked to considerable quantities of greenhouse gases emissions and to energy and water consumption.

The stabilization of greenhouse gas atmospheric concentrations needs emission reduction actions to be realized in an integrated and synergic way in all the key sectors of society: energy production and use, transports, buildings, industrial systems, land use and human settlements. It is possible to drastically reduce greenhouse gases emissions in the next decades but only with a wide range of already available technologies in all sectors.

A silver bullet, a miracle technology to solve rapidly the problem doesn't exist; but several different actions and technologies that allow us to face global energy needs for the next decades, avoiding CO_2 emissions increase, do exist. Some of these actions are already a routine in some countries, where they are considered, at this point, as taken for granted. Those who build houses with high efficiency in holding heat in winter and cold in summer, after a while consider it as natural and would be amazed about buildings wasting half of the energy they consume. Those people also get used to separating waste collection and find it unnatural to throw all the garbage in one only bag. Those who usually commute by bike in the city centre, find the use of car uncomfortable and frustrating.

Renewable energies are at the core of change, and among them solar and wind energy will have a crucial role in the next years; their development in the last 10 years has been overwhelming; it has gone beyond the most optimistic previsions of all the research centres, included the environmental ones. Many works pointed out the technical, geographical, and economic feasibility of replacing the present fossil fuel energy infrastructure with solar power and other renewables, without a significant increase of costs (Jacobson and Delucchi, 2011). Due to this substantial reduction of electric renewable sources, the fast scale-up of mitigation action in many sectors will start from early reductions in the electricity sector, and later will spread in other sectors.

Mitigation of climate change is not a matter of the available technologies, but of finding the way to put technology and capital together in a timely manner, all over the world. To have epochal changes, as the ones needed to scrap a widespread fossil energetic system, we need resolute legislative actions, coherent industrial policies, adequate subsidies and prohibitions. Policy decisions, strategic choices on infrastructures, public and private investments and urban planning are also important.

There is something to do for everyone, both at individual level and at the level of administrative and legislative actions of municipalities, regions, national governments and international organisms like World Bank, World Trade Organization, and International Monetary Fund. They will have to change rules and procedures, which have fostered fossil industry so far.

If the important choices on technologies and infrastructures depend on decisions made in global agreements or in the parliaments, they have to be actualized at local level by a myriad of concrete actions and measures. Most of emissions arise from individual behaviours. A strong push to reduce emissions can come from the bottom-up, but it is often slowed by a lack of economic resources due to inconsistent policies.

It must be reiterated that actions to reduce greenhouse gases emissions also have many co-benefits, and this means benefits and profits on other levels. Many actions with a positive impact on climate are immediately pleasant and convenient. Sometimes the profits are immediate, some other times they are visible a little bit after; but they are always very concrete. For example, if we adopt modern thermal isolation systems in a house, heating the house will be less energy-consuming: there will be an initial cost (the purchase and installation of thermal insulating materials), but in the following years we will save on energy bill. Thanks to public subsidies, in the form of deduction from taxes, finally the operation is often convenient, namely it is not a cost but an investment, also profitable by the merely economical point of view.

Other benefits are indirect and have an impact on the whole society. If in order to reduce greenhouse gases emissions we burn less fossil fuels (in thermal power plants, industries, cars and trucks), we reduce at the same time the emission of other substances that are harmful for public health and vegetation, as particulate, nitrogen and sulphur oxides and carbon monoxide. Thus, there will be fewer sick persons and fewer premature deaths due to air pollution; in global economic terms, there will be fewer lost working days for respiratory diseases and less health costs. Vice versa, several actions foreseen today to fight air pollution, like improving public transports and buildings energy efficiency, are useful for climate.

There are only few conflicting points between the two policies: for example, small domestic wood appliances, fireplaces and stoves, which emit a lot of particulate, but which are zero-CO_2 on the long period, because emitted CO_2 is absorbed by the atmosphere during the growth of the tree providing wood. Or diesel cars, which are more efficient than gasoline cars, because with the same displacement they emit less CO_2 but more sulphur oxides and particulate. These few contrasts have to be carefully evaluated, weighing up costs and benefits, considering specific local situations.

There are then individual behaviours, which can start immediately to demonstrate the reality of the feasible change. Even with efforts and thousand incoherences, each one can play his part.

2.7 No clear threshold for the "dangerous interference with the climate system"

Although one of the milestones of the United Nations Framework Convention on climate change (UNFCCC) is the objective "*to achieve stabilization of greenhouse gas concentrations in the atmosphere at a level that would prevent dangerous anthropogenic interference with the climate system"*, no political consensus has been reached about what this "dangerous interference" is, and therefore what threshold level of global warming could be considered "acceptable".

The Paris Accord, signed in December 2015 by nearly all the 195 countries represented within the UNFCCC, has set as the objective of international climate policies, to hold "*the increase in the global average temperature to well below 2 °C above pre-industrial levels and to pursue efforts to limit the temperature increase to 1.5 °C above pre-industrial levels, recognizing that this would significantly reduce the risks and impacts of climate change*".

This ambitious goal raised an important discussion within the negotiation. It is worth remembering that the target of limiting the global average temperature increase to 2°C above pre-industrial levels has been identified as a climate policy objective since the middle of 1990s, and it was subsequently recognized and adopted in the international negotiations in 2009 in the Copenhagen Accord.

Scientific evidence has successfully shown that no clear threshold for the "dangerous interference with the climate system" exists. Furthermore, the different version of the "burning embers" diagrams, that summarize the relationships between various impacts reflected in five "reasons for concern"[4] and increases in global average temperature, from the first published in the Summary for Policymakers of the IPCC's Third Assessment Report (TAR)-WG2 to the update in 2011 by Smith et al, to the last version in the IPCC-AR5 (Figure 2.4), point out that there would be significant residual impacts even with a warming of 1.5°C.

Experts emphasized the meaningful differences between 1.5°C and 2°C of warming regarding the level of risk from ocean acidification and from extreme events or tipping points. The conclusion of the "expert dialogue" within the UNFCCC concluded that

> *Some benefits of scenarios with 1.5°C instead of 2°C of warming were identified and include the following: most terrestrial and marine species would be able to follow the speed of climate change; up to half of coral reefs may remain; sea level rise may remain below 1 m; some Arctic sea ice may remain; ocean acidification impacts would stay at moderate levels; and more scope for adaptation would exist, especially in the agricultural sector.*
>
> (Climate Analytics, 2015)

The scientific comprehension that many impacts projected for a global warming level of 2°C relative to pre-industrial levels may exceed the coping capacities of particularly vulnerable countries helped many countries in advocating limiting warming to below 1.5 °C, and the term *target requested by science*, although not precise, has become a *leitmotiv* in the climate change debate.

Although no safe zone exists, it is worth remembering that the quick reduction of greenhouse-gas emissions to limit the average global temperature rise to about

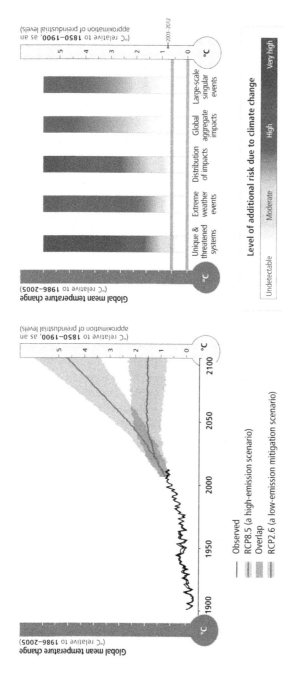

Figure 2.4 Risks associated with reasons for concern are shown at right for increasing levels of climate change. The colour shading indicates the additional risk due to climate change when a temperature level is reached and then sustained or exceeded.

Source: IPCC, AR5-WG2, Fig. SPM2 (IPCC, 2014b).

1.5–2°C could just reduce the so-called "long term commitment" of global warming, avoiding major catastrophic consequences that may change the face of our planet; i.e., this is considered as the only possibility to avoid the destabilization of the Antarctic ice sheet and the sea-level increase of several meters in the next centuries.

2.8 The long-term commitment

As mentioned before, there is a clear the link between the causes (greenhouse gases emissions and deforestation) and the consequences (the warming of the atmosphere and oceans, ice melting, sea level rise, impacts on ecosystems and human activities) of climate change. But there are two factors which make the link between causes and effects different from the one of other environmental issues, also on a global scale, which humanity has dealt with.

The first factor causing the long-term commitment is the long permanence of CO_2 in the atmosphere: this gas is highly stable in the atmosphere, and unlike the other GHGs it can be removed from the atmosphere in the very long term, only through the slow deposit in the ocean floor; consequently, roughly one-fifth of the emitted CO_2 stays in the atmosphere for thousands of years, and it is fundamentally perennial on a human lifetime time-scale. Other gases as methane and nitrous oxide have a shorter lifetime in atmosphere; but CO_2 has this peculiarity, so the impact of today's human activities on climate affects hundreds future generations.

Since a relevant part of anthropogenic climate change is due to CO_2 emissions (about 80 percent of the anthropogenic forcing in the climate system since pre-industrial times), a part of the climate change of the next decades will be irreversible on time scale of millennia, unless CO_2 is removed from the atmosphere through carbon capture and storage (CCS), a solution technologically and economically unfeasible today at the required large scale.

The increased confidence that the projected impacts of anthropogenic climate change due to GHGs, emitted in the next decades, will persist for a time frame of many millennia, is at odds with most of scientific and policy debate on climate change, based on climate projection and socio-economic evaluation of impacts for the twenty-first century.

The second factor making global warming so dangerous is the inertia of the climate system and of some of his relevant component such as the Greenland and Antarctica ice sheets. Once the ocean warms up, these colossal ice sheets loose mass, but it takes decades to reach a level that could induce destabilization and irreversible melting. The loss of ice lasts long after emission are stabilized or start to decline, or after the energy imbalance of the planet starts to reverse. Recent studies, developing a better understanding of how the ocean and atmosphere affect the ice sheet, concluded that continued growth in GHGs emissions over the next several decades could trigger an unstoppable collapse of Antarctica's ice, raising sea levels by more than a meter by 2100 and more than 15 meters by 2500 (DeConto and Pollard, 2016); the ice sheet will not be able to recover until the oceans cool back down, a process that could take thousands of years. As stated by

Clark et al. (2016) *"many key features of future climate change are relatively certain in the long term, even if the precise timing of their occurrence is uncertain"* (Clark et al., 2016).

Although the long-term commitment of anthropogenic climate change induced by emissions in this century has already been pointed out by research published in the previous decade, and summarized in the Chapter 12 of the IPCC-AR5-WG1 (Collins et al., 2013), the improved understanding of the ice sheet dynamics allows a better understanding of sea-level change over the next 10,000 years, as shown in Figure 2.5 for a medium-low emissions scenario (Clark et al., 2016). Sea level continue is raising long after emissions are stopped and CO_2 concentrations in the atmosphere decrease.

This leads to the necessity to view near-term climate changes in the context of a long-term perspective, to address the possibility that human actions may initiate future global climate change on a geological time-scale rather than on a scale of a few human generations.

Only a very low emission pathway for the next three to four decades allows to avoid significant ice-sheet disintegration and to contain the sea level increase to few meters (DeConto and Pollard, 2016). Policy decisions made during this time-frame are likely to result in changes to earth's climate system measured in millennia rather than human lifespans, along with associated socioeconomic and ecological impacts that will exacerbate the risks and damages to society and ecosystems projected for the twenty-first century and propagate into the future for many thousands of years.

The very long-term effect induced by CO_2 implies that policy decisions made in the next few decades will have impacts on global climate, ecosystems and human societies for the next ten millennia and beyond.

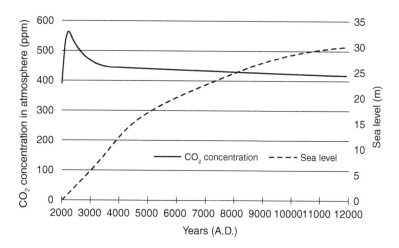

Figure 2.5 Temporal evolution of atmospheric CO_2 concentration and sea level in a scenario with a total emission of 1260 GtC.

Adapted from data in Clark et al., 2016. CO_2 data from model ensemble; sea level from Uvic 2.8.

2.9 The carbon budget and the carbon bubble

By now, one clear hint is that the amount of global carbon emissions (in form of CO_2) released in the atmosphere determines the level of global temperature increase: the more emissions, the more emissions accumulate in the atmosphere, the temperature will increase. Thus, wishing to limit the global temperature increase to a predefined level (for instance 1.5°C or 2°C higher than in the pre-industrial era), the almost linear relation between global temperatures and accumulated CO_2 emissions identifies an overall budget of CO_2 emissions that cannot be surpassed. A part of this budget has already been used by the emissions released so far, while the remaining part is still available for the emissions of coming years and future generations. Uncertainty in the evaluation of the link between emissions and temperature makes the relation a bit more complicated, because it requires the introduction of emission intervals or probabilities of overshooting a given temperature increase threshold. Yet this approach is useful to clarify the terms of the climatic change problem: an upper limit to the temperatures of our planet implies a limit to the emissions; higher emission rates in the coming decades entail lower emissions afterwards.

For example, in order to have at least a 66 percent probability of keeping the global warming within 2°C higher than in the 1860–1880 period (used as a reference time for the pre-industrial era), the accumulated emissions from all anthropogenic sources must be less than 790 billion tons of carbon (Gt C) (2,890 Gt of CO_2). This limit compares with the amount of approximately 515 Gt C (1,890 Gt CO_2) already emitted by human activities (since 1870 to 2011). In other words, if we aim to limit, with a good probability, the global temperatures increase to 2°C, roughly 65 percent of the available carbon space has already been exhausted; the consequence is that the present and the future generations will have to share the residual 35 percent. A lower warming limit, or a higher probability of staying below the limit, implies a smaller budget of CO_2 emissions, thus a smaller supply for present and future activities.

Since the cumulative carbon emissions between 2016 and 2050 need to be limited to around 1,000 Gt CO_2, the reduction of the present emissions, roughly corresponding to 9.8 Gt C (36 Gt CO_2) per year, turns then to be unavoidable. At the present emission rate, the available budget would be completely exhausted in less than 30 years. Considering that the emissions in the last decade have grown at approximately the rate of 2 percent per year, the challenge is clearly tremendous. A substantial cut of global emissions is needed, in a few decades.

There is much more coal, oil or gas underground than what is enough to damage the climate of our planet. In order not to trespass the 2°C limit, a first reference point for the international negotiation on climate, we need to leave at least three quarters of the known fossil fuels underground.

An integrated assessment model considering estimates of quantities, locations and nature of the world's oil, gas and coal reserves and resources, has shown the implications of carbon budget on fossil fuel production in different regions. According to recent studies (McGlade and Ekins, 2015), *"globally, a third of oil reserves, half of gas reserves and over 80 per cent of current coal*

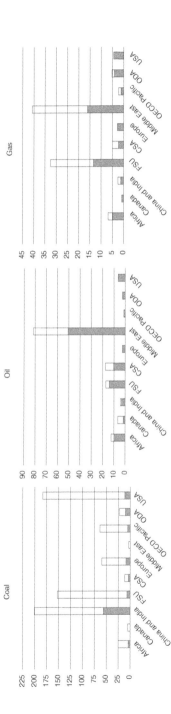

Figure 2.6 Regional distribution of burnable and unburnable carbon reserves before 2050 for the 2°C scenarios, without CCS.

Source: Elaborated from Table 1 in McGlade and Ekins, 2015; an average carbon content in coal, oil and gas have been assumed.

reserves should remain unused from 2010 to 2050 in order to meet the target of 2°C"; in area such as United States and Former Soviet Union more than 90 percent of coal reserves should remain below ground and about 40 percent of oil and 60 percent of gas reserves in the Middle East should remain unburned. All Arctic resources and a large percentage of unconventional oil and gas should not be exploited.

The comprehension that unabated use of all current fossil fuel reserves is incompatible with a warming limit of 2°C has profound consequences on energy strategies that financial investors have begun to discuss.

Looking at the percentage of carbon stored in proven reserves of each fossil fuel, it becomes clear that limiting the use of coal plays a major role in reducing emissions. As shown in Figure 2.6, the major portion of carbon that should be kept in the ground is in the coal reserves of China, India, former Soviet Union and United States.

Keeping emissions within an appropriate carbon budget means that the current financial system needs to face a growing risk to waste capitals and strand carbon assets, known as the "carbon bubble" (Carbon Tracker Initiative, 2013). To minimize the risks for investors and savers, capital investment in the energy sector needs to be redirected away from high-carbon options. There is a growing understanding that regulators and investors need to review their approach to systemic risks, as conventional business model of recycling fossil fuel revenues into replacing reserves should be no longer valid: capitals should not be used for fossil fuel exploration and developing more reserves, they should be invested in low-carbon

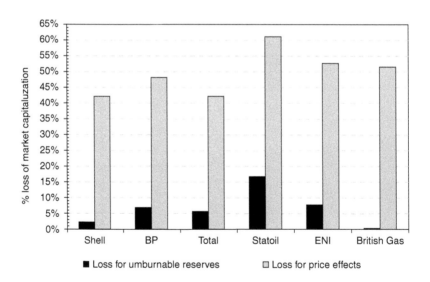

Figure 2.7 Loss of value for European oil and gas companies due to unburnable reserves and price effect.

Source: Elaborated from Spedding, Mehta, and Robins, 2013.

opportunities. In a carbon-constrained world, any new discovery could not lead to increased aggregate production.

Many financial analysts in the last years rise the concern on the risk posed by the carbon bubble to the market capitalization value of coal, oil and gas companies. The collapse of major coal producer in 2015 shows the concreteness of the threat. For example, Figure 2.7 shows the assessment made by HSBC of the value of the reserves potentially at risk due to "unburnable" carbon for the major European oil and gas industries. Although not directly linked to the need to restrict carbon emissions, there is an additional risk of loss due to a price effect: even though some existing assets may be still commercial, their value would fall if weaker demand led to lower oil and gas prices.

2.10 Conclusions

Even if scientific uncertainties haven't all been solved and human activities are not the only responsible of all climate changes, the knowledge of the climatic system and the large amount of fossil reserves available imply a strict emission budget for the next decades. Although the Paris Accord has been signed by nearly all the heads of States and is widely recognized as a success, many decision makers at different administrative levels fail to acknowledge the consequences of the Accord, the striking timing of the change that it requires. The timing implied by the carbon budget is that the transition to net zero carbon emissions worldwide has to be achieved between 2045 and 2060 (Rogelj et al., 2015).

Pursuing the objective of the Paris Accord, to limit global temperature increase "well below 2°C", requires thus a significant deviation from the policy trend of the last decades, characterized by lack of ambition, limits of scope and shameful delays. Immediate actions and profound transformations in every individual sector of the economy are needed. Emissions reduction should be very fast, much faster than what imposed by previous commitments. Only in a few decades it will be necessary to change the present energy system, to deliver a profound near-term de-carbonization of energy supply and simultaneously to satisfy the growing energy demand.

The next decades are a brief window of opportunity to minimize large-scale and potentially catastrophic climate change that will extend longer than the entire history of human civilization. If the pathways of the international effort to limit the increase in global temperature will stop, there will not be another option, it will not be possible to try again later with the same objectives.

Notes

1 IPCC reports can be fully consulted and are downloadable for free at the web site: www. ipcc.ch.
2 See for example: Kahan et al., 2012.
3 A review is available in different reports, accessible on web-sites: UCS, 2007; Greenpeace, 2010; IFG, 2011.

4 The five reasons for concern considered are: (1) Unique and threatened systems, including ecosystems and cultures. (2) Extreme weather events, such as heat waves, extreme precipitation, and coastal flooding. (3) Distribution of impacts: risks are unevenly distributed and are generally greater for disadvantaged people and communities in countries at all levels of development. (4) Global aggregate impacts, on Earth's biodiversity, ecosystem wealth and services and the overall global economy. (5) Large-scale singular events, risk of abrupt and irreversible changes to physical systems or ecosystems, such as warm-water coral reef, Arctic ice and ecosystems, or irreversible sea level rise from ice sheet loss.

References

Carbon Tracker Initiative (2013). *Unburnable carbon 2013: Wasted capital and stranded assets*. http://carbontracker.live.kiln.digital/Unburnable-Carbon-2-Web-Version.pdf

Clark, P., et al. (2016). Consequences of twenty-first-century policy for multi-millennial climate and sea-level change. *Nature climate change*, 6, 360–369.

Climate Analytics (2015). *1.5°C risks and feasibility*. http://climateanalytics.org/files/1o5_key_points.pdf

Collins, M., Knutti, R., Arblaster, J., Dufresne, J.-L., Fichefet, T., Friedlingstein, P., Gao, X., Gutowski, W.J., Johns, T., Krinner, G., Shongwe, M., Tebaldi, C., Weaver, A.J., and Wehner, M. (2013). Chap. 12: Long-term climate change: Projections, commitments and irreversibility. In T.F. Stocker, D. Qin, G.-K. Plattner, M. Tignor, S.K. Allen, J. Boschung, A. Nauels, Y. Xia, V. Bex and P.M. Midgley (eds.), *climate change 2013: The Physical Science Basis. Contribution of Working Group I to the Fifth Assessment Report of the Intergovernmental Panel on climate change*, Cambridge and New York, Cambridge University Press.

DeConto, R.M., and Pollard, D. (2016). Contribution of Antarctica to past and future sea-level rise. *Nature*, 351, 597–601.

Doran, P.T., and Zimmerman, M.K. (2009). Examining the scientific consensus on climate change. *EOS*, 90(3), 22–23.

Forster, P., Ramaswamy, V., Artaxo, P., Berntsen, T., Betts, R., Fahey, D.W., Haywood, J., Lean, J., Lowe, D.C., Myhre, G., Nganga, J., Prinn, R., Raga, G., Schulz, M., and Van Dorland, R. (2007) Chap. 2: Changes an Atmospheric constituents and in radiative forcing. In S. Solomon, D. Qin, M. Manning, Z. Chen, M. Marquis, K.B. Averyt, M. Tignor and H.L. Miller (eds.), *climate change 2007: The Physical Science Basis. Contribution of Working Group I to the Fourth Assessment Report of the Intergovernmental Panel on climate change*, Cambridge and New York, Cambridge University Press.

Greenpeace (2010). *Dealing in doubt: The climate denial industry and climate science*.

IFG (2011) *Outing the oligarchy: Billionaires who benefit from today's climate crisis*, International Forum on Globalization.

IPCC (2013). Summary for Policymakers. In: *Climate change 2013: The Physical Science Basis. Contribution of Working Group I to the Fifth Assessment Report of the Intergovernmental Panel on climate change* [Stocker, T.F., D. Qin, G.-K. Plattner, M. Tignor, S. K. Allen, J. Boschung, A. Nauels, Y. Xia, V. Bex and P.M. Midgley (eds.)], 15.

IPCC (2014a). *Climate change 2014: Synthesis Report. Contribution of Working Groups I, II and III to the Fifth Assessment Report of the Intergovernmental Panel on climate change*, Core Writing Team, R.K. Pachauri and L.A. Meyer (eds.), Geneva, Switzerland, IPCC, 151.

IPCC (2014b). *Fifth Assessment Report (AR5) climate change 2014: Impacts, adaptation, and vulnerability*. Intergovernmental Panel on climate change. www.ipcc.ch

Jacobson, M., and Delucchi, M. (2011). Providing all global Energy with wind, water and solar power. *Energy Policy*, 39(3), 1154–1169.

Jansen, E., J. Overpeck, K.R. Briffa, J.-C. Duplessy, F. Joos, V. Masson-Delmotte, D. Olago, B. Otto-Bliesner, W.R. Peltier, S. Rahmstorf, R. Ramesh, D. Raynaud, D. Rind, O. Solomina, R. Villalba and D. Zhang, 2007: *Palaeoclimate. In: Climate change 2007: The Physical Science Basis. Contribution of Working Group I to the Fourth Assessment Report of the Intergovernmental Panel on climate change* [Solomon, S., D. Qin, M. Manning, Z. Chen, M. Marquis, K.B. Averyt, M. Tignor and H.L. Miller (eds.)]. Cambridge University Press, Cambridge, United Kingdom and New York, NY, USA.

Kahan, D., et al. (2012). The polarizing impact of science literacy and numeracy on perceived climate change risks. *Nature climate change*, 2, 732–735.

McGlade, C., and Ekins, P. (2015). The geographical distribution of fossil fuels unused when limiting global warming to 2 °C. *Nature*, 517, 187–190.

NSIDC (2012). *Arctic sea ice extent settles at record seasonal minimum*. National Snow and Ice Data Center. http://nsidc.org/arcticseaicenews/2012/09/

Rogelj, J., Luderer, G., Pietzcker, R.C., Kriegler, E., Schaeffer, M., Krey, V., and Riahi, K. (2015). Energy system transformations for limiting end-of-century warming to below 1.5 °C. *Nature climate change*, 5, 519–528.

Spedding, P., Mehta, K., and Robins, N. (2013) *Oil & Carbon Revisited: Value at Risk From "Unburnable" Reserves*, HSBC Global Research.

UCS (2007) *Smoke, Mirrors & Hot Air*, Union of Concerned Scientists.

University of Queesland (2015). Making sense of climate science denial. *edX Course*. www.edx.org/course/making-sense-climate-science-denial-uqx-denial101x-0#!

3 Limits for a growing complexity system

Angelo Tartaglia

Generally, the public awareness about the physical constraints on a pretendedly ever growing economy is concentrated on the issues of the finiteness of the physical resources available on the planet earth and on the impact of human activities on the environment, in terms of pollution and climate changes. These are indeed the topics that have been addressed in the previous two chapters of this book.

There is, however, an aspect which is largely overlooked, though being of paramount importance, as we shall see. It concerns the issue of the *complexity* of our society and of our economic system and especially the fact that such complexity, if the system grows, will also grow.

Definitions

In order to consistently speak about *complexity*, we must start defining what complexity is. Unfortunately, there is no unique definition beyond the intuitive meaning of the word, so I shall try the simplest and resort to graphs and networks. A quantitative formulation of the complexity of a system, implicitly defining what I mean, can be the number of relations or links, L, in a network where the number of interconnected nodes or poles is N. A definition like this is a bit fuzzy, because I have not specified whether the reference is to the active links or to the totality of possible links. For the moment let us maintain this ambiguity, which will be removed case-by-case when needed.

We are of course interested in physical systems, so, even though at the beginning a number of abstract considerations will be done, all our case studies and examples will be on material situations. When mentioning "links", I always mean channels along which something tangible flows. Provided that there is a material basis, the arguments will not be different for bits or tons or kWh or cubic meters and so on. In this respect, the complex system we will be considering may well be an economy interpreted as a network of exchange relations between different actors.

An important aspect to be taken into account is that the system under analysis is assumed to be growing, because this is the feature that, according to classical economy and political refrains, must be insured and kept for the health of our societies. Even though, listening to non-technical speeches and reading newspapers, we could sometime be led to think that the term *growth* simply is some synonym of welfare, happy life and similar concepts, it must be stressed that the economic growth in our present world always has a material basis. Most often facts about economy are expressed and measured in terms of money, but we should remember that money is a human convention essentially accounting for the relative (buying) power of different persons within a given society; in other words, money expresses differential access rights to the *existing* wealth. In the real world, no stock exchange "miracles", creating and annihilating in one day enormous fortunes, happen: before and after a sudden rise or collapse of the stock market, the material wealth in the world is exactly the same. Any real growth has consequently a material basis and can and must be measured in physical units: tons, kWh, cubic meters, etc.

After this premise, let us consider a network where the number of nodes increases with time and have a look to the number of possible links among the nodes. The progression is sketched in Figure 3.1, where it is clearly visible that the number of connections grows faster than the number of nodes. The relation is simply obtained counting the number of independent pairs which can be identified in a set of N objects; i.e.,

$$L = \frac{N(N-1)}{2} \qquad \text{(Eq. 3.1)}$$

We have implicitly assumed that all nodes are equivalent and any of them can be connected with any other; furthermore, no upper limit to the number of connections which can be harboured by a single node has been considered. These assumptions, but especially the last one, are unphysical, but the example clarifies the simplest dynamics of complexity.

In a real network, be it a computer web or a commercial set of exchanges or a transportation system or else, the poles are specialized and grouped into

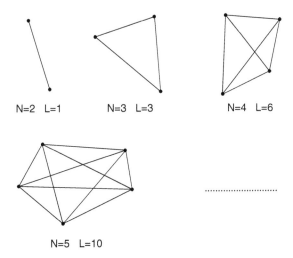

N=2 L=1   N=3 L=3   N=4 L=6

N=5 L=10

Figure. 3.1 A series of graphs showing that, when the number of nodes grows, the number of relations grows faster.

different classes; what matters more is that they have a finite capacity of physical connections. In any case, the message is that when the net grows the complexity grows faster.

Saturation

An additional consideration that looks trivial, given its obviousness, is that all exchange channels are subject to physical saturation. You may think of a road, a canal, a duct, a band for communication of electromagnetic signals, an optical fibre, an electric wire; in short, of any means allowing for transfer from an origin to a destination. Depending on the physical nature of the link, you know and verify that there is an upper limit to the flux it can carry. If there is any reason for the flow to try and continue to grow, the actual transfer rate will necessarily tend to saturation; when starting for the first time to use the channel the flux will be small, then gradually increasing, until the expansion rate will be obliged to decline and the conveyance to stabilize. This well-known behaviour id described by a *logistic* curve like the one shown in Figure 3.2.

The functional form of a logistic is:

$$f = \frac{F}{1 + e^{-ht}}$$
(Eq. 3.2)

Far in the past (time $t \to -\infty$) the flux f is negligible; far in the future (time $t \to +\infty$) the flux saturates to a maximum F; parameter h determines the "stretching" of the curve; time $t = 0$ is assumed to be at the moment when the flux is midway between 0 and the maximum.

Of course, the real world is more complicated than that and the actual evolution in time of the flow will be more irregular than shown in Figure 3.2. External

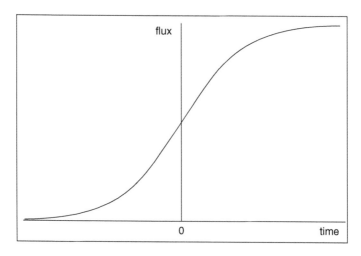

Figure 3.2 Typical logistic curve displaying the behaviour of a growing flux along any finite channel.

perturbations may force the traffic to slow down and reduce for a while, then growing again or oscillating a bit. What matters, however, is that any long-term push towards growth, in the mean, will engender a tendential saturation.

These considerations hold for links, but they may be applied to nodes too. Consider for example a crossroads: the maximum number of converging roads depends on the allotted size of the junction and the average breadth of the roads. Think of an Internet router: it has a maximal number of possible connections depending on the physical properties of its electronic components. We could develop more detailed descriptions distinguishing between upper limits to the number of simultaneous connections and maximum number of manageable exchanges per unit time; the outcome would however be the same: nodes also have saturation.

If then some cursed or blessed push toward growth is unavoidable, even more unavoidably: first, the activated links will tend to the totality of possible links; then the links will tend to individual saturation. To counteract saturation, people will strive to enhance the maximal capacity of the links (for instance, widening the roads, replacing copper wires with optical fibres, broadening the band used for wireless communication, etc.). Eventually, however, the nodes, hubs, crossroads . . . will get saturated. Approaching that condition, the push will be transferred on the nodes and their number will start to grow. However, we have seen above that increasing the nodes will provide a number of new links exceeding by far the number of new nodes. In short, growth will imply a faster growing complexity.

When speaking of nodes, we end up with individual human beings, but actually there is room for even more than the human population. Think to social networks or to professional, religious, sport, recreational . . . communities: each individual may be a member of many independent such groups, acting as a multiple communication pole. The idea of saturation is here easily exemplified when referred to time. In old times, messages were exchanged through messengers who took a long time for their journeys, travelling at most at the speed of a horse (I am not considering visual signalling by fires or flags and the like); between dispatch and reception there was plenty of time for anything else. The introduction of engines, public surface mail service, the telegraph, allowed people to exchange messages within one single day. In Conan Doyle's London and later in Agatha Christy's novels you have the morning and the afternoon mail: still Sherlock Homes and Hercule Poirot had the opportunity to carefully read letters and thoughtfully write answers saving time to ponder the mysteries they were involved in. An enormous revolution happened when electronic mail was introduced, making communication at any distance almost instantaneous. At the beginning, this innovation incredibly enhanced the efficiency of information exchange: you could acquire missing knowledge in real time, reduced dead times and had more ease for thinking and working. However, the system also increased the number of connectable origins and destinations of the messages (the nodes of the net) and the number of incoming mails started to grow faster than the number of prospective interlocutors. The avalanche of messages is now exploding, so that one has to contrive defence strategies and in general the time allotted to select, sort and read mails is much more than it was for Sherlock Holmes; globally we have today less time for activities other than handling the mail, than in the past. So much so that even reading long mails is a disturbingly time-consuming activity and new forms of short messaging have been introduced, such as tweeting.

The above is a typical example of progressive saturation, overwhelming the advantages initially brought in by the growth of the system.

Combining the saturation of the links with that of the nodes, the system, if it has to grow, *must* keep on growing also in complexity at a rate in the order of the square of the increase of its physical size.

Wealth and growth

In an economic system, the network described above is destined to produce an ever growing wealth which is made of things and services evaluated by their price. What is intended to grow is that money valued set of things and services. I am not claiming I can provide here a global credible model of an economy, but I can try to introduce a reasonable link between economy and the exchange network mentioned in the previous section. Whatever flows along the links of the net is manifested as and converted into wealth (possibly additional wealth) in the nodes of the grid. This is easy to understand in the case of a factory: inflowing raw materials are converted into goods at the factory and the products are then conveyed to the markets through the same connections that allowed the arrival of the materials needed to feed the activity of the factory.

Oversimplifying, we may assume that the production of "wealth" is proportional to the number of nodes. It is at the "nodes" that we tally incomes and losses, actually converting the incoming and outgoing fluxes into real wealth. The exchange along the links does not produce anything *per se*; it is in the knots that row materials, information, intermediate products, are converted into new additional riches. I should add that the whole machinery is kept working by a continuous extraction of primary resources from the surrounding environment. The extraction is reasonably and more or less linearly related to the number of nodes. This relation is what matters here, without calling in directly the finiteness of all natural reservoirs, which is the subject of the first two chapters. The reality is much more complicated than what is outlined here, since a node needs the exchange flows in order to work, however, in a bird's eye view, and disregarding the details, the idea of a direct connection between the number of nodes and the wealth being produced looks reasonable.

On the other side, a communication and exchange network needs maintenance in order to insure efficiency. Now it is reasonable to expect that the cost for that maintenance be proportional to the number of links in the network. Summing up, the riches produced by the system are more or less proportional to the number of nodes N, whereas the cost of maintenance (and failures, as we shall see shortly) is, roughly speaking, proportional to $N(N-1)$ (see Eq. 3.1).

Among the desiderata of classical economists (and traditional rulers), is a steady rate growth of wealth. The corresponding time dependence of riches is represented by an exponential:

$$W = W_0 e^{kt}$$

(Eq. 3.3)

W_0 is the existing wealth at time $t = 0$; k is the growth rate, usually expressed as a fraction of W.

It is well known that an exponential growth has no ceiling, then it is unphysical, but this is not the issue now. According to the gross description above, a consequence of (3.3) is that N should also grow more or less at the same rate, and a consequence of the consequence is that the cost C of maintenance is expressed by

$$C \propto N_0 e^{kt} \left(N_0 e^{kt} - 1 \right)$$ (Eq. 3.4)

As anticipated (and obvious), C grows faster than W. We may visually render the situation plotting (3.3) and (3.4) under the assumption that both wealth and cost are expressed in the same units. The resulting graph is shown in Figure 3.3a. Figure 3.3b presents the difference between gross wealth and costs of maintenance of the network. As it is clearly seen, after an increasing return phase a shorter and steeper descent follows, ending in the annihilation of the net gain.

The curve in Figure 3.3b is, in a sense, universal, at least in its shape. It is indeed found in different fields, but always related with something trying to grow against material constraints. Something like that describes the rise and fall of ancient civilizations, from Sumerians to the Roman Empire, and has been described by sociologists, archaeologists and historians; see for instance the book by one of the co-authors of the present work, Joseph Tainter (Chapter 4) (Tainter, 1988). Another of our authors, Ugo Bardi (Chapter 1), nicknamed graph (3.3b) "Seneca's curve", from the *Epistulae morales ad Lucilium* (moral letters to Lucilius, written by Seneca in the first century A.D.), letter 91.6, where one reads "*incrementa lente exeunt, festinatur in damnum*" (improvement comes slowly, one hurries in harm).

Just to have an idea also of the quantities, let me specify that the diagrams in Figure 3.3 have been obtained assuming that initially the cost of "maintenance" in the exchange process be 1 percent of the gross income and that the steady growth rate

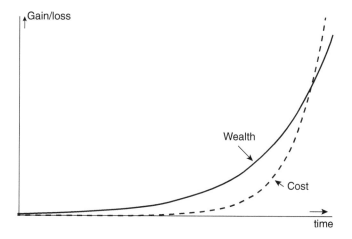

Figure 3.3a Time evolution of wealth and cost of maintenance, in a steadily growing system.

56   *Angelo Tartaglia*

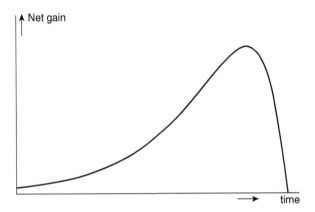

Figure 3.3b Time evolution of the net gain in the system shown in Fig. 3.3a.

of the economy be 2 percent per year. In that case, the time to reach the top of the net gain would be approximately 200 years, with a duration of the whole process of 230 years. Of course, the assumptions are arbitrary but not completely unrelated with reality. If the initial cost is 30 percent of the gross product, everything lasts 60 years.

Safety and control

It is the case to try and say something more about "maintenance" of the network. In fact, within the expenditure related to the links we may easily recognize two components. One is simply due to the fact that any physical process controlled by technology is of course subjected to the risk of failure and along the links of our (economic) network physical processes travel and happen. Any engine, any road, any device (be it mechanical or chemical or electronic, etc.) can undergo malfunctions, breakdowns, accidents. Whenever such an event happens there is also an economic loss, a cost. The total number of failures, being the rest unchanged, is proportional to the total flux through the link; if the flux grows the same happens to the number of "accidents". An easy example are car crashes: their expected number per year is proportional to the traffic density on the road.

The first component is then an obviously unwanted damage, i.e., a loss. Even damages in our peculiar system may be accounted on the positive side, corresponding to specialized jobs for repairs and recovery from "failures", but undoubtedly it means that part of gross wealth is tied to maintenance of the system and diverted from the production of new riches. As we have described it, the global damage D may be expressed by means of a rule of thumb formula:

$$D = \delta \varepsilon f L = \delta \varepsilon f \frac{N(N-1)}{2}$$

(Eq. 3.5)

where, besides the total number of links and the average flux per link f, the conversion factor to the units for wealth, δ, and the average failure probability ε appear.

So far, this little analysis does not modify the information contained in (3.4), but we have to consider a second component of the maintenance cost announced above. In general people want to prevent failure and damage and this may, in principle, be achieved acting on the value of ε in order to make it as small as possible and keep it stable. An interesting quantity to consider is the ratio of the total "damage" D to the total "wealth" W; recalling Eq. (3.5) and remembering that W is proportional to N we see that:

$$\frac{D}{W} \propto \varepsilon f(N-1) \tag{Eq. 3.6}$$

In times of growth the ratio of D to W grows at the same rate as N, provided the average flux through a link, f, and ε stay constant. However, the damage D corresponds not only to a negative accounting item in the calculation of wealth. It has a counterpart in accidents, annoyances, malfunctions which have a social impact. The social demand and pressure is then to keep it under control and even, especially while the average income grows, to reduce it or at least maintain it under some absolute tolerable level D_M. If so, from Eq. (3.6) we deduce that, in order to insure the stability of D/W, it should be $\varepsilon \propto e^{-kt}$; we know, however, that the failure rate ε cannot physically be reduced to zero. Calling ε_* the asymptotic minimum value and ε_0 the value at time $t = 0$ it could be at most:

$$\varepsilon = \varepsilon_* + (\varepsilon_0 - \varepsilon_*)e^{-kt} \tag{Eq. 3.7}$$

So, sooner or later, D/W would start to grow at the same rate as N grows, i.e., the losses from damage would grow much faster than the riches the system produces. Furthermore, the reduction of ε has a cost which must be considered and represents the second component of the total required expense for keeping the system working.

The role of technology

As already stressed many times, the description in the previous section is an oversimplified one. It treats all nodes and links on the same footing, whereas in the real world strong differences and hierarchies exist. Without underrating this fact, we have seen that we could, however, think of reducing somehow, at least for a while, the damage from "failures" and/or their occurrence frequency, acting on ε; but is it possible? The answer is yes: resorting to technology, optimal management and various measures to improve the efficiency of the exchange across the network.

In fact, car crashes in analogous circumstances are today less dangerous than, say, 50 years ago, because contemporary cars are safer than in the past; road traffic is better organized and controlled than decades ago. Another simple example are LED lamps that do last much longer than old incandescent bulbs and are much less subject to failure; and so on.

However, as already said, technology has a cost. This trivial remark must be considered with care. Technological improvements easily appear as investments which lead to enhancements in productivity, then in the growth of global wealth. The productivity affecting the way nodes work may reduce a bit the growth rate of the number of nodes, making it somewhat milder than in (3.4). Technology is then a factor driving growth, but in the same time it is a price paid to safety.

In the previous section we assumed, for the sake of simplicity, to be trying to keep the ratio between damage and wealth constant, at a socially accepted level, while maintaining a growing trend in the total revenue. As a consequence, the risk of failure per exchange event (per single journey, per transmitted bit, etc.) had to gradually diminish, as in (3.7), in order to compensate for the increasing complexity of the system. The problem is that the cost of improvements is in turn not fixed. When the efficiency of a device is very low, a little enhancement (and little expenditure) produces great results; however, when the efficiency is already good, in order to ameliorate it further you have to spend much more. "Failures" are less and less dangerous; socially this is good, but you have to account elsewhere for the cost of the control of safety and this is more and more relevant. This trend is a peculiar manifestation of what economists call the diminishing return law.

Let us try to write down some formal expression of the link between the probability of accident, malfunctioning, etc. during one transfer through any link, ε, and the amount spent to reduce failures and prevent damages. Even though both the occurrence of damages and the expenditure for improving safety are discontinuous processes, we suppose to spread them continuously. Considering the already mentioned fact that ε has an asymptotic lowest value ε_*, similarly as for the time evolution, the dependence of ε on the expenditure for safety will be like the one shown in Figure 3.4.

As it is clearly seen, the cost per unit improvement increases progressively and diverges, while tending to the asymptote. Many different formulae can describe

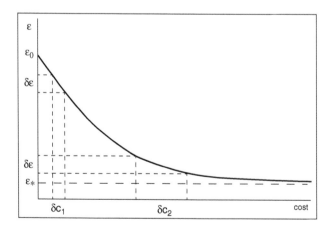

Figure 3.4 Reduction of risk as a function of cost. It is graphically shown that the same improvement has a greater cost when the risk is already small, than when the safety is poor.

such behaviour; let us try the same functional form as for time, Eq. (3.7), and write:

$$\varepsilon = \varepsilon_* + \left(\varepsilon_0 - \varepsilon_*\right)e^{-q(k-k_0)} \tag{Eq. 3.8}$$

The cost of innovation for safety (per year) is κ (κ_0 is the value at $t = 0$) and the evolution of ε towards the asymptote is controlled by the parameter q. Under these conditions we have a cost growing linearly with time. This expense, summed to (3.5), gives the total cost associated to the way the global network operates.

A simple model

We have worked out four elements that contribute to the way social and economic machines work, according to the prevailing ideology. They are the growth of the gross wealth, the growth of complexity, the damage from faults of the exchange along the network of links, the expenditure for improving the efficiency and safety of the exchange.

It is time to try and sew the elements together in order to build a model, whose purpose is not to provide detailed predictions, as rating agencies use to do with disastrous reliability rates that nobody cares to verify. The aim is to confirm or disprove evolution trends and, at most, to point out orders of magnitude of critical times.

Recall then the intention, mentioned above, of keeping the global occurrence of "failures" under a socially acceptable threshold and to hold it fixed. As we have seen, the total loss or damage D has been expressed in formula (3.5) and we have seen that the "safety" demand would require a decreasing value of ε according to (3.7). To insure the attainment of that aim the expenditure for safety κ should increase linearly with time:

$$k = k_0 + \frac{k}{q}t \tag{Eq. 3.9}$$

Feeding this and (3.8) into Eq. (3.7), then adding again (3.9), the total cost/loss (per annum) is:

$$C = k_0 + \frac{k}{q}t + \frac{\delta f}{2}\left(\varepsilon_* + \left(\varepsilon_0 - \varepsilon_*\right)e^{-kt}\right)N_0e^{kt}\left(N_0e^{kt} - 1\right) \tag{Eq. 3.10}$$

Qualitatively this total cost confronted with W reproduces a trend similar to the one shown in Figure 3.3, but shortening the time required to reach the zero-gain condition.

Differences

The network we have considered so far is alive because of the fluxes going back and forth along its links, but it is now time to call in a new physical analogy. A current flows along a channel only when there is a difference in height at the ends. In the case of electric currents, this elementary rule has the form of the simple Ohm's law: the current is proportional to the potential difference applied to the wire. For what concerns us here, let us say that the drivers of an economy based on exchange are differences. The nature of the differences is varied and not as immediate as for Ohm's law, but the principle is clear. Still using an electric similarity, we must consider that the same difference can move opposite mutually compensating flows (opposite "charges"), but in this case there is no added value. The economy we are analyzing and criticizing in this book assumes growth as a "must", which means that differences must be dynamical and essential to the working of the machine: steady state and compensation of fluxes are banned.

When writing about differences in an economy, the situation is not as simple as in the case of electric potentials or level drops for water channels. Now social issues are involved and differences are perceived both as a stimulus to compete (this is what usually maintain those who already have advantages from a given social order) and as something bad to be overcome in order to offer fair conditions to anybody. The prevailing ideology tries to reconcile the two faces of differences by continuous growth; the idea is simple: if the total wealth grows there will always be something for everybody, even at the bottom of the social hierarchy. The point is, however, as we know, that the material wealth is necessarily limited for physical reasons; what about growth, then?

Is it possible to keep fluxes growing in a finite primary resources world? Yes, it is indeed possible. The mechanism is explained once more by Ohm's law. You may increase the current across a wire even when the number of available electrons cannot increase; you just may speed up the flux increasing the potential difference at the ends of the wire. Coming back to our economic and social system, the analog of the above says that, in a materially constrained world, the insisted upon growth is progressively transferred from the global wealth to the differences. This phenomenon is already visible around us; even though the situations are different in different parts of the world and, as always, the machinery is quite complicated, Gini's coefficient[1] is worsening in most countries starting from the richest ones. The example of the United States has been acutely described and discussed in (Gordon, 2016). Of course, one has to look over two or three decades in order to evaluate the real trend. There are many examples where transients produce an amelioration over a few years, soon converted into its opposite. Better than by formulae or verbal explanations, the way differences grow in an economic system is perfectly well illustrated by the Monopoly game: at the beginning all players have equal shares of the existing assets; the latter and the playground are finite: at the end of the game one player has everything and the others nothing.

By the way, in an electric network a continuous increase of potential differences among the nodes produces, as said, a generalized augmentation of currents, but sooner or later it leads to disruptions, discharges and fires. The corresponding phenomena on the human side are social unrest, troubles, conflicts and violence. A peculiar form of human "currents" are mass migrations inescapably driven by economic differences and we have clear examples all around the world but especially across the southern borders of Europe.

Economy and thermodynamics

Any economic system, even the one I have schematized as a simple network, is made up of a great number of mutually interacting elements at a scale that calls in the tools of thermodynamics to be described and analyzed. This idea is not new and has been used, in the twentieth century, especially in the works of Georgescu-Roegen (Georgescu-Roegen, 1971). Of course, one must be prudent when translating physical into human concepts. Classical thermodynamics is based on strictly deterministic elementary interactions, which is not the case of a human society; certainly, the laws of thermodynamics ruthlessly apply to the material basis and enveloping contour of any economy. One so arrives, in spite of the stubborn and silly denials of the advocates of the omnipotence of mankind, to the raise of the average temperature of the planet, to the irreversible dispersion of useful materials and to the even more irreversible depletion of any material stock or extra energy source, besides what enters the human layer of the planet from outside.[2]

Here however the most appropriate form of thermodynamics is the statistical one, dealing with probabilistic laws and big numbers. The foundation of this branch of science was laid by Boltzmann at the end of the nineteenth century and the discipline applies at a perfect gas as well as to a human crowd.

Thermodynamics can indeed provide useful insights in the dynamics of a socio-economic system, but a warning is in order. Such fundamental laws as the first and second principles, or powerful concepts such as statistical temperature, internal energy and entropy are all formulated and defined with reference to an equilibrium condition. Our ailed global economy is, by ideological definition and insisted will, out of equilibrium and in a proclaimed state of perpetual growth.

Out of equilibrium thermodynamics has also been developed, but it is less simple to apply than the classical equilibrium version. For our purposes, the most appropriate applications have to do with the propagation and growth of noise in a communication network with respect to the signals one wants to transmit. Furthermore, of paramount importance is the order/disorder dynamics which has to do, in the language of thermodynamics, with *entropy*. We are used to think of a society as being an ordered system, where different functions are well identified and guaranteed in order to keep the system working; order is a necessary condition for the control and governance of any system. Now, in a finite and isolated system, the evolution is necessarily towards increasing disorder: entropy tends to be maximized and in the final equilibrium condition everything tends to have the same relevance and all roles are uniformly mixed up (second principle of thermodynamics). If we want to keep hierarchies, different functions, and, in one word, the control of what happens, the system cannot be isolated and we need to exploit an incoming external flow of energy and to dump the excess entropy outside. This is well known: the dynamical equilibrium of nature in the surface layers of the earth has been insured for millions of years by the incoming solar energy and the thermally radiated out degraded energy, being the control parameter the thermodynamical temperature of the surface, seen from the outer space.

A system trying to perpetually and materially grow does not fit the above scheme. Non-equilibrium thermodynamics is an evolving domain, but it is not the case here to try and discuss very complicated problems related to transients. We simply suppose, as it is often done, that the time evolution be slow enough to allow for the use of concepts typical of the ordinary equilibrium theory, with just an additional time parameter. Furthermore, in the present approach the aspects I am interested in are not the physical ones, undoubtedly of paramount importance, but those having to do with disorder and control. The description I have been using for the economic system is based on a grid where the points of interest are the nodes and the dominant sources of troubles and losses are the links. Let me add now what initially had been left aside: if the network has to be an ordered one there must be a different classification of the nodes, which have to be differently specialized. If they were really equal and undistinguishable from one another, the system would not work and everything would lie in a perfect disorder condition; in other terms, the statistical entropy would be maximal. In order not to be so, we need a permanent flow of resources through the network allowing us to control the processes under way. However, as I always remind, the system wants to grow and we would like to maintain everything under control; let us see whether and to what extent it is possible.

The most appropriate definition of entropy S for our problem is the one of Bolzmann. In formulae it is:

$$S = k_B \ln \mathcal{n} \tag{3.11}$$

Boltzmann's constant k_B is used to convert the result in thermodynamical units; $\mathcal{n}$ is the number of equivalent configurations of the system. In our network we have N nodes, but we expect them to be subdivided into various groups, differing by function and hierarchical position. We may suppose that, within each group, the nodes are equivalent; if so, the number of equivalent configurations in the i_{th} group is given by the number of permutations among the elements of the group, i.e., it is $\mathcal{n}_i = N_i!$.[3]

Considering the whole network we have:

$$N = N_1 + N_2 + N_3 + ... = \sum_1^n N_i$$
$$\mathcal{n} = N! = N_1! N_2! N_3! ..... N_n! \tag{3.12}$$

We suppose N to be growing and the same will be true for the addenda, N_i's, even though we may expect the proportion to be evolving too. In order to make some calculation it is convenient to approximate the factorial by means of the Stirling formula:

$$N! \cong \sqrt{2\pi N} \left(\frac{N}{e} \right)^N \tag{3.13}$$

The next step is to write down the time derivative, $\dfrac{dS}{dt} = \dot{S}$:

$$\dot{S} \cong k_B \left(1 + 2N + 2N \ln \frac{N}{e} \right) \frac{\dot{N}}{2N}$$

The relevant quantity is the relative growth:

$$\frac{\dot{S}}{S} \cong \frac{1+2N+2N\left(\ln N-1\right)}{\ln 2\pi+\left(2N+1\right)\ln N-2N}\frac{\dot{N}}{N} \tag{3.14}$$

The factor multiplying $\dot{N}/N$ is always bigger than 1, tending to 1 when N→∞. In practice, we see that the entropy production is faster than the growth of the system. In other words, if we want to keep the system under control (or in order, which means the same) and growing, we have to dispose of a faster growing amount of entropy to be discharged "elsewhere".

We may think of the entropy issue as a different way to state the same as already evidenced in the previous sections, or we may assume it is an additional contribution. In any case, the fraction of the total wealth to be diverted to the maintenance and control of the system has to grow and the typical evolution of the real advantages earned by keeping the machine working is represented by "Seneca's curve" of Figure 3.3b.

Epilogue

In this chapter, we have introduced some hints to a face of the sustainability problem generally overlooked; i.e., the one related to the control of the economic and social system, which the dominant way of thinking and power structure of contemporary mankind would like to keep growing forever. The inconsistency of this pretense is by now well known in connection with the finiteness of the environment from which we draw all material resources we need for our life style. Equally known, though still sporadically challenged by a few stubborn partisans of business as usual, are the side effects of our growth on the surface of the earth, in terms of climate changes and related consequences.

Here however I have brought to the attention of the reader the fact that in a materially growing system inconveniences of different nature grow usually faster than the system does. This phenomenon remains initially unperceived, so much so that everything looks prosperous and all possible critical comments are shunned as grumbles of jinx; after reaching an optimal condition, however, the degradation of the system falls rapidly eroding and finally nullifying all advantages.

This raise and steep fall behaviour may be recognized in a number of apparently different situations and systems, including living beings. The detailed description of the evolution of an economy is a very difficult task; it may be tried by complicated, highly non-linear, barely reliable mathematical models. One should always be extremely prudent while using such models. I have not tried to build up a formal model, but, rather, I have isolated a small number of structural aspects, which are decisive for the general trend, beyond any detail.

In the last more formal section, everything has been connected to the universal laws of thermodynamics and in particular to the second law, governing the production of entropy, i.e., of disorder, necessarily coupled to any physical process. Growing entropy production here has been interpreted in terms of progressive loss of control of the system. The related phenomenology is made out of social instability, uneven distribution of the advantages, unrest, mass migrations and conflicts: exactly what is under our eyes every day.

Notes

1 Gini's coefficient is a simple index expressing the inequality of the distribution of income in a given society.
2 Geothermal heat from below and solar energy (plus the sun-earth and moon-earth gravitational energy) from above.
3 It is $N! = N \times (N–1) \times (N–2) \times \ldots \times 3 \times 2 \times 1$.

References

Georgescu-Roegen, N. (1971). *The Entropy Law and the Economic Process*, Cambridge, MA, Harvard University Press.
Gordon, R.J. (2016). *The Rise and Fall of American Growth: The U.S. Standard of Living Since the Civil War*, Princeton, NJ, Princeton University Press.
Tainter, J.A. (1988). *The Collapse of Complex Societies*, Cambridge, Cambridge University Press.

4 Depletion *vs.* innovation

The fundamental question of sustainability

Joseph A. Tainter, Deborah Strumsky, Temis G. Taylor, Michelle Arnold, and José Lobo

Near the end of World War II, President Franklin Roosevelt asked Vannevar Bush, director of the wartime Office of Scientific Research and Development, to prepare a report on the post-war role of government in promoting science. In his famous report, Bush wrote: "Advances in science will . . . bring higher standards of living, will lead to the prevention or cure of diseases, will promote conservation of our limited national resources, and will assure means of defence against aggression" (Bush, 1945: 10). This statement, so characteristic of our faith in science, became the basis for the emphasis on innovation that we know today. It is a system that has brought material prosperity in the industrialized countries and high levels of employment. Innovation has fostered the complexity of modern societies. Bush's statement reflects what is called *technological optimism*, a faith in technology to solve problems.

Technological optimism lies at the heart of contrasting narratives about sustainability, and about how our future might emerge. The following quotations are representative of our cultural belief in technology:

> No society can escape the general limits of its resources, but no innovative society need accept Malthusian diminishing returns.
>
> (Barnett and Morse, 1963: 139)

> All observers of energy seem to agree that various energy alternatives are virtually inexhaustible.
>
> (Gordon, 1981: 109)

> By allocation of resources to R&D [research and development], we may deny the Malthusian hypothesis and prevent the conclusion of the doomsday models.
>
> (Sato and Suzawa, 1983: 81)

The alternative view, expressed, for example, by Jared Diamond, is that innovation will not offset resource depletion. Diamond states: A modern societal collapse would be "triggered ultimately by scarcity of environmental resources" (Diamond, 2005: 7). There are significant literatures concurring with technological optimism (e.g., Chu, 2009), and with the contrary view that human activity is approaching earth's limits (e.g., Röckstrom et al., 2009; Brown et al., 2011).

The contrasting narratives of technological optimism and earth limits illustrate the fundamental dilemma of sustainability. This dilemma is: Will we *always* be able to offset resource depletion with innovation? If the answer is yes, then the technological optimists are correct, and sustainability is less of a concern than many believe. If the answer is no, there is indeed reason to be concerned about our future. Our purpose here is to explore whether we can confidently expect that innovation will forever offset depletion.

Certain biases obscure the nature of innovation, and prevent us from understanding it. To explore something that is so fundamental to our lives, it is important to understand these biases. The biases are:

1   Since we live in a period of institutionalized innovation, we assume unconsciously that high-frequency innovation is normal and intrinsic to humanity. That is, we are blind to the fact that innovation as we know it today is solely a phenomenon of modern times.
2   We have developed ideologies to legitimize innovation in our way of life, exemplified in terms like *progress* and *opportunity*.

In contrast, our main points are:

1   Human history has not been characterized by high rates of innovation. Furthermore, we are blind to the historical contingency of innovation.
2   Today's high societal complexity and institutionalized innovation are facilitated by specific external conditions.
3   Our system of innovation is self-perpetuating under those conditions.
4   The continuity of today's system depends on the continuity of those conditions.

We will address these points systematically. First, we assess the narrative of technological optimism.

Resources and technological optimism

Technological optimism incorporates the belief that resources are never scarce, they are just priced wrong. That is, as resources do become less immediately available they will rise in price. The market then signals that there are new opportunities for innovation. Innovation produces new resources or technologies, more efficient ways of using existing resources, or better ways of extracting lower quality deposits. Supply and demand always find balance. Sustainable resource production is automatic, and need never be a concern. Recent examples include the expansion of food production through the Green Revolution and the development of technologies to extract petroleum from deposits that are increasingly difficult to access.

If the technological optimism narrative is correct, an examination of price trends in non-renewable commodities should reveal one or both of two outcomes. One outcome is that, over the long term, prices should remain constant or even fall. It is important to investigate this with a long time series since, as discussed later, various factors may influence prices in the short term. To technological optimists, fluctuations in price should always revolve around a fairly constant mean (or even fall), reflecting the likelihood that innovation has offset depletion, and markets have cleared. An alternative outcome is that prices are observed to rise, but this can be attributed to factors other than scarcity. We investigate this below with data on commodity prices over 55 years.

Non-renewable commodities are obtained from the earth's natural resources. As easily obtained and higher quality ores and deposits are depleted, we must dig deeper and work in more difficult conditions to maintain production levels. In practice, this "best first" principle (Cleveland, 2008) means that, once the best sources of a resource raw material have been tapped, deposits become progressively of lower grade, smaller or more inaccessible. As extraction becomes increasingly difficult, more overburden must be moved, more ore matrix processed, wells drilled deeper and more waste disposed of in order to provide an equivalent amount of a non-renewable commodity (Hall and Klitgaard, 2012). Often resources must be sought in places that are politically unstable. Increasing inputs of labour and capital must be added to the production chain to continue to provide non-renewable commodities to society.

Production of commodities has become more difficult and costly in other ways as well. Stricter requirements for control and mitigation of pollutants and site restoration make the increasing output of waste and other liabilities ever more expensive. Apprehension over atmospheric carbon has prompted a discussion of the limits to fossil fuels that we can afford to burn if we are to keep climate change at a manageable level (Leggett, 2014; McGlade and Ekins, 2015). Local communities have demanded more power in decision making. As a result, ideas such as Social License to Operate and Corporate Social Responsibility require producers to attend to questions of sustainability, quality of life, ethical issues, moral and equity concerns and increasingly, the recognition of indigenous rights (Prno and Slocombe, 2012; Owen, 2007). Furthermore, domestic unrest and geopolitics complicate efficient extraction and movement of resources around the globe (Nunn, Schlesinger, and Ebel, 2000).

While these dynamics seem to predict rising global commodity prices, other factors can be expected to produce mixed results. Where technology improves efficiency or allows unused resources to be recovered, prices may decrease for a time. Yet changes that reduce the cost of using a resource can increase consumption of that commodity through the rebound effect. William Stanley Jevons observed this pattern in the use of coal in the nineteenth century (1866), and it was evident more recently among American automobile drivers (Tainter and Patzek, 2012: 93). We see similar patterns in the optimism over inexpensive natural gas produced by hydraulic fracturing from previously unusable shale deposits (U.S. Energy Information Administration, 2015; Joskow, 2013).

Commodity pricing

Using data from the industrial commodity-price index of *The Economist* for the period from 1862 to 1999, Cashin and McDermott (2002) found that for the period from 1862 to 1999, real commodity prices declined about 1 percent per year. Some studies concur that prices generally decline (e.g., Grilli and Yang, 1988), while others conclude that prices have shown slight increases or mixed results (e.g., Jacks, 2013; Kellard and Wohar, 2006; León and Soto, 1995). Findings of changes tend to be small, and depend on the commodities, indices, methods and time periods under scrutiny.

Despite this uncertainty, some trends are apparent. Figure 4.1 shows the World Bank Global Economic Monitor Commodity Indices for non-renewable (energy, fertilizers, metals and minerals) and renewable resources (represented collectively by the agriculture index) for the period between 1960 and 2014 (World Bank, 2015). There are fluctuations around negligibly changing mean prices. Variability has been increasing in terms of greater amplitude of fluctuations and shorter cycles, which create a more frequent boom-bust cycle. Cashin and McDermott (2002), and Jacks (2013), suggest that changes in exchange rate regimes may be in part responsible for the wider variation seen in recent years.

Externalized costs may also play a role in keeping prices down. These may take the form of environmental degradation or socioeconomic impacts. In a study of peak mineral production in Australia, Prior et al. (2012) suggest that the costs of production from lower grade resources may be offset by intensification of labour, capital and other resources such as water and energy.

It is important to consider non-geological components at work in commodity prices. First among these are deliberate attempts to stabilize prices through policy and production management. Higher social and environmental costs are less acceptable to the public, and there is a decreasing willingness to accept risks associated with industrial production (Beck, 1992). This has the effect of pushing production into places with fewer regulations to protect people and the environment. While these factors may help explain why prices have not increased significantly, they do not serve to refute the technological progress narrative.

Notwithstanding the uncertainties in determining the causes of long-term price trends, it is worth examining these trends in terms of the sustainability conundrum. If the resource limitations argument is correct, the price of commodities should rise over time. This should be true especially of non-renewable resources, which are progressively depleted as they are used. If the technological optimism argument is correct, innovation (combined with other factors, as discussed) should reduce or even offset the price effects of depletion. Renewables do not appear in Figure 4.1 to perform differently from non-renewables, although his may be in part due to the nature of modern agricultural methods, which demand high mineral and hydrocarbon inputs.

Overall, Figure 4.1 shows that as the world economy grew since 1960, the prices of many commodities, adjusted for inflation, have been fairly constant. Prices fall, then rise, then fall again. This seems to be the case in the metals and agriculture indices. For these indices, prices for the most recent year, 2014, are similar to those 55 years earlier (1960). The indices for energy, fertilizers and

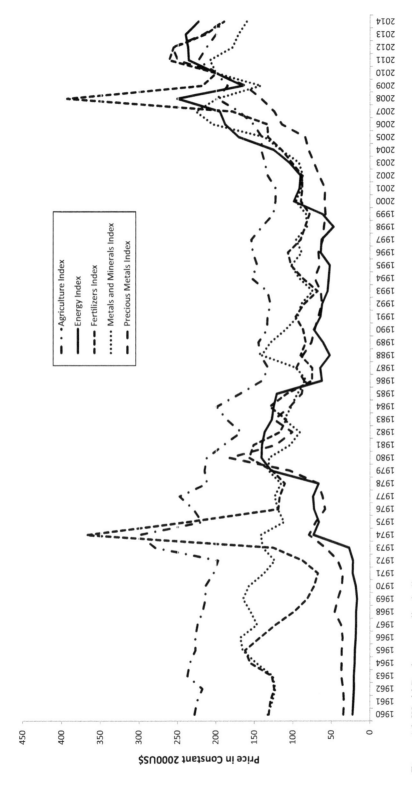

Figure 4.1 World Bank commodity indices.

Source: World Bank.

precious metals were, in contrast, higher at the end of the period. All indices showed increasing prices during China's growth years after 2000, but all were falling again after the recession of 2008–2009. A few more years of data might show that all indices would fall further in price. Overall, the trends evident in the chart do not strongly contradict the view espoused by technological optimists. It appears that innovation has offset depletion. The fundamental question then becomes: Can our ability to offset depletion through innovation continue indefinitely?

History and rates of technical innovation

Two key assumptions underlying technological optimism are that our contemporary system of innovation is intrinsic to humanity, and that this will ensure innovation in the future. Yet one significant difference between the ancient and modern worlds is how few innovations past people produced. Human ancestors can be traced perhaps 4 million years. We know these ancestors in part from the stone tools that they produced, a major part of their technology. During this time, there were periods of hundreds of thousands of years with little technological change (Ambrose, 2001).

Our own species of humans, *Homo sapiens*, has existed for about 200,000 years. During these 200 millennia there have been periods of tens of thousands of years with little technological change. In Africa, early humans sometimes invested in more complex kinds of tools, then would revert to simpler tools when the more complex ones were no longer needed (Shea, 2011a, 2011b). This suggests that innovation was based on benefit-cost evaluations, rather than being an intrinsic impulse.

The same has been true more recently. There have been periods of hundreds to thousands of years with little technological change in many areas of life. Agriculture in 800 B.C., for example, was not much different from agriculture in 800 A.D. For that matter, agriculture in some parts of the world is practiced today as it has been for centuries. We marvel at the technical inventions of ancient societies (e.g., Landels, 2000), forgetting that these technologies were developed over periods of centuries to millennia. For a given period of time in the ancient world, innovations came infrequently.

This seems odd to us today, accustomed as we are to high-frequency innovation and short produce cycles. Why was innovation so rare in the past? A major reason is that, before the era of fossil fuels, energy and power production constituted about 90 percent of economies (Jones, 1964: 465; Fouquet, 2010: 269). This was mainly in the form of agricultural products, and in a year of bad harvests, power production could be all of an economy (Fouquet, 2010: 269). Elites, the military and religious specialists would take up the remaining 10 percent. When energy is so dominant, an economy has little surplus to support innovators, or even for education.

One might ask why ancient people did not perceive that innovation could increase trade, and therefore well-being? Whether they perceived this or not (and most didn't), the problem was that the cost of transport was so high that trade was possible only in high-value goods. The exception was that trade in low-value commodities was possible where there was access to water transport. In the Roman Empire, transport by road was 28 to 56 times more costly than by sea. A wagon load of wheat would double in value in 480 kilometres, a camel load in 600 kilometres. It was less expensive to ship grain to the other end of the Mediterranean than to carry it 120 kilometres by land (Jones, 1964: 841–844). Most people could not afford high-value goods transported over land, so trade in early societies was little developed. Not only was there little economic capacity to support entrepreneurial innovators, there was also little incentive to innovate.

Ancient states often encouraged agricultural expansion and population growth. Populations were low (compared to today) and there was much land. Ancient states needed food for the cities, sons for the army and taxes for the state. All of these were produced by peasant farmers, who are typically reluctant to adopt risky innovations or to intensify production (Boserup, 1965).

Thus, before the Industrial Revolution (that is, before fossil fuels were used in large quantities), innovation was rare compared to more recent times. This is illustrated in patents sealed in Great Britain before and after the Industrial Revolution (Figure 4.2). There were consistently few patents per year until the early years of industrialism. Thereafter patenting grew, leading to the high-frequency innovation that we know today.

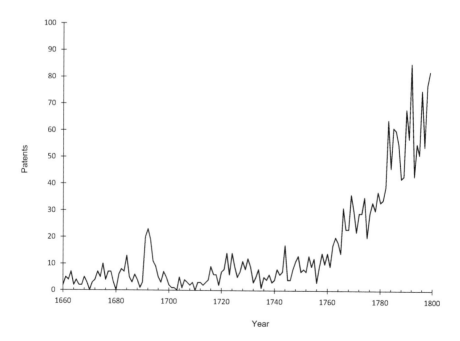

Figure 4.2 Patents sealed in Great Britain, 1616–1800.

Source: Data from MacLeod (1986: 150).

We can conclude from these examples that high-frequency innovation is *not* an innate characteristic of human societies. High-frequency innovation is a historical anomaly, and can exist only in specific circumstances. We turn next to understanding the modern pressures to innovate.

Conditions of innovation today

Today's system of high-frequency innovation is a historical aberration. It exists, and can only exist, in a narrow set of historical conditions. These conditions are:

1   Inexpensive and abundant energy, permitting high complexity in our way of life (Tainter and Patzek, 2012), discretionary consumption, widespread education, profit seeking and investment in research; and
2   Competition forcing continual innovation.

Within these conditions, innovation appears commonplace and inevitable. Novelty and revenue growth are necessary for businesses to survive.

Energy availability

As energy has grown less expensive, it has become a smaller part of the economy. Figure 4.3 shows non-domestic power expenditures in England from 1500 to 2000. In the early sixteenth century, power (energy applied to work) constituted the bulk of the economy. As previously noted, this is characteristic of subsistence economies that lack fossil fuels. Power expenditure then fell to a little over 20 percent of the economy by 1600. Since energy actually increased in price during the sixteenth century (Figure 4.4), it appears that power expenditure fell as

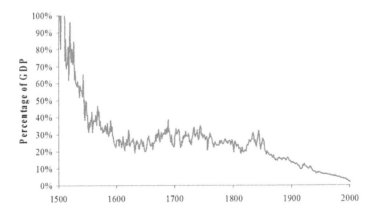

Figure 4.3 Non-domestic power expenditures in England relative to GDP, 1500–2000.

Source: (Fouquet, 2008: 269). Chart provided courtesy of Roger Fouquet.

Reproduced with permission.

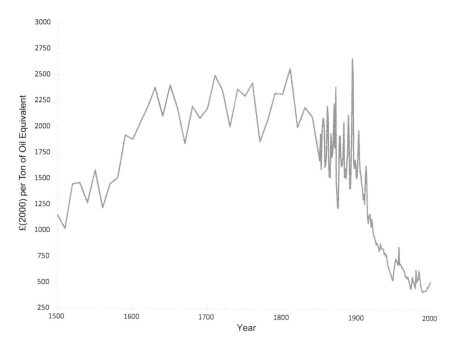

Figure 4.4 Average price of energy in England, 1500–2000.
Source: Data from Fouquet, 2008: 413–417.

a fraction of the economy because the economy was expanding. This may have been due to the influx of New World gold and silver into the European economy. Whatever the reason, the relative cost of power then remained steady until the middle of the nineteenth century, when it began to fall again. The last decline came about from the diffusion of fossil fuels and new technologies. These allowed the price of energy to fall while the economy expanded. This expansion allowed increased investment in education and research.

Figure 4.4 shows that in England the price of energy declined as the Industrial Revolution got underway. This drop in the price of energy was made possible by innovations, first the Newcomen and later the Watt steam engines, which facilitated pumping water from coal mines, and thus reduced the cost of producing coal. By excavating canals and putting steam engines on rails, England had most of the elements of the Industrial Revolution (Wilkinson, 1973). These elements were inexpensive and abundant energy; high-capacity, standardized and mechanized production; and a distribution system for moving raw materials and finished products inexpensively.

Fossil fuels are the basis of the Industrial Revolution, and thus of our system of innovation (Ayres, Ayres, and Warr, 2003; Wrigley, 2010). The classical economists of the eighteenth and early nineteenth centuries, living at the end of the era of solar energy, could not envision growth as we know it today. The balance

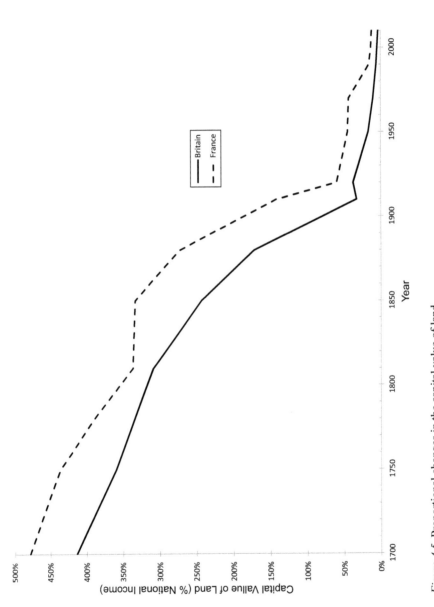

Figure 4.5 Proportional changes in the capital value of land.

Source: Data from Piketty, 2014: 116–117 (www.piketty.pse.ens.fr/en/capital21c).

among land, labour and population in subsistence societies, as well as shifts in trade, meant that while there might be growth, it would be intermittent and reversible (Fouquet and Broadberry, 2015). Material well-being would be limited for most people. Fossil fuels changed that by allowing us to tap stored solar energy from the past (Wrigley, 2010).

Fossil fuels facilitated continuing economic growth through positive feedback. Industrial growth demanded agricultural growth, since workers needed to be shifted from agriculture to industrial production. In England, agricultural output expanded greatly, doubling between the late sixteenth and the early nineteenth centuries (Wrigley, 2010). There was then more feed for farm animals. Horses supplied with oats could perform more work than those fed on grass, and the same with better-fed oxen. The late seventeenth and eighteenth centuries saw a massive increase in turnpikes, giving more work for those horses to do. More goods and passengers could be transported, feeding back into the industrialization process, the latter requiring and increasing the need for more coal. Coal facilitated a reduction in the age of marriage by relieving the necessity of subsistence farming. The resulting population increase meant demand for more agricultural produce, industrial goods and coal (Wrigley, 2010).

Improvements in agricultural production and transport facilitated growth of cities, providing customers for industrial output (Wrigley, 2010: 29–37, 55–90). As the economy grew beyond energy production, more could be invested in education and innovation. None of this growth would have been possible when energy was 90 percent of the economy. Furthermore, each of these developments stimulated demand for yet more coal. By 1850 England was consuming a quantity of coal that, if it were wood instead, would have required 150 percent of the area of the country (Wrigley, 2010: 99). The economy grew correspondingly, increasing demand and rewarding innovation.

As energy production became a smaller part of economies, the relative capital value of land decreased as a proportion of national income (Figure 4.5). Land was no longer the most valuable asset.

Profit seeking and continuity of innovation

Provided that energy remains a small part of an economy, our system of innovation should be self-perpetuating, at least in the near term. Innovation is driven today by competition and profit seeking, which are unlikely to decline. As long as competition and profit seeking remain in force, firms will employ innovation to position their products in the market. Automobile manufacturers, for example, often employ a yearly product cycle. Apple keeps a cycle of 12 to 16 months for successive generations of the iPhone. Such short product cycles are now common.

Future energy and innovation

The continuation of our system of innovation requires abundant and inexpensive energy. That is, we need energy to continue to be a small part of the economy, allowing for discretionary spending and high complexity in our way of life. The ability to engage in discretionary spending means that we can continue to invest in research and development.

As noted, fossil fuels permit us to have an economy that is not dominated by the energy sector. When energy is the primary product of an economy, and the cost of transport is high, it is neither possible nor profitable to invest much in innovation. Moreover, when the majority of a population is impoverished peasants (as is the case in solar energy subsistence societies), there is little payoff to investing in commercial innovation. Most people are too poor to buy much beyond basic commodities.

Fossil fuels changed these constraints through two factors. The first is that fossil fuels are abundant, concentrated and energy dense. They came from the accumulation of millennia of past solar energy and photosynthesis. An economy based on fossil fuels is freed from the constraints of annual solar energy. Wealth can accumulate and be spread more widely. It becomes worthwhile to invest in education and innovation. Moreover, as abundant energy causes a society to complexify (Tainter, 2011: 91–92), education and innovation become necessary. Positive feedback emerges among energy, wealth, education and innovation.

The second factor in economic growth depends on the concept of energy returned on energy invested, denoted by the acronym EROI. It takes energy to get energy. The utility of an energy source derives in part from its energy density, its abundance per unit of land area, and its EROI. The problem of resource extraction is that we tend first to pluck the low-hanging fruit (Cleveland, 2008). That is, using the best knowledge and technology of the time, we first exploit resources that are most profitable to find, acquire, and/or distribute. As these are exhausted, we shift to sources of supply that are harder to find, acquire in the desired quantities, and/or distribute, so that the net energy profit declines. In petroleum production in the US, for example, the highest EROI came from drilling into the great, shallow pools of oil in California, Louisiana, Oklahoma and Texas (Yergin, 2009). These pools yielded high EROI. In 1940 the United States produced oil and gas at an energy profit (EROI) of 100:1 (Cleveland, 2005). For every barrel of oil that we invested in finding and producing oil, we got 100 barrels back. Inevitably, as the best sources of oil were tapped fully or depleted, production shifted to sources that have been less productive, difficult to access, difficult to extract and/or difficult to process. As the easiest sources of oil have been tapped, the technology to produce petroleum grows correspondingly complex and costly. The first well in Titusville, Pennsylvania, drilled in 1859, hit oil at a depth of 21 meters (70 feet). By the 1920s, wells were being drilled to 2,500 meters (8,200 feet). Today wells can be drilled as deep as 12,000 meters (40,000 feet), and require complex technology and equipment (Yergin, 2009).

Producers now face further problems of being unable to situate drilling rigs in a desirable place or in enough places, perhaps because of environmental concerns, or (especially at sea) because of cost. The solution is horizontal drilling. Horizontal holes can now be bored to distances of nearly 13 kilometres (8 miles). All of this comes at a price, of course. While today's rigs can drill up to 80 percent faster than those of the 1920s, the scale of the effort has grown exponentially. In 2013, global oil and gas investments came to $900 billion (The Economist, 2016: 67). As the process of finding and extracting oil grows complex and costly, EROI declines. Today the US produces petroleum at an EROI of 15:1 (Cleveland, 2005). The downward trend is irreversible.

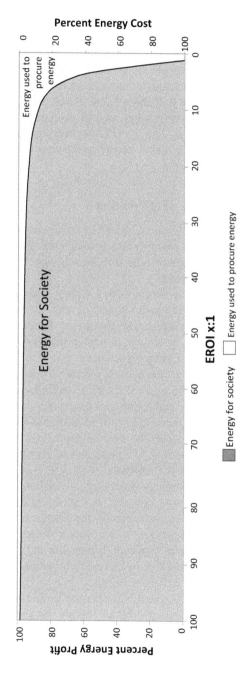

Figure 4.6 The energy cliff.

The graph in Figure 4.6 is known as the energy cliff. It shows the energy profit of producing energy on the y-axis as EROI declines from left to right on the x-axis. The noteworthy aspect of this chart is that the cliff becomes pronounced when EROI reaches about 8:1. As EROI declines after this point, as inevitably it will, the energy profit of producing energy falls rapidly. When EROI on fossil fuels falls below 8:1, an increasing share of our economies will again be allocated to producing energy. Other sectors of the economy will proportionately contract, leaving less economic surplus to invest in education and innovation. Already Canadian tar sands yield an EROI of about 3:2 (Cleveland and O'Connor, 2011).

Declining EROI, an inevitable process, will in time constrain the resources available to support innovation. This means that barring the development of energy supplies that can provide higher energy profits, our system of innovation will in time be forced to contract.

Evolution and productivity of innovation

Continuous innovation must provide constant or increasing returns to innovative efforts. Our investments in research and development (R&D) must yield the results we want. Should this cease to be the case, the incentive to continue to invest in innovation would diminish.

Innovation is a complex system embedded within other complex systems. Complexity is here defined in the anthropological sense of increasing differentiation and specialization in structure, combined with increasing integration of parts (Tainter, 1988). Complex systems have evolutionary histories, and innovation is no exception. The popular image of science is that of the lone-wolf scholar, an idiosyncratic but persistent genius peering through a microscope or trekking through unexplored jungles (Toumey, 1996). This was indeed how science was conducted through most of the eighteenth and nineteenth centuries, the age of naturalists such as Charles Darwin and Gregor Mendel. Yet the naturalists made themselves obsolete as they depleted the stock of general questions that an individual, working alone, could resolve. The principles of gravity, natural selection and inheritance no longer wait to be revealed.

The point overlooked by technological optimists is that knowledge production, like other human activities, grows complex and produces diminishing returns (Tainter, 1988). Innovation grows in complexity and costliness, and exhausts easy solutions to problems. The productivity of innovation is therefore not constant. Research problems over time grow increasingly complex and difficult to solve. In response, research and development grow increasingly complex, and correspondingly more costly.

In every scientific field, early research plucks the lowest fruit: the questions that are least costly to resolve and most broadly useful. As general knowledge is established early in the history of a discipline, that which remains axiomatically becomes more specialized. Specialized questions become more costly and difficult to resolve. Research organization moves from isolated scientists who do all aspects of a project, to teams of scientists, technicians and support staff who require specialized equipment, costly institutions, administrators and accountants. The size of research teams grows, as illustrated in the increasing size of science authorship teams (Wuchty, Jones, and Uzzi, 2007; Jones, Wuchty, and Uzzi, 2008). Thus fields of scientific research follow a characteristic developmental pattern, from general to specialized; from wealthy dilettantes and lone-wolf scholars to large teams with staff and supporting institutions; from knowledge that is generalized and widely useful to research that is specialized and narrowly useful; from simple to complex; and from low to high societal costs.

It has long been known that within individual technical sectors, the productivity of innovation reaches diminishing returns. Hornell Hart (1945) showed that innovation in specific technologies follows a logistic curve: patenting rises slowly at first, then more rapidly and finally declines. Rostow (1980: 171) extended this observation in his attempt to explain why economic growth slows in developed countries. The question before us is: does the phenomenon of diminishing returns to innovation in individual sectors apply to innovation as a whole?

Nicholas Rescher has addressed this question. Paraphrasing Max Planck, Rescher observed that "with every advance [in science] the difficulty of the task is increased" (1980: 80). Writing specifically in reference to natural science, Rescher suggested:

> Once all of the findings at a given state-of-the-art level of investigative technology have been realized, one must move to a more expensive level. . . . In natural science we are involved in a technological arms race: with every "victory over nature" the difficulty of achieving the breakthroughs which lie ahead is increased.
>
> (1980: 94, 97)

Rescher terms this "Planck's Principle of Increasing Effort" (1978: 79–94). Planck and Rescher suggest that *exponential* growth in the size and costliness of science is needed just to maintain a *constant* rate of innovation. Science must therefore consume an ever-larger share of national resources in both money and personnel. Jacob Schmookler, for example, showed that while the number of industrial research personnel increased 5.6 times from 1930 to 1954, the number of corporate patents over roughly the same period increased by only 23 percent (1966: 28–29). Such data prompted Dael Wolfle in 1960 to pen an editorial for *Science* titled "How Much Research For a Dollar?" Derek de Solla Price observed in the early 1960s that science even then was growing faster than both the population and the economy and that, of all scientists who had ever lived, 80 to 90 percent were still alive at the time of his writing (Price, 1963).

In academic research, Wuchty, Jones, and Uzzi (2007), and Jones, Wuchty, and Uzzi (2008), have shown that the ongoing challenges of research have been met by increasing complexity in the form of larger research teams. These teams are complex in that they are differentiated – incorporating diverse specialties – and require the organization of any differentiated system.

The possibility that innovation overall may produce diminishing returns on knowledge capital calls into question the narrative of technological optimism. As Price (1963: 19) pointed out, continually increasing the allocation of personnel to research and development cannot continue forever or the day will come when we must all be scientists. It is therefore important to determine whether the research enterprise overall produces diminishing returns.

To assess the productivity of innovation, Deborah Strumsky of our team constructed a database of all US patents, and patents issued in specific fields of technology, between 1974 and 2012. These dates were chosen to ensure high quality data. The database consists of just under 3 million patents. About half of United States patents are granted to non-US applicants, so the data reflect global innovation.

The process foreseen by Rescher and others is underway in the research that leads to patents. Figure 4.7 shows that, from 1974 through 2012, the number of authors per patent has consistently increased, from 1.7 in 1974 to 2.6 in 2012. It is taking more and more innovators to achieve a patentable invention. Moreover, as we argue later, the complexity of patenting teams is growing.

Corresponding to the increase in size and complexity of patenting teams, the productivity of those teams, measured as patents per investor, has been declining. Over the 39 years shown in Figure 4.7, the productivity of innovation declined by 22 percent. That is, the productivity of innovation is declining at a rate of about 0.56 percent per year. Our data do not allow us to say when the decline in productivity began. Huebner (2005) concludes that major innovations peaked in the 1870s. The problem of increasing complexity in the research enterprise has been suspected since the same period (Peirce, 1879).

New fields of innovation are thought to be more productive than old ones, since in new fields simpler, basic discoveries can still routinely be made. It is appropriate therefore to ask whether there are increasing returns to innovation in newer technical fields and, if so, whether these offset diminishing returns in older fields. Figures 4.8 and 4.9 show patents per inventor in several technical sectors that are long-established, and in which there are still active research programs. While each field shows short-term fluctuations, the trend in several of them is a decline in patents per inventor, mirroring the overall trend seen in Figure 4.7. Since these are older fields, this finding would be expected.

Figure 4.10 combines several energy technologies; most sectors (except solar energy since the mid 1980s) show declining patents per inventor. The most disturbing aspect of this chart is that solar and wind power technologies show in part the same trend as the older gas and power system sectors. It is widely believed that solar and wind energy will be needed to power industrial societies in the future. Yet it appears that some of our investments in improving technologies in these sectors are producing diminishing returns, and that these sectors may be approaching technical maturity. Again, solar energy shows increasing productivity since about 1986.

Figure 4.11 tracks patents per inventor in the relatively newer fields of information technology, both hardware and software. These are some of our most dynamic technical sectors, and the sources of much recent economic growth. Yet each of these technical sectors shows a long-term trend of declining productivity per inventor.

Even the newest technical fields, biotechnology and nanotechnology, show this trend (Figure 4.12). Inventive efforts in these sectors are producing declining rates of innovation. If this is characteristic of newer fields more broadly, then in industrial economies there may no longer be increasing returns in newer sectors to offset diminishing returns in older ones.

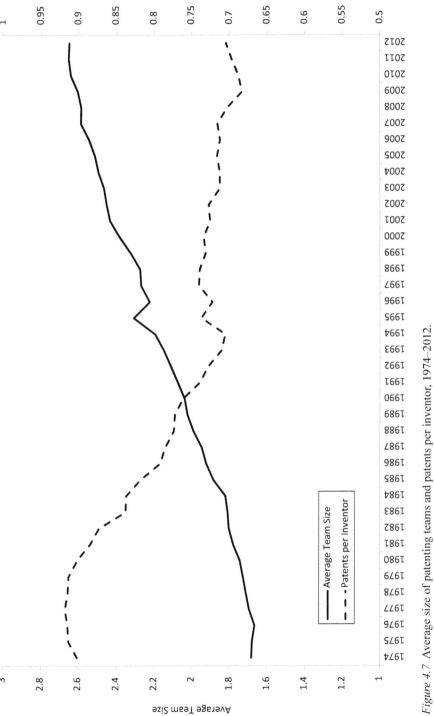

Figure 4.7 Average size of patenting teams and patents per inventor, 1974–2012.

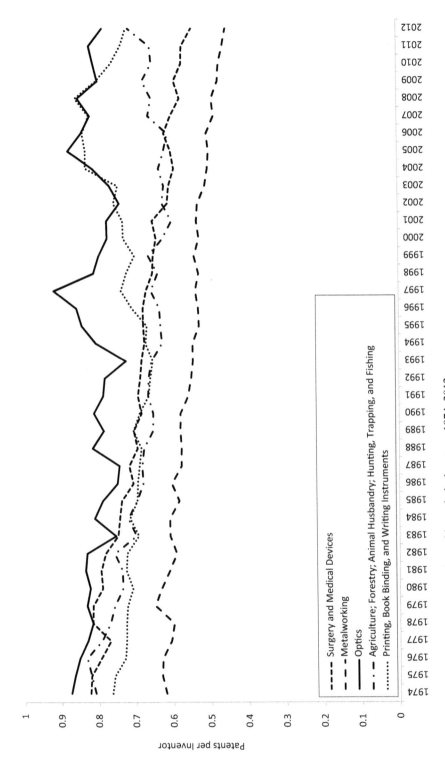

Figure 4.8 Patents per inventor in various older technical sectors, 1974–2012.

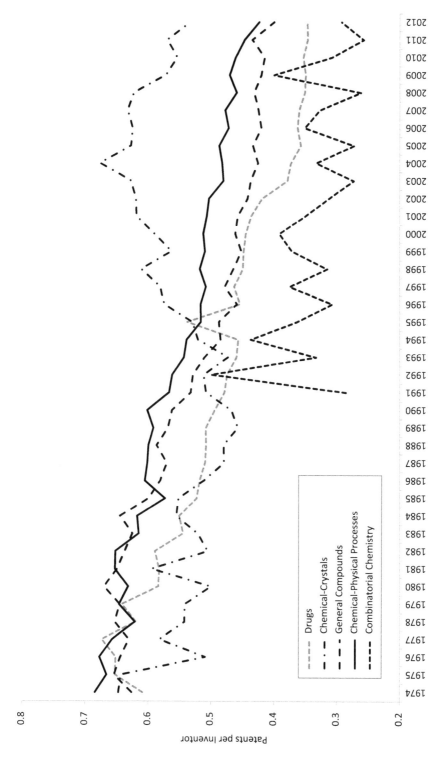

Figure 4.9 Patents per inventor in drugs and chemicals, 1974–2012.

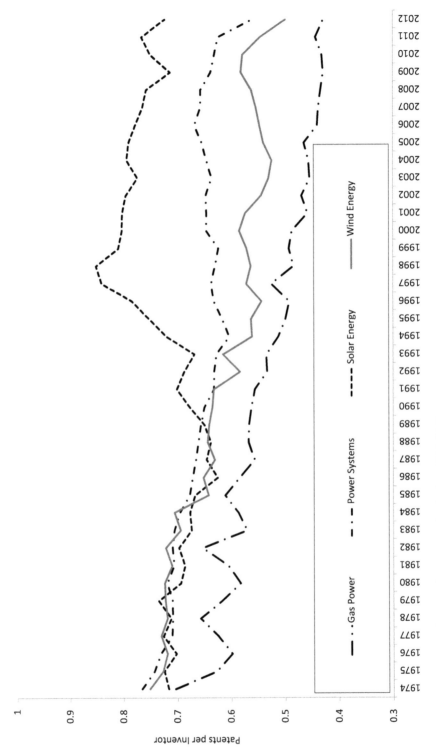

Figure 4.10 Patents per inventor in energy technologies, 1974–2012.

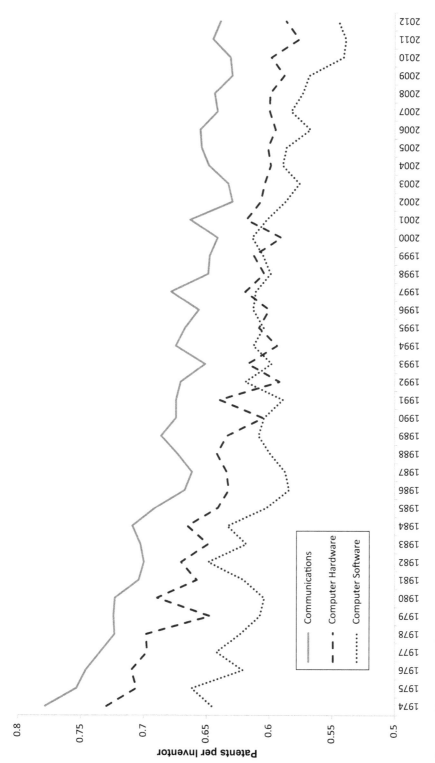

Figure 4.11 Patents per inventor in information technologies, 1974–2012.

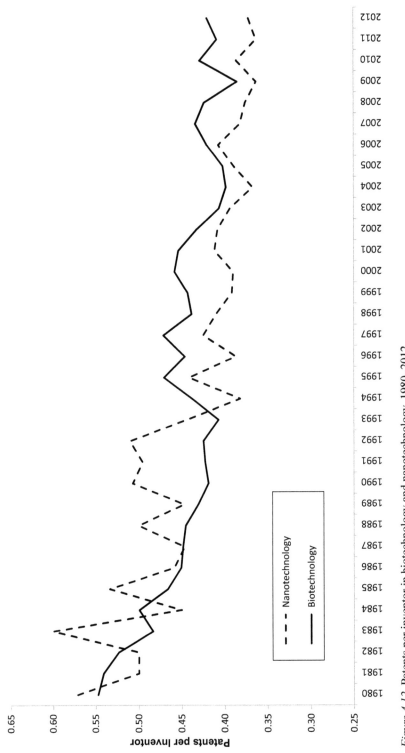

Figure 4.12 Patents per inventor in biotechnology and nanotechnology, 1980–2012.

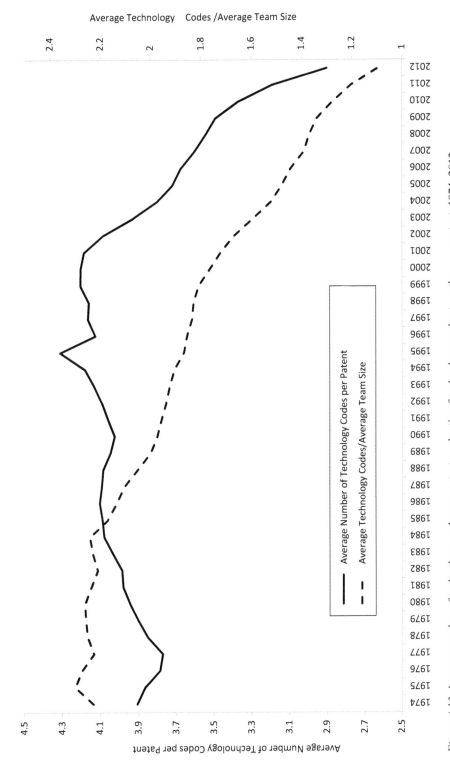

Figure 4.13 Average number of technology codes per patent, and ratio of technology codes to authors per patent, 1974–2012.

Finally, in an attempt to measure complexification, Figure 4.13 shows the average number of technology codes per patent and the ratio of technology codes to authors per patent. Technology codes are used by the US Patent and Trademark Office to classify a patent's technology, and represent distinct technological capabilities. The results show an increasing number of technology codes per patent through 1995, a slight contraction and approximately a plateau through 2000, followed by a decrease through 2005. The results need clarification. Patents with more technology codes need longer than the average three to five years to process, and are harder to get awarded. Furthermore, many patents today are imitations or repeated refinements of previous patents. These patents rely on fewer technology codes. Thus, the decline in the last few years of this chart is partly an artefact of the increased evaluation time needed for more complex patents, and partly a change in patenting strategy. With this caveat in mind, the chart shows a trend of increasing complexity per patent through 2000, with incomplete results thereafter. At the same time, technology codes per patenting author declined throughout this period.

We suggest some interpretations based on this graph, acknowledging that these require further investigation. It seems that firms are increasing the size of innovation teams faster than they are increasing the technical diversity of such teams. This suggests that firms are adding more of the same kind of specialist in preference to more kinds of specialists. It may be that firms or the members of research teams don't recognize the need for more specialties, or that firms are resisting further complexification. It is also likely that technology codes per patent are holding roughly steady or increasing but that, along with the rest of science, innovations are becoming more technically narrow. Part of firms' strategy to avoid increased processing time for more complex patents is to break these innovations down into narrower claims.

The fundamental conclusion to be drawn from these charts is that it is requiring the investment of more and more resources to innovate in the technical arena. This appears also to be the case in academic research. The productivity of innovation is declining, as the authors cited above foresaw. This calls into question the suitability of relying on innovation to ensure future sustainability.

Assessment

Innovation is part of the cosmology of industrial societies. We believe it to be innate, immutable and inevitable. We have fetishized innovation, and consider it a primordial characteristic of our species. It takes on a religious character when we place our faith in it as the ultimate source of material salvation.

Our belief in innovation places it at the centre of sustainability debates. The debate is between technological optimists, who believe that resource constraints can always be overcome by innovation, and those who believe that resource constraints are pressing and cannot be overcome forever.

Technological optimists believe that resources are never scarce, just priced wrong. As long as markets are unfettered and there is a price mechanism, rising costs of resources from a scarce supply should spur innovation. Innovations would come in the forms of finding new sources of the resource, developing technical approaches to using the resource more efficiently or finding substitute resources. Our analysis of price trends in non-renewable commodities suggests that technological optimists have largely been correct *to this point*. As resource stocks have been drawn down, their prices have not risen permanently. The key question is whether technological optimism will be correct forever.

Projecting technological optimism into the future requires certain assumptions. The most basic assumption is that there is an innate human tendency to innovate. Optimists must make this assumption, even if they are unaware of doing so. If innovation is not an innate tendency, then it must be historically contingent. A second assumption is that we will always have the resources to innovate. A third assumption is that investment in innovation will yield constant or increasing returns into the future. If these assumptions are incorrect, the case for optimism is diminished.

The first assumption, that innovation is primordial and innate, can be evaluated indirectly. We cannot, of course, look into most past minds to know if they had innovative thoughts. We have only written and physical remains of innovations. These tell us that, for most of human history, innovation has been rare compared to its frequency today. Humanity has experienced spans of hundreds, to thousands, to tens of thousands of years in which there were few to no innovations in various sectors of activity. High-frequency innovation such as we experience it today is the product of unique historical conditions.

Today's system of innovation emerged in specific historical conditions, exists because of them, and can continue only in those conditions. Those circumstances include fossil fuels and industrialization. Together these started a positive feedback loop that made industrial societies wealthy, and that reduced the role of energy in the economy. Fossil fuels made it possible for humans to do much more work than they had ever done before. With wealth, and with energy a small part of an economy, there are opportunities for discretionary consumption that include investing in research. Discretionary consumption makes possible the existence of industries to meet consumption potentials, thereby ensuring that the majority of workers who once produced energy can find other employment, and earn salaries, to fund their consumption demands. In turn, competition among firms impels continued investment in R&D, provided that there are incentives to invest and energy costs allow it.

The first fault with technological optimism is declining EROI on our energy sources. Our system of innovation depends on energy being inexpensive and a small part of the economy. This permits discretionary consumption and investment in education and innovation. Yet as EROI declines, as it has done and will continue to do, energy will become a larger part of our economies. This will curtail discretionary investments.

Technological optimism will also, in time, falter over the matter of incentives. Firms and governments will invest in R&D provided that the costs are affordable and the returns are constant or increasing. If investment in innovation yields diminishing returns, the outlook is less favourable. Yet diminishing returns are precisely what our data reveal. Over a period of 39 years, the productivity of innovation, measured as patents per inventor, declined at a rate of 0.56 percent per year even as investment in research has increased.

This trend is driven by increasing complexity and costliness in the research process and cannot be reversed. As the trend continues, within one or two generations our system of innovation will become too expensive and/or too unproductive to continue in its present form. Firms and governments will be forced to curtail investment in innovation. In some areas of research this is happening already.

One can always hope that the trend of declining productivity of innovation will not continue. That can only be a hope (or a matter of faith), for the evidence points in the other direction. The reason underlying the declining productivity of innovation – complexification of the research process – will not change. As we answer questions in science, subsequent questions are more difficult to resolve. As research questions grow more challenging, the research enterprise grows larger, more complex and more costly. As research grows complex and costly, it produces diminishing returns. This process is inexorable.

Conclusion: innovation *vs.* depletion

Much of the debate about sustainability boils down to the question whether innovation can always outrun depletion. Our assessment of commodity price trends suggests that, to this point, it has. Until now the technological optimists have been correct. Yet the energy profit on the fossil fuels that are needed to support innovation, and the productivity of investment in innovation, are declining. These trends suggest that innovation will not forever offset depletion. If so, then the continuation of our way of life into the indefinite future is uncertain. As the productivity of innovation declines, technological optimism will be less and less defensible, and innovation less and less effective at solving resource constraints. Technological optimism will come more and more to resemble what Richard Feynman (1974) described as "cargo cult science."

The future of innovation will not be a linear extrapolation of the present. Increasing complexity of innovation and diminishing returns to research investments, combined with declining EROI, mean that, within a few decades, our system of innovation will be very different. It will be more expensive and less productive. The English novelist L.P. Hartley once wrote that "The past is a foreign country; they do things differently there" (1953). To paraphrase Hartley: The future is a foreign country. We will do things differently there. Among many other changes, if present trends continue, we will have a system of innovation that is less capable of solving problems and ensuring supplies of resources than we have been accustomed to.

Acknowledgements We are pleased to express our appreciation to Angelo Tartaglia for the invitation to present this work at the conference "Science and the Future," Politecnico di Torino, 28–31 October 2013, to Roberto Burlando for the invitation to submit the paper to this volume, and to Roger Fouquet for providing us with Figure 4.3.

References

Ambrose, S.H. (2001). Paleolithic technology and human evolution. *Science*, 291, 1748–1753.

Ayres, R.U., Ayres, L.W., and Warr, B. (2003). Exergy, power and work in the US economy, 1900–1998. *Energy*, 28, 219–273.

Barnett, H.J., and Morse, C. (1963). *Scarcity and Growth: The Economics of Natural Resource Availability*, Baltimore, MD, Johns Hopkins Press.

Beck, U. (1992). *Risk Society: Towards a New Modernity*, M. Ritter (trans.), Newbury Park, CA, Sage Publications.

Boserup, E. (1965). *The Conditions of Agricultural Growth: The Economics of Agrarian Change Under Population Pressure*, Chicago, Aldine.

Brown, J.H., Burnside, W.R., Davidson, A.D., DeLong, J.P., Dunn, W.C., Hamilton, M.J., Mercado-Silva, N., Nekola, J.C., Okie, J.C., Woodruff, W.H., and Zuo, W. (2011). Energetic limits to economic growth. *BioScience*, 61, 19–26.

Bush, V. (1945). *Science, the Endless Frontier*, Washington, DC, U.S. Government Printing Office.

Cashin, P., and McDermott, C.J. (2002). The long-run behavior of commodity prices: Small trends and big variability. *IMF Staff Papers*, 49(2), 175–199.

Chu, S. (2009). *Statement of Steven Chu, Secretary, U.S. Department of Energy, Before the Senate Committee on Appropriations, Subcommittee on Energy and Water Development and Related Agencies, FY 2010 Appropriations Hearing*, Washington, DC, U.S. Department of Energy.

Cleveland, C.J. (2005). Net energy from oil and gas extraction in the United States, 1954–1997. *Energy*, 30, 769–782.

Cleveland, C.J. (2008). Natural resource quality. In C.J. Cleveland (ed.), *The Encyclopedia of Earth*. www.eoearth.org/view/article/154798/, accessed 21 May 2014.

Cleveland, C.J., and O'Connor, P.A. (2011). Energy Return on Investment (EROI) of oil shale. *Sustainability*, 3, 2307–2322, doi:10.3390/su3112307.

Diamond, J. (2005). *Collapse: How Societies Choose to Fail or Succeed*, New York, Viking.

The Economist. (2016). Oiling the wheels. *The Economist*, 418(8981), March 19–25, 67.

Feynman, R.P. (1974). *Cargo cult science*. Commencement Address at the California Institute of Technology, Pasadena. Online: http://calteches.library.caltech.edu/51/2/CargoCult.htm, accessed 29 March 2016.

Fouquet, R. (2008). *Heat, Power and Light: Revolutions in Energy Services*, Cheltenham, Edward Elgar.

Fouquet, R., and Broadberry, S. (2015). Seven centuries of European economic growth and decline. *Journal of Economic Perspectives*, 29, 227–244.

Gordon, R.L. (1981). *An Economic Analysis of World Energy Problems*, Cambridge, MA, Massachusetts Institute of Technology Press.

Grilli, E.R., and Cheng, Y.M. (1988). Primary commodity prices, manufactured goods prices, and the terms of trade of developing countries: What the long run shows. *The World Bank Economic Review*, 2(1), 1–47.

Hall, C.A.S., and Klitgaard, K.A. (2012). *Energy and the Wealth of Nations: Understanding the Biophysical Economy*, New York, Springer.

Hart, H. (1945). Logistic social trends. *American Journal of Sociology*, 50, 337–352.

Hartley, L.P. (1953). *The Go-Between*, London, Hamish Hamilton.

Huebner, J. (2005). A possible declining trend for Worldwide innovation. *Technological Forecasting & Social Change*, 72, 980–986.

Jacks, D.S. (2013). From boom to bust: A typology of real commodity prices in the long run. *National Bureau of Economic Research Working Paper Series* 18874. doi:10.3386/w18874.

Jevons, W.S. (1866). *The Coal Question: An Inquiry Concerning the Progress of the Nation and the Probable Exhaustion of Our Coal-Mines* (2nd edition), London, Macmillan.

Jones, A.H.M. (1964). *The Later Roman Empire, 284–602: A Social, Economic and Administrative Survey*, Norman, University of Oklahoma Press.

Jones, B.F., Wuchty, S., and Uzzi, B. (2008). Multi-university research teams: Shifting impact, geography, and stratification in science. *Science*, 322, 1259–1262.

Joskow, P.L. (2013). Natural gas: From shortages to abundance in the United States. *American Economic Review*, 103, 338–343. doi:10.1257/aer.103.3.338.

Kellard, N., and Wohar, M.E. (2006). On the prevalence of trends in primary commodity prices. *Journal of Development Economics*, 79, 146–167.

Landels, J.G. (2000). *Engineering in the Ancient World* (2nd edition), Berkeley, CA, University of California Press.

Leggett, J.K. (2014). *The Energy of Nations: Risk Blindness and the Road to Renaissance*, New York, Routledge.

León, J., and Soto, R. (1995). *Structural Breaks and Long-Run Trends in Commodity Prices*, Washington, DC, World Bank.

MacLeod, C. (1986). *Inventing the Industrial Revolution: The English Patent System, 1660–1800*, Cambridge, Cambridge University Press.

McGlade, C., and Ekins, P. (2015). The geographical distribution of fossil fuels unused when limiting global warming to 2° C. *Nature*, 517, 187–190. doi:10.1038/nature14016

Nunn, S., Schlesinger, J.R., and Ebel, R.E. (2000). *The Geopolitics of Energy Into the 21st Century*, Washington, DC, CSIS Press.

Owen, D.P. (2007). *Beyond Corporate Social Responsibility: The Scope for Corporate Investment in Community Driven Development*, Washington, DC, The International Bank for Reconstruction and Development/The World Bank.

Peirce, C.S. (1879). Notes on the theory of the economy of research. In C. P. Patterson (complier), *United States Coast Survey, Showing the Progress of the Work for the Fiscal Year Ending June, 1876*. Washington, DC, U.S. Government Printing Office, 197–201.

Piketty, T. (2014). *Capital in the Twenty-First Century*, A. Goldhammer (trans.), Cambridge, Belknap Press.

Price, D.d.S. (1963). *Little Science, Big Science*, New York, Columbia University Press.

Prior, T., Giurco, D.P., Mudd, G.M., Mason, L., and Behrisch, J. (2012). Resource depletion, peak minerals and the implications for sustainable resource management. *Global Environmental Change*, 22, 577–587. doi:http://dx.doi.org/10.1016/j.gloenvcha.2011.08.009.

Prno, J., and Slocombe, D.S. (2012). Exploring the origins of "Social License to Operate" in the mining sector: Perspectives from governance and sustainability theories. *Resources Policy*, 37, 346–357. doi:http://dx.doi.org/10.1016/j.resourpol.2012.04.002.

Rescher, N. (1978). *Scientific Progress: A Philosophical Essay on the Economics of Research in Natural Science*, Pittsburgh, PA, University of Pittsburgh Press.

Rescher, N. (1980). *Unpopular Essays on Technological Progress*, Pittsburgh, PA, University of Pittsburgh Press.

Röckstrom, J., Steffen, W., and 27 others. (2009). A safe operating space for humanity. *Nature*, 461, 472–475.

Rostow, W.W. (1980). *Why the Poor Get Richer and the Rich Slow Down*, Austin, TX, University of Texas Press.

Sato, R., and Suzawa, G.S. (1983). *Research and Productivity: Endogenous Technical Change*, Boston, MA, Auburn House.

Schmookler, J. (1966). *Invention and Economic Growth*, Cambridge, MA, Harvard University Press.

Shea, J.J. (2011a). *Homo sapiens* is as *Homo sapiens* was. *Current Anthropology*, 52, 1–15.

Shea, J.J. (2011b). Refuting a myth about human origins. *American Scientist*, 99, 128–135.

Tainter, J.A. (1988). *The Collapse of Complex Societies*, Cambridge, Cambridge University Press.

Tainter, J.A. (2011). Energy, complexity, and sustainability: A historical perspective. *Environmental Innovation and Societal Transitions*, 1, 89–95.

Tainter, J.A., and Patzek, T.W. (2012). *Drilling Down: The Gulf Oil Debacle and Our Energy Dilemma*, New York, Copernicus Books.

Toumey, C.P. (1996). *Conjuring Science: Scientific Symbols and Cultural Meanings in American Life*, New Brunswick, NJ, Rutgers University Press.

U.S. Energy Information Administration (2015). *Annual Energy Outlook 2015*, Washington, DC, U.S. Energy Information Administration.

Wilkinson, R.G. (1973). *Poverty and Progress: An Ecological Model of Economic Development*, London, Methuen.

Wolfle, D. (1960). How much research for a dollar? *Science*, 132, 517.

World Bank (2015). *World Bank Global Economic Monitor*, Washington, DC, The World Bank. Online: http://data.worldbank.org/data-catalog/global-economic-monitor, accessed 21 February 2016.

Wrigley, E.A. (2010). *Energy and the English Industrial Revolution*, Cambridge, Cambridge University Press.

Wuchty, S., Jones, B.F., and Uzzi, B. (2007). The increasing dominance of teams in production of knowledge. *Science*, 316, 1036–1039.

Yergin, D. (2009). *The Prize: The Epic Quest for Oil, Money, and Power*, New York, Free Press.

5   Strategies for an economy facing energy constraints

Ian Schindler and Julia Schindler

1.1 Introduction

This chapter will be incomplete as the subject is quite vast, nor is there a unique strategy. The best we can do is give the reader directions of thought, establish some basic principles and give references for further study. This work differs from the works of Rob Hopkins[1,2] in that we spend more time trying to understand qualitatively the eminent contraction phase of the economic (or business) cycle of fossil fuels from both empirical and theoretical standpoints. We feel this is necessary because many people make the mistake of thinking that the peak oil problem (and more generally the problem of peak extraction rate for all fossil fuels) will be characterized by high prices which will lead to market solutions to the energy shortage, while empirical and theoretical results indicate that peak oil extraction will be the market solution to low prices. That is, market prices will not increase as fast as extraction costs causing extraction rates to fall. This consideration changes the strategies we advocate. This period is a time of many challenges but also a time of opportunity. We have the opportunity of rethinking our goals, monetary system, political and judicial systems, and we can attempt to transition to a sustainable economy. Today we have advantages such as better communication systems and more data than former citizens had facing similar problems.

While modern economists study the ways people make choices on the production and allocation of goods, we go back to the etymological roots of the word which mean management or administration of the home. Managing the home goes beyond the study of choices, it addresses the organization of society and its relationship with the ecosystem of which it is a subsystem.[3]

In Section 1.2, we review the way we measure economic output. Current measures are too narrow. Measuring monetary output alone can lead to very misleading measures. For many economists, the twentieth century was a very positive period because of the growth in economic production. However using other metrics, the twentieth century was a disaster because of the loss of biodiversity, habitat and the depletion of mineral resources. The perspective of broader measures helps in defining goals.

Understanding secular or long economic cycles as described in Turchin and colleagues in 2009[4] is an important step in developing strategies because the dynamics of these cycles are similar to the dynamics of economies facing energy constraints today. Understanding these dynamics not only enables us to assess current conditions but give insight into how to use the dynamics to attain goals. In Section 1.3 we give a brief summary of the cycles and provide a theory to explain them based on results on economic production functions proved in the appendix.

In Section 1.4 we look at some strategies used by countries faced with energy constraints in the twentieth century in order to explore more modern dynamics. These dynamics lead to consideration of important sectors of the economy affected by energy constraints.

The permaculture movement began thinking about strategies for an energy challenged world in the 1970s. In Section 1.5, we summarize the core principles of this movement which were conceived of primarily with the goals of sustainability and using natural ecological systems to human advantage. The concept of design is critical to this approach.

We then review some contrasting twenty-first-century strategies and look at some technology that is currently not implemented on a significant scale which could be used to maintain aspects of our culture in the face of energy constraints.

1.2 Measuring economic output

In order to mathematically describe the dynamics of the economy, we need some measure of economic output. A standard measure is Gross Domestic Production or GDP (one can replace *domestic* with *world*) measured in units of currency. One must be careful in interpreting the significance of this measure.[5] All measures of economic output have limitations. Of interest to us is the relative size of sectors of the economy. With respect to GDP (or any measure in units of currency) this is called "cost share", or the size of a sector divided *be* the overall size of the economy (see Equation [A.1.2] for a precise definition).

Units are a major problem in measuring economic production. If all economic production were apples, one could count the apples to evaluate economic production. But in an economy which produces apples, oranges, computers, software and mathematical theorems among many other things, each unit one uses has its specific problems.

Different units have been studied by different authors to measure the economy. We feel each of the units have different advantages and disadvantages. Studying different units gives different insights into how the economy functions.

1.2.1 Currency

The major success of currency as a unit is that it is common to all things measurable (objects with a price), allowing us, for example, to compare software production to apple production. The unit of currency does have drawbacks.

Money or currency is many things. A monetary system is a social contract for the distribution of goods produced by the society. One aspect of money is that it is a measure of value on measurable objects. The so-called market compares the price of computer software and apples allowing us to compare the relative values of very diverse objects. The value system is not democratic, as persons controlling large relative amounts of money have more votes in determining the value of an object than a large number of people without money. For example, if a large part of the population is starving, one might expect the price of food to be high, but this is not necessarily the case if the people who are starving have no money. The distribution of money or wealth thus significantly affects the price of goods.

Another aspect of money is that as it is a man-made construct, it can be manipulated so that there are distortions. Economists attempt to see through these distortions, for example, by adjusting for inflation, using discount rates and factoring in subsidies. It is nonetheless impossible to account for all distortions in a satisfactory manner. The success of the website Shadowstats attests to the intensity of this debate with respect to inflation. One can also attempt to broaden the scope of currency by using monetary incentives to encourage "good behaviour" with respect to other units, for example, by taxing pollution. Such changes are often difficult to implement because they require political consensus.

Many authors[6,7,8,9] have worked on Energy Return on Energy Invested, or EROEI

$$EROEI \underset{=}{\operatorname{def}} \frac{E_0}{E_i},$$

(1.2.1)

where E_i is the energy invested to obtain the output energy E_0. Rather than using currency, these authors use units of energy to measure economic activity. Energy as a unit, is known very well in all the physical sciences. It is impossible to manipulate (though energy statistics can and are manipulated). The drawback of energy is that one does not consider what the energy is used for and how well it is used for that purpose, primary concerns for those wishing to understand the economy. EROEI is the equivalent of cost share in units of energy.

Energy balance equations are fundamental to understanding all sciences. We feel that this should be an important area of future research.

When measured with the unit of energy, the economy resembles one or more electric circuit(s) in parallel with a power supply(s). Each good can be traced back to the origin of the energy that permitted its manufacture. Energy, or more properly, exergy, is different from money in that it is exhaustible. Exergy cannot circulate forever, spent exergy never comes back. It needs to be produced from a power supply. To people measuring the economy with energy, exergy production is the most fundamental aspect of the economy. The IEA has recently made interactive Sankey diagrams available, a valuable tool for people studying energy and the economy.

1.2.3 Useful work I

Ayres and Warr[10] have introduced the idea of useful work

$$U \underset{=}{\operatorname{def}} eE$$

(1.2.2)

where E is energy production and e is efficiency. Since efficiency is a dimensionless proportion, U has the units of energy so it is really just an aid to study the unit of energy rather than an entirely new unit. Essentially, U represents energy production less the energy lost in (non-useful) heat. Note that $0 < e < 1$ so that e is bounded.

This variable has the advantage of adding a measure of technological progress to measures of energy production. It also has the advantage of attempting to measure what is actually done with the energy, an improvement over just measuring energy production alone.

We define Useful Work Return on Energy Investment in a similar way to EROEI:

$$UWROEI \underset{=}{\operatorname{def}} \frac{U_0}{E_i} = eE_0 / E_i \qquad (1.2.3)$$

We do not divide by e in the denominator, as we assume that this is accounted for in the computation of EROEI.

1.2.4 Useful work II

One can take the idea of useful work a step further by measuring precisely what we do with energy in the economy. For example, one can measure vehicle×kilometres travelled, Ton×kilometres of freight transported, person×kilometres travelled, processor cycles cycled, or page views on the web. Such measures are direct measures of economic activity, but unfortunately one loses a uniform unit and it becomes difficult to compare different activities. One obtains measures of different parts of the economy with incompatible units. If the goal is to transport people or goods one can also talk about efficiency, though it is not as well defined as in Section 1.2.3. One can measure, for example, ton×kilometres per kilowatt hour. The larger the quotient, the greater the efficiency.

1.2.5 Labour and food

Marx[11] noted the importance of hours of person work in measuring value added. Again, different work requires different accounting methods. The amount of training and skill of workers varies. However, we can make meaningful averages based on population among other statistics. In order for people to work, they must be fed, so methods of food production must be considered. We believe that food production is the origin of labour specialization, and hence modern economies.

Because food is an essential ingredient of labour, we may substitute food production for labour. With food and labour, we can do analysis similar to EROEI analysis done with energy. Knowing the percentage of the population engaged in food production tells us how much labour is available for producing other things. In the United States, approximately 1 percent of the population is directly employed in agriculture, leaving 99 percent of the population available for other work.

In Burundi, 93 percent of the population is in agriculture leaving a mere 7 percent available to do other things. More generally, one can divide the number of person hours required to feed a population by the total number of person hours worked to obtain a measure of the diversity of the economy.

1.2.6 Ecological measures

Mollison and Holmgren[12] studied human systems with standard measures of species robustness. Economic activity cannot be positive if it destroys our ecosystem. The success of industrial agriculture can be relativised by ecological measures. Industrial mechanized agriculture has the advantage that few people can produce food for many permitting labour specialization. With the aid of chemicals and pest control, a very large percentage of the biomass produced is for human consumption. From an ecological point of view however, the biomass produced by industrial agriculture is frequently less than the biomass produced by wild systems, with great cost to natural ecological systems. Notably soil quality is destroyed and biodiversity is lost.[13,14,15,16]

1.2.7 Social measures

Economists have begun studying well being to enhance other measures of economic output.[17,18] Understanding factors influencing well being can be important in establishing strategies for an energy constrained economy. Energy constraints may make growing GDP impossible, but perhaps there are strategies for living well despite a stagnant or decreasing GDP.

In conclusion, different units give different points of view of the economy. A single measure will not reflect the full spectrum of economic activity. Mathematical models require measurements in order to be useful.

1.3 Secular cycles

1.3.1 Empirical description

Turchin and Nefedov empirically identified recurring secular or economic cycles in agrarian societies. The cycle begins with a period of growth, in population and living standards lasting on the order of a hundred of years. Then comes a period of stagflation in which population density approaches the carrying capacity of the land (one says increased population pressure) lasting on the order of half a century. During the stagflation period, peasants leave the countryside for cities, the difference in wealth between the elite and the commoners increases and the price of food rises relative to wages. Population ceases to grow because food production ceases to grow. At first the elite are somewhat better off in the stagflation period because wages are low and they can employ a larger number of former peasants who have left the countryside. As the stagflation period progresses, the ratio of elite population to working class population rises (the working class have a lower birthrate and a higher mortality rate due to malnutrition and cramped living conditions in cities), creating competition among the elite. Social mobility increases, mostly downward as elites lose their status. The inter elite competition creates fissures which lead to civil war and the final crisis stage lasting a few decades in which population decreases and the state breaks down. There follows an inter-cycle lasting several decades before a new growth period ensues.

1.3.2 The cost share theorem

Many empirical studies[19, 20, 21, 22, 23, 24, 25] show that food and energy are key quantities to consider when evaluating economic production. The "Cost Share Theorem" from neoclassic equilibrium theory [3, Appendix A] says that for an economy in equilibrium, cost share is proportional to the elasticity or scaling factors of the variables in the production function equation. Because the cost share of labour is almost 10 times the cost share of energy in the economy, many economists discount the idea that energy is important for economic production. In Appendix A, we prove Theorem A.1.1 which characterizes the dynamics of important factors in the economic production function whether the economy is in equilibrium or not. Theorem A.1.1 shows that the cost share theorem is extremely speculative in either a growing or shrinking economy. We make the following remarks relative to the cost share theorem and Theorem A.1.1:

Remark 1.3.1

1   *Theorem A.1.1 shows that in a growing or shrinking economy, the dynamics of the cost share is the important consideration, not the size. For important quantities, the derivative of the cost share is small or negative; that is, in a growing economy the cost share of important quantities decreases or remains constant while the cost share of unimportant quantities increases. This makes sense. Important quantities such as oil permit the growth of less important parts of the economy such as art or competitive sports.*

2   *Empirical results from Meadows and colleagues in 2009 (previewed in Schindler in 2016[26]) are consistent with very strong (super-linear) dependence of economic production on oil extraction.*

3   *Equilibrium theory studies steady states. The economy is dynamic.[27] A dynamical system might converge to a steady state but one does not expect a dynamical system to be in a steady state while it is changing. We feel that a dynamical system approach to modeling the economy would be more useful.*

4   *In the previously-cited articles, empirical evidence did not support the Cost Share Theorem. Rather than question the hypotheses on which the theorem is based, the authors attempted to save equilibrium theory by introducing constraints (thus introducing a Lagrange multiplier to explain the importance of energy in the economy). We believe these attempts are artificial and think a dynamical system approach to understanding economic production and prices would be more useful as in Meadows in 1974,[28] Meadows and Meadows in 2005[29] and Bardi in 2011.[30]*

5   *Theorem A.1.1 says that the scarcity rent of an important item in the economic production function will be lower than that of an item of less importance in some sense. This can be understood by the fact that scarcity of an*

important item causes the economy to decline, decreasing the market for the good. On the other hand, the cost share of the item will increase, decreasing ecodiversity.

There is a high probability that the hypotheses on which the Cost Share Theorem is based are not verified. The Cost Share Theorem says that a large cost share corresponds to importance in the economic production function. Theorem A.1.1 says that increasing cost share is a sign of unimportance in economic production, however a large cost share frequently translates into political power. This dynamic can induce governments to embrace counterproductive policies as during the stagflation period, they might focus on large sectors of the economy which are unimportant in economic production rather than important areas of the economy with smaller cost shares.

1.3.3 An economic theory of secular cycles

Secular cycles can be seen as a business, or economic cycle in food production, that is, food is the key economic motor (as defined in Definition A.1.1) of growth. We see modern economies as a superposition of interacting business cycles where the motors of growth of the cycle are the key quantities to study.

We present a theory to explain these cycles which we hope will be useful to foresee problems and elaborate procedures to mitigate the ill effects. We make the following hypotheses:

(H1)   Profits are spent on culture and growth.
(H2)   The principle of conatus.

Hypothesis (H1) is to be understood quite broadly. It is in fact similar to Darwin's theory of natural selection. Darwin felt that populations grew creating a diversity of traits and species until resources constrained the growth. This resulted in a competition which the species with the best adapted traits survived.

Hypothesis (H1) says that businesses with profits will grow, but will also create ecodiversity by investing in culture. This growth continues, if unchecked, until limits are attained.

Hypothesis (H2) is Spinoza's principle that all things strive to continue their existence promoted for economic entities by Frédéric Lordon.[31,32]

The business cycles of several energy sources will go into contraction in the twenty-first century. According to Uppsala Global Energy Systems, the first of these will be oil, which in fact comports several different business cycles classified by the means of extraction. With the above hypotheses, and Theorem A.1.1 one can qualitatively describe the economic cycle of oil as follows:

The growth phase

Extraction of oil is profitable. From Hypothesis (H1) this encourages the production of oil consuming capital: internal combustion engines, oil burning turbines, space heaters, etc. If the price of oil drops, extraction rates stagnate but oil consuming capital grows, creating more demand, which increases prices. The increase in price causes an increase in extraction rates. Because oil is an economic motor, its cost share decreases, thus there is an increase in ecodiversity. This creates many opportunities for work, and in general salaries are high. Abusive employers do not find quality workers willing to work for them.

People are in general happy with political leaders because their conatus is in general satisfied.

The stagflation phase

This phase is characterized by increasing oil prices relative to wages while quantities increase marginally due to the decreasing quality of oil reserves (the sweet spots are produced first). The phase is also characterized by decreasing profits both in oil extraction (the cost of oil extraction increases) and consuming industries. In this phase, the motivating factor shifts to Hypothesis (H2). Economic agents attempt to prolong their existence and the status quo, that is to say increased production and profits. The cost share of oil increases (in family budgets). The economy loses ecodiversity due to less excess profits to spend on culture. Wages fall as the choice in jobs falls and decreasing wages are used as a tool to maintain profits. Stress and competition increases.

From Theorem A.1.1 we anticipate that prices do not increase as much as anticipated because the oil economy ceases to grow and some parts begin to contract. Oil becomes less and less affordable through higher oil prices and lower incomes due to less ecodiversity. In other words, the concentration of wealth leads to lower incomes and puts downward pressure on oil prices. People can fall out of the oil economy either through unemployment or through joining parallel non-oil-based economies. The difference between the elite class and ordinary workers increases. As stagflation continues, competition to remain in the elite class increases.

Politically, people are less happy with leaders because their conatus is less satisfied. Initially this dissatisfaction occurs only in the lower classes, but as stagflation continues, the dissatisfaction spreads to higher classes.

Contraction phase

In this phase, the feedback cycle that characterized the growth phase goes into reverse. High prices will reduce the market for capital transforming oil into useful work with stagnant production. Low prices reduce production and people will use the remaining oil transforming capital to prepare for a future with less oil.

We then reach a bifurcation point in history. The solution is not unique. Civil war is a possibility. Substitution of energy sources is a possibility, (as the oil-based economy replaced the whale economy of the nineteenth century[33]). We discuss this in greater detail in the next section.

Current assessment

Between 1998 and 2005 the price of oil quadrupled (from about half its twentieth-century average). The extraction rate rose by 14 percent. Between 2005 and 2014 the price doubled. Wages in OECD countries fell. The extraction rate rose by 5 percent. Concurrently, we have a concentration of wealth.[34] Empirically, we can put the beginning of stagflation for the oil cycle in 2005.

According to Uppsala Global Energy Systems, excluding Light Tight Oil (LTO) extracted using fracking, the contraction phase in oil extraction should have started in 2015. A fall in commodity prices beginning in 2014 rendered two-thirds of global coal extraction unprofitable in 2015 according to the energy consulting firm Wood Mackenzie. A large proportion of global oil extraction was also unprofitable in 2015, including most LTO extraction. The oil extraction industry reacted by sacrificing future production in favour of current production,[35] in other words, beginning a price war. If one considers the oil extracting industry to be the elite class, today's price war is similar to the civil wars described by Turchin and Nefedov.

The price war has come at the expense of an increase in debt by the oil extraction industry.[36] The debt of the industry will hamper future development. Bankruptcy frees the industry from debt at the expense of the financial sector of the economy so that further inter-elite competition is to be envisioned. We are approaching the end of the stagflation period.

1.4 Twentieth-century strategies

Several countries were confronted with energy shortages in the twentieth century, giving us the opportunity to have an empirical view of the dynamics of energy constraints on an economy.

Japan 1918–1945

In the face of fuel shortages between 1918 and 1945, Japan embarked on several military campaigns. Japan's leaders aspired to be a global power and thought that military conquest was the best means of assuring the raw materials necessary. Mistakes were made in the choice of targets and the attempt ultimately failed. Japan's oil consumption could only increase after the World War II once the US embargo had ended.

North Korea 1990s

North Korea has no oil reserves. After the fall of the Soviet Union, oil shipments to North Korea fell by 90 percent.[37] This caused a cascade of industrial failures. Transportation was curtailed, as a consequence, electricity generation fell because transportation of coal to power plants was hampered. Food production fell for lack of electricity for irrigation pumps and fertilizer. Increased use of biomass for energy exacerbated food problems. An estimated 3 percent to 5 percent of the population died of hunger. The elite class clamped down on the population and switched from Stalinian industrialization to politics of systemic scarcity. Petroleum products were reserved for military use and other parts of the industrial economy declined sharply. Outside of food production, the North Korean government has been relatively successful at running the country and maintaining power. There is still an endemic food scarcity in the country and a danger of famine. We note that the fuel shortage in North Korea was not like the typical secular cycle described by Turchin and Nefedov because there was no stagflation period and the shortage comes from an exterior source. In such a case, it is easier for governments to remain in place and manage the shortage.

Cuba

Like North Korea, Cuba has no oil reserves. Cuba suffered perhaps a greater industrial collapse than North Korea when the Soviet Union collapsed. Both the Cuban government and people managed the situation far better than North Korea, in part because the Cuban government was more humanitarian.

The key to Cuban adaptation was local resilience. Cuban agriculture had been mostly industrial production of sugar cane for the export market. Without fuel, fertilizer or pesticides, production dropped precipitously. Per capita caloric intake fell in a like manner. The government requisitioned all available plots of land in the cities and obliged people to begin producing food. Australian permaculture designers showed Cubans ecoagricultural techniques allowing the Cubans to raise food production to pre-Soviet collapse levels with a twentieth of the pesticides. Cuba was able to attain the highest standard of living for a country living with the sustainable criteria established by the Global Footprint Network. Rather that cut access to foreigners, Cuba opened up tourism.

The Soviet Union

The Soviet Union was the largest oil producer in the world in 1985 when oil prices began to collapse. The low price caused Soviet oil production to peak in 1986. This is exactly the scenario that our theory of secular cycles predicts. Adapting to lower oil production in a major oil producing nation is perhaps more difficult than in a non-producing nation because of Hypothesis (H2). Because oil production and use is so entrenched in the culture, it is very difficult to imagine a different scenario. The oil extraction industry will suggest state aid to boost extraction rather than policies aimed at adjusting to declining production.

Dmitry Orlov[38] has described the Soviet leadership blindness to the meaning of destruction of natural resources, outsized military expenditures and encroaching insolvency. Hypothesis (H2) is the basis of all sorts of false justification for continuing non-sustainable practices. Because of diminishing returns on investments, the Soviet economy collapsed. Soviet citizens typically lost about 90 percent of their savings after the collapse. When a state is collapsing, much analysis is done as to what went wrong. The people of the Soviet Union had parallel local economies that functioned outside of the main economy. These parallel economies helped people to adapt when the main Soviet economy collapsed. Unlike many authors, we expect the same fate as the Soviet Union to befall oil-extracting countries.

A slow decline in energy production is harder to manage politically than a fast collapse as in the case of Cuba and North Korea. A fast collapse in a non-oil-producing region can be seen as a problem coming from outside, while a slow contraction following a stagflation period uncovers corruption and flaws in the political system exacerbated by increased wealth inequality. As Turchin and Nefedov observe, governments collapse only when fissures appear in the elite class. That is only when the elite class runs up against limits.

1.4.1 Interactions

From these case histories, we see that energy shortages interact with other areas of the economy. At the same time that we are facing a crisis in energy shortages, we are facing other critical issues and interactions with the oil economy.

Food

Industrial agriculture, which has enabled an extraordinarily small percentage of the population to produce food for a great number, is unsustainable and the food cycle will roughly coincide with the oil cycle. Nitrogen fertilizers are reduced from fossil fuels (usually natural gas). Phosphorous comes from mines in North Africa. Ploughing the earth destroys the organisms of the soil and its natural robustness leading to soil degradation and reduced yield.[39] The system is unsustainable even with the required inputs of fossil fuels and fertilizers.

Financial system

The current international financial system was designed for constant economic growth. In the US, the cost share of the financial sector of the economy increased from about 2.25 percent of the economy in 1950 to over 8 percent in 2000 and thus has a positive derivative. Stagflation is already straining the system. In the event of a prolonged energy contraction, the system will cease to function. Local currencies can play a role in maintaining economic activity in case mainstream currencies break down. For example, the Swiss WIR Bank began issuing the WIR Franc in 1934 due to world financial instability.

The WIR Franc is still in circulation today and insulates the Swiss from global depressions as people can exchange WIR Francs in case there is a lack of normal Swiss Francs.

Climate change

Declining fossil fuel production is excellent news for climate change. Man has been affecting climate for millennia. A sustainable economy means implementing robust systems mitigating climate change. A key feature in climate change mitigation overlooked until recently is ecoagricultural techniques. The best indicator of high-quality soils is carbon. Industrial agricultural techniques decrease soil quality liberating carbon dioxide into the atmosphere whereas ecoagricultural techniques increase soil quality sequestering carbon. The French minister of agriculture launched the 4 for 1,000 campaign at the COP 21 climate talks promoting agricultural techniques that sequester carbon. It is estimated that 80 percent of current global carbon emissions could be sequestered in the soil.[40]

Loss of biodiversity and habitat We are experiencing the sixth great extinction of the planet.[41] Such a development cannot be deemed an economic success. Measures of the biosphere must be incorporated into measures of economic production.

Increased military tensions We see that shortages often increase military tensions and activities.

1.5 Permaculture

Permaculture is an increasingly popular strategy to prepare for an energy constrained future, though it is often not understood that permaculture was specifically designed to reduce problems associated with an energy constrained future.[42] Permaculture sees society as a subset of an ecosystem. A healthy society can only survive in a healthy ecosystem, so the economy must respect the ecosystem which sustains it. This is a common perspective of ecologists.[43]

We review the ground-breaking work of Mollison and Holmgren and its evolution.

Fundamentals Underlying assumptions of permaculture.[44, 45]

- The environmental crisis is real and of a magnitude that will certainly transform modern global industrial society beyond recognition. In the process, the well-being and even survival of the world's expanding population is directly threatened.
- The ongoing and future impacts of global industrial society and human numbers on the world's wondrous biodiversity are assumed to be far greater than the massive changes of the last few hundred years.
- Humans, although unusual within the natural world, are subject to the same scientific (energy) laws that govern the material universe, including the evolution of life.
- The tapping of fossil fuels during the industrial era was seen as the primary cause of the spectacular explosion in human numbers, technology and every other novel feature of modern society.
- Despite the inevitable unique nature of future realities, the inevitable depletion of fossil fuels within a few generations will see a return to the general patterns observable in nature and pre-industrial societies dependent on renewable energy and resources.

Permaculture is a creative design response to building new sustainable societies in a world of declining energy and resource availability.

When the US oil production peaked in the 1970s, affecting the world's economy, people started realizing how Western societies were dependent on oil and looking at ways we could lessen our dependency on it. Bill Mollison and David Holmgren, two academics in Tasmania, worked precisely on tackling what they considered the two biggest threats we are facing: climate change and peak oil (peak resources in general).

They considered that the first aspect to living with these challenges is local production of food and basic raw materials. So they looked for answers to the question: how can a group of people live sustainably on the same piece of land? In other words, how should land be cultivated for it to be able to provide food and raw materials as long as possible?

This led them to develop the concept of "permaculture" with the idea that a society could cultivate the same piece of land almost indefinitely to sustain their needs (permanent agriculture). After years of research and personal experiments, they imagined this "permanent agriculture" to represent an "integrated, evolving system of perennial or self-perpetuating plant and animal species useful to man".[46] Finding their inspiration by the observation of natural ecosystems, and researching for existing sustainable human societies, they outlined the basic principles and laws characterizing an agrarian system able to sustain itself. In short, they tried understanding how the resources should be managed, leading to the conceptualization of resource optimization in a human made ecosystem.

A more current definition of permaculture given by David Holmgren,[47,48] which reflects the expansion of focus, is "Consciously designed landscapes which mimic the patterns and relationships found in nature, while yielding an abundance of food, fibre and energy for provision of local needs."

People, their buildings and the ways they organize themselves are central to permaculture. Thus, the permaculture vision of permanent (sustainable) agriculture has evolved to one of permanent (sustainable) culture. Regenerative is implicit in Holmgren's understanding of "sustainable".

Ethics "are culturally evolved mechanisms that regulate self-interest, giving us a better understanding of good and bad outcomes. The greater the power of humans, the more critical ethics become for long-term cultural and biological survival".[49] Permaculture ethics have been inspired by the ethics commonly found in indigenous tribal cultures, having existed in relative balance with their environment:

- Care for earth: ensure abundant resources for survival and continuation of all life on earth, with perhaps an emphasis on the life in the soil.
- Care for people: respect and value humanity, communities and oneself.
- Fair share: Set limits to consumption and reproduction and redistribute surplus to those in need. Value staying within limits.

The design system Permaculture is an innovative concept that leads to creating sustainable societies based on the functioning of natural ecosystems. It has many similarities and overlaps with Lovins's emphasis on design processes drawn from nature.[50]

For many people, myself included, the above conception of permaculture is so global in its scope that is usefulness is reduced. More precisely, I see permaculture as the use of systems thinking and design principles that provide the organizing framework for implementing the above vision. It draws together the diverse ideas, skills and ways of living which need to be rediscovered and developed in order to empower us to move from being dependent consumers to becoming responsible and productive citizens.[51]

The permaculture vision differs from most traditional societies that mostly evolve through trial and error by better focusing on understanding the interrelationships between things and using them to human advantage. This is called design: how to place different elements of the system in space and time in order to optimize the beneficial relationships. In short, it is thinking of energy optimization. This is the key tool of permaculture systems enabling a decrease in energy use while still maintaining a comfortable and healthy lifestyle.

Permaculture is a new paradigm for creating new civilizations. Permaculture seeks to build a new way of thinking, but is also cantered on key values. It approaches the world with a different way of viewing things. The point of view shares more with the ecologist than with current neoclassic economic thought. Basically, it is a mode of viewing the world which underlies the theories and methodology of science in a particular period of history, that is to say a paradigm.

1.5.1 Strategies for change embedded in permaculture

"[T]he values to which people cling most stubbornly under inappropriate conditions are those values that were previously the source of their greatest triumphs".[52] Many people who are aware of our high energy lifestyles stay optimistic and believe in a "technology miracle", that is to say we will discover some way of "green tech" that will enable us to continue our current growth.[53] Permaculture more fundamentally, was predicated on the likelihood of some degree of collapse and breakdown in technology, economics and even society, which is actually a current reality for many people around the world. Going to a less energy intensive lifestyle is both inevitable and desirable if caring for the earth is part of our value system.

Bottom-up redesign processes

When one thinks of change, there are different levels of action, because the powers to drive things are dispersed in governments, markets, economy, society, international treaties, lobbies, scientific research, technologies, communication, etc. Most countries, even those classified as "democratic", are actually run by relatively small groups of politicians, which makes it hard for simple electors to communicate their ideas. One has to clearly identify our different means of action and estimate the degree of efficiency of each. A citizen can invest in government propositions, lobbies, but can also choose to change his or her buying habits, communicate in his or her neighbourhood or simply change his or her living choices. All level of actions are important to investigate. But ideally, following the design principle "start small", permaculture emphasizes bottom-up "redesign" processes, starting with the individual and household as the drivers for change at the market, community and cultural level. Change is more a matter of changing individual psychology and reflexes. Local resilience is the priority. Rather than having a centralized food production system with few farmers, a system of local production with many part-time farmers is a primary goal of the design process.

Build on new myths and values

"We can't solve problems by using the same kind of thinking we used when we created them" Albert Einstein.

"Two types of choices seem to me to have been crucial in tipping the outcomes [of the various societies' histories] towards success or failure: long-term planning and willingness to reconsider core values. On reflection we can also recognize the crucial role of these same two choices for the outcomes of our individual lives" Jared Diamond

Societies are built on myths and conceptions that are vehicles for values. The main obstacle of change is the way people think and conceive of things. In other words, the conatus principle (H2).

The permaculture flower that symbolizes the movement consists of the core values at the centre with sustainable techniques and technologies represented by the petals used to realize those values.

Use existing wealth to rebuild natural capital

"Natural capital is easy to overlook because it is the pond we swim in. One can live perfectly well without ever giving a thought to the sulfur cycle or wetland functions. Only when the benefits nature provides are disrupted do we take notice."[54]

"The economies of the Earth would grind to a halt without the services of ecological life-support systems, so in one sense their total value to the economy is infinite".[55]

Soil fertility is the key to a healthy ecosystem,[56,57] thus a healthy society. That is why when one thinks of strategies to build a new society that would live sustainable, it is most important to consider the land uses and farming practices.

Permaculture gives priority to using existing wealth to rebuilding natural capital, especially trees and forests, as a proven storage of wealth to sustain humanity into a future with less fossil fuel. The first rule of sustainability is to align with natural forces, or at least not try to defy them.

Holistic management: assure long term investments Pre-industrial societies are design models for resilience. Pre-industrial sustainable societies provide models that reflect the more general system design principles observable in nature and relevant to post-industrial systems. For example, fields were cultivated in China for 4,000 years without loss of yield.[58]

The inefficiency of the current dominant system is masked because growth and progress are measured in money, and money does not give us information about ecological systems, it only gives information about financial systems. Permaculture emphasizes holistic management techniques which include broader measures of human activity than currency (see Section 1.2).

1.6 Twenty-first century strategies

In the twenty-first century, we have seen the US invade Iraq possibly in anticipation of eminent oil shortages as Japan did in the twentieth century. We have seen political uprisings in Tunisia, Egypt and Syria where local oil production has peaked and oil is becoming increasingly unaffordable.

The town of Güssing, Austria population about 4,000 transitioned to 100-percent renewable energy sources between 1994 and 2001. They did not institute a carbon tax, nor did they sign any international treaties. In the 1990s the price of fossil fuels was relatively low. Güssing was in one of the poorest regions of Austria with few local jobs. Many people who lived in Güssing worked in Vienna. The local authorities considered how they could revitalize the local economy and create jobs. They decided a transition to 100-percent renewable energy would save money and create jobs. The plan worked. Not only were local jobs created, but Güssing acquired technology which today is exported by the firm Güssing Renewable Energy GmbH. Güssing benefited from subsidies from the European Union for regional development. There was a strong collaborative effort by the villagers. What they could not pay for, they did themselves.

Güssing's example shows that it is possible to transition to renewable energy sources, it suffices to make renewable energy the goal and perhaps accept different lifestyles. More generally, we could use peak fossil fuel production as a catalyst for transitioning to a sustainable economy in the spirit of permaculture. By this we mean that we would like to transition to a society which damps large secular cycles. This entails transitioning to a society which stays away from limits. Therefore, a cultural change is necessary because the natural tendency of Hypothesis (H1) must be restrained. Cultures exist in which (H1) is restrained. For example, hunter–gatherer societies handle constraints in food and resources by voluntarily reducing population in times of resource stress (frequently through infanticide). Thus, the aborigines of Australia have maintained an oral tradition that is 15,000 years old. In the Pyrenees, a culture without growth existed for many centuries based on primogeniture. Only the eldest son in a household was permitted to marry and procreate. His brothers and unmarried sisters were expected to work for the family without reproducing.

To transition to a sustainable economy, there are two key points we emphasize: The first is that there is not a unique solution. The second is the local nature of solutions. Solutions will change with respect to the local climate, terrain, culture and resources.

We believe that the primary difficulty in transitioning is fighting those who would like to continue on the current trajectory of fossil fuel production and use along with the goal of economic growth. Homer-Dixon notes in a 2006 publication[59] that the masters of the dominant energy form of an age dominate that age. In the eighteenth century, the Dutch mastered wind. The nineteenth century was dominated by the coal-powered British and the twentieth century was dominated by petroleum-powered US and Soviet Union. Why didn't the Dutch quickly adopt coal or the British adopt petroleum? Homer-Dixon attributes the lack of change to installed capital which would have had to be changed, another version of the conatus principle.

1.6.1 Technology

There is much technology available today, or which could be available shortly, that would mitigate an energy shortage and some of the associated problems.

We stress that any use of technology will reach limits if population continues to expand. Therefore, there is no technological fix. The only fix can be cultural in that we change our culture to a culture without growth.

Composting toilets

One of the most important aspects of ecoagriculture is dry toilets which conserve fresh water, improve soil quality, replace chemical fertilizers and when combined with composting can odourlessly sanitize and destroy toxic chemicals.[60]

Negawatthours All forms of energy production have drawbacks. Güssing's first step in attaining 100-percent renewable energy production was to reduce consumption by 50 percent. Currently, an astonishing proportion of energy is wasted. The most environmental form of energy production is the negawatt, that is, producing less energy.

According to the US Energy Information Administration (EIA), 48 percent of household energy consumption in the US for 2009 was used for space heating and cooling. We know how to weatherproof buildings using green architectural techniques which could reduce the quantity of energy spent on space heating and cooling considerably.

Electrical storage

A frequent objection to renewable power generation is that the source is intermittent, therefore is not feasible to use renewable power as the unique power source because electric power cannot be stored cheaply. This is not true. It is true that batteries which currently offer the highest energy density have high cycle cost. Technologies that have low cycle cost are:

- Pumping water. About 70-percent efficient but requires a great deal of space.
- Fly wheels. Today they spin in a vacuum and have magnetic bearings. Very flexible to use, but require a large initial investment.
- Heat pumped electrical storage. A relatively recent idea which should be relatively cheap. Energy is stored using a temperature difference. To store electricity, a heat pump uses a gas to create a temperature difference between two insulated containers, one hot high pressure container, the other a cold low-pressure container. To recover the energy, the system works in reverse: the gas expands from the high-pressure tank into the low-pressure tank driving a gas turbine (or the equivalent) creating electric power. Thermal mass is added to the containers to reduce temperature extremes.

High-altitude wind power

Wind is both stronger and more regular at high altitude. High altitude wind has the potential of being cheaper and more respectful to other species than terrestrial wind turbines. The challenges to implementing high-altitude wind power are to teach computers how to fly kites or gliders. Contraction in oil production will undoubtedly reduce aircraft orders creating a glut in airospace engineers. These engineers would be well suited to find commercial solutions to high-altitude wind power production.

1.6.2 Marketing

Combining concerns about climate change and an energy constrained future leads to very persuasive marketing if symptoms of peak fossil fuels are correctly communicated. Articulating the future lack of ecodiversity and increased competition from continued dependence on fossil fuels as an energy source and the possibility of a dynamic local economy based entirely on renewable energy. The price of renewable energy has been falling relative to that of fossil fuels, and if Uppsala Global Energy Systems predictions are even close to being believed, this trend will continue.[61] From a climate change point of view, the goal is to decrease the price of fossil fuels below their production cost which will decrease the financial and political clout of the fossil fuel industry.

Güssing's example is being followed by many so-called transition towns. These towns are in advance. Anticipating future changes facilitates transformations. When considering which energy source is the cheapest, one must consider how relative prices will evolve in the future. Since a coal _red power plant lasts about 40 years, one should seriously consider how the price of coal (and its transport) will evolve relative to a renewable source in the next 40 years before deciding whether the choice is really cheaper than renewable energy.

At this writing, since January 2015, Haynes and Boon LLC has reported 69 bankruptcies in the North American oil extraction industry. Informing investors of the risks of investing in the extraction business can steer funding away from non-sustainable solutions.

As renewable resources become the dominant energy source during the twenty-first century, many twentieth-century myths will be shattered. This will create an opportunity to change cultures and economic goals.

Permaculturists' emphasis on food seems quite relevant as many farms require subsidies, either government or private, in order to produce.[62] This means that our food supply is much more fragile than the relative cost of food suggests. People should be informed that producing and consuming food produced with ecoagricultural techniques is important not for personal health, but rather for the health of the planet and to provide food security.

1.6.3 Crises and opportunities

We believe the probability that the current financial system collapses to be high. As an insurance policy, parallel local economies should be developed, with local currencies, that are able to provide essential services such as food and transportation in the event of a collapse. Perhaps such things as education could be provided in a parallel setting as well. For example, permaculture design courses could be organized. Workshops in constitutional law should also be organized. Étienne Chouard correctly advocates practicing writing constitutions in the case of a government collapse. Usually when a government collapses people are not ready with a new constitution and politicians whose policies failed are able to seize power on their own terms.

Many ways of reaching collective decisions are being actively studied in academia.[63, 64] People should be actively thinking about new financial systems adapted to economic stagnation or contraction. Transparent ways of incorporating broader economic measures into our economic decision making must be thought out.

1.7 Conclusion

Many strategies for an energy-constrained future are being actively carried out today, sometimes unknowingly. The most constructive are those implemented by transition towns strongly motivated by permaculture design concepts. Many people are not aware that much current social stress is caused by the current stagflation phase of petroleum extraction and even less aware that these forces will accentuate in the coming years as we move into contraction. In order to transition to a sustainable economy, cultural change is required. Currently we respect and praise a person who achieves great personal wealth. We must learn to respect and praise those who live rich and fulfilling lives without excessive use of resources. We are living in a time of great challenges, but opportunities are opening for redesigning our economy with more holistic goals in mind.

Appendix A

We prove some basic results about general economic production functions and cost share.

A.1 Economic production functions

A.1.1 Definitions and hypotheses

Let $Y(t)$ be the economic production of an economy expressed in currency where t denotes time. We make no assumptions about the structure of the economy other than the existence of a well-developed monetary system to determine the distribution of wealth. Let $q(t) \epsilon R^d$ be the measurable quantities in the economy (quantities with a price). We will make use of the following assumptions:

H1

$$Y(t) = Y(\mathbf{q}(t), t) \tag{A.1.1}$$

is a locally $C^1(R^d \times R \mapsto R)$ with $\mathbf{q}(t) = (q_1(t), \ldots q_d(t))$ R^d. Prices are locally $C^1(R^d \times R \mapsto R)$ functions of quantities.

H2 Over short periods of time the economic production function depends more on $\mathbf{q}(t)$ than on the time variable, therefore, for short periods of time $Y(\mathbf{q}(t), t) \approx \tilde{Y}(\mathbf{q}(t))$, $\mathbf{q}(t) \in R^d$.

H3 For short periods of time we have $\dfrac{\partial Y}{\partial q_i} \neq 0$ for $i = 1, \ldots, d$.

Remark A.1.1

1 The regularity assumptions are not essential to the theory developed below, their purpose is to simplify notation.

2 In the real world, $d = d(t)$. Care must be taken when applying results to new quantities or disappearing quantities.

H1 is not a strong assumption, as the very fact that GDP is measurable means we measure certain quantities and use prices to evaluate the value added by the domestic economy.

H2 essentially says that we assume it takes time for the economy to change. Certain quantities are fungible, but we assume it takes a certain amount of time to switch from one item to the other.

H3 is not a strong assumption, as we are eliminating only quantities that have a small effect on the economy at any given time.

Let $p_i(t)$ be the cost per unit of $q_i(t)$ and let c_i be the *cost share* or *intensity* of q_i in the economy,

$$c_i(t) \underset{=}{\mathrm{def}} \frac{p_i(t) q_i(t)}{Y(t)}. \tag{A.1.2}$$

We make the following definitions.

Definition A.1.1

1   We will say that a currency is adjusted for inflation with respect to the variable q_i if $\dfrac{\partial p_i}{\partial q_i} = 0$.

2   A quantity q_i is called a super linear motor of economic growth if $\dfrac{\partial q_i}{\partial c_i} < 0$ in a currency adjusted for inflation with respect to q_i.

3   A quantity q_i is called a drag on economic growth if $\dfrac{\partial c_i}{\partial q_i} < 1 / q_i$ in a currency adjusted for inflation with respect to q_i.

Remark A.1.2

The cost share of economic motors decreases in times of economic growth and increases in times of economic contraction.

Definition A.1.1 is an artificial construct to simplify the proof and statement of Theorem A.1.1. However, during the twentieth century, adjusted for inflation in the standard way, the price of oil and other commodities were highly volatile around a constant average,[65] while their cost shares decreased and the economy grew, making them strong candidates for being economic motors.

We will denote by $Y_{q_i} = Y_i(\bar{q}_i(t), t, u)$, with $\bar{q}_i(t) \in R^{d-1}$, consisting of $q_j, j \neq i$, the quantity

$$Y_{q_i}(u) \underset{=}{\mathrm{def}} \int_0^u \frac{\partial Y}{\partial q_i} q_i{}'(s)\, ds. \tag{A.1.3}$$

We denote by $Y_u(u)$ when the above integral is with respect to the last variable. We define the functions $p_{qiu}(u)$ and $C_{qi}(u)$ similarly.

The function $Y(t)$ can also be seen as a function of the prices $Y(\mathbf{p}(t), t)$, $p \in R^d$ When the above derivatives and integrals are with respect to p_i, they will be denoted $Y_{qi}(u)$, etc.

For any function $x(t)$ and $(t_0, t_1) \in R^2_+$, we define the index of x:

$$I_x(t_0, t_1) \underset{=}{\mathrm{def}} (t_1) / x(t_0) \tag{A.1.4}$$

A.1.2 Elasticity

Elasticity, or how quantities scale in the economic production function, is very important. Suppose $d = 1$. One can write $Y(t)=Cq^{\alpha(t)}$. If $\alpha(t) \equiv \alpha$, a constant, then the production function is homogeneous of degree α and we call α the elasticity or scaling factor. If $\alpha = 1$ Y is linear in q, if $\alpha < 1$, Y is *sub-linear* in q, otherwise, Y is *super-linear* in q. Scaling factors are important in many sciences and mathematics. One looks for constant or average scaling empirically by normalizing quantities at a start date, taking logs and performing linear regression.

A.1.3 Main theorem

We prove
   Theorem A.1.1. *Assume (H1), then*

1   *If $\alpha_i(t)$ is the scaling factor of q_i, then $\alpha_i(t) - 1$ is the scaling factor of p_i/c_i.*
2   *Assume that c_i is constant. Then sublinear scaling of Y in q_i occurs if and only if $p_i(q_i)$ is monotone decreasing, linear scaling implies price is independent of q_i, and super-linear scaling occurs if and only if $p_i(q_i)$ is monotone increasing.*
3   *Super-linear economic motors have super-linear scaling in Y, economic drags have sublinear scaling in Y.*
4   *The greater $\dfrac{\partial Y}{\partial q_i}$, the smaller the scarcity rent in the sense of (A.1.8) (see discussion later).*
5   *The quantity $\dfrac{\partial Y}{\partial q_i}$ is negative if and only if q_i is a drag on economic growth. If q_i is a motor of economic growth, $\dfrac{\partial Y}{\partial q_i} > 0$.*
6   *The index of $Y_{qi}(u)$ for any $(t_1,t_2) \in \mathbb{R}_+^2$ is given by*

$$I_{Y_{qi}} = I_{q_{p_i}}(t_1,t_2)I_{c_{qi}}(t_2,t_1)I_{q_i}(t_1,t_2).$$ (A.1.5)

7   *The index of $Y_{pi}(u)$ for any $(t_1,t_2) \in \mathbb{R}_+^2$ is given by*

$$I_{Y_{pi}}(t_1,t_2) = I_{q_{p_i}}(t_1,t_2)I_{c_{qi}}(t_2,t_1)I_{q_i}(t_1,t_2).$$ (A.1.6)

Proof.   From (A.1.2) one immediately obtains

$$p_i(t) = c_i(t)Y(t)/q_i(t).$$ (A.1.7)

Properties (1) and (2) can be read directly from (A.1.7). Property (3) is also clear from (A.1.7) since for an economic motor, a negative cost share derivative means the cost share decreases with constant price implying superlinear scaling in Y. A similar statement holds true in the case of an economic drag.
   Taking the derivative of (A.1.7) one obtains

$$\frac{\partial p_i}{\partial q_i} = \frac{Y}{q_i}\frac{\partial c_i}{\partial q_i} + \frac{c_i}{q_i^2}\left(\frac{\partial Y}{\partial q_i}q_i - Y\right).$$ (A.1.8)

The scarcity rent of a quantity varies inversely to its importance in the economic production function in the following sense. The more important a quantity in the economic production function, the greater the partial derivative of Y with respect to that quantity. But from (A.1.8), we see that the price is an increasing function of the partial derivative of Y with respect to q, or price decreases as quantity decreases, a negative scarcity rent.[66] This proves (4).

Solving (A.1.2) for Y, taking logs, and then the partial derivative with respect to q_i, one obtains

$$\frac{\partial Y}{\partial q_i} = Y\left(\frac{1}{p_i}\frac{\partial p_i}{\partial q_i} - \frac{1}{c_i}\frac{\partial c_i}{\partial q_i} + \frac{1}{q_i}\right).$$

(A.1.9)

The sign of the left-hand side of (A.1.9) is the same as the sign in parentheses on the right-hand side. Using a currency adjusted for inflation with respect to q_i the first term in parentheses is 0, this proves (5). To obtain (A.1.5), we multiply (A.1.9) by $\frac{dq}{dt}/Y$ and integrate from t_1 to t_2 and take the exponential of the resulting equation. The proof of (A.1.6) is similar.

Remark A.1.3

1   *Equation (A.1.8) should not be considered a precise model because different quantities in the equation move at different speeds. Prices move more quickly than does the reaction of the economy to price changes.*
2   *Equation (A.1.5) can provide a method for measuring the relative contribution of a quantity in $I_Y(t_1, t_2)$ in cases where $c_{q_i}(t)$ or $c_{p_i}(t)$ can be estimated. Note that*

$$I_Y\left(t_1,t_2\right) = I_{Y_u}\prod_{j=1}^{d} I_{Y_{q_j}}\left(t_1,t_2\right).$$

(A.1.10)

Note also that the order in which $I_{Y_{q_j}}\left(t_1,t_2\right)$ is computed in (A.1.10) can change i's value because this changes the values of the $q_i(t)$, $i \neq j$ in (A.1.5).

3   *In most cases one has*

$$I_{c_{q_i}}\left(t_1,t_0\right) \leq I_{c_i}\left(t_1,t_0\right).$$

(A.1.11)

In order for the inequality to be strict in (A.1.11), another independent quantity must increase. See Section A.2.

4   *If useful work $U = eE$ is used as a variable, we can write $Y(U(t)) = Y(e(t)E(t))$ (A.1.7) becomes $p_E = c_E Y(eE)/q_E$. One sees that energy efficiency increases the price per unit of energy assuming $c_E(t)$ remains constant and Y is an increasing function of U. We thus have a very simple explanation of the empirically observed Jevons paradox or the rebound effect.[67,68]*

5   The "cost share theorem" from neoclassic equilibrium theory [3, Appendix A] says that cost share is proportional to the scaling factors of the variables in the production function equation. Equation (A.1.9) suggests strongly that in a growing economy a large scaling factor should be associated with a shrinking cost share, thus the interaction between variables gives some variables larger scaling. We can think of many reasonable scenarios in which this theorem is not verified (see Section A.2). We believe that the hypotheses from which the cost share theorem is derived are speculative and that empirical evidence should be inspected carefully before accepting this theorem.

A.2 An example

We suppose a very limited economy produces three quantities: $q_1 = E$, $q_2 = G$, and $q_3 = F$. We assume prices are adjusted for inflation for the three quantities and we normalize all prices to 1. The size of this economy is

$$Y(t) = \sum_{i=1}^{3} p_i q_i$$

(A.2.1)

$$= E + G + F .$$

(A.2.2)

Now suppose that E is a motor of economic growth in the following sense, when E grows 10 percent this produces a growth of 5 percent in both G and F in the next time period. Growth in G has no effect on E or F. However F is a drag on economic growth since a 10 percent growth in F causes a 5 percent contraction in E and G.

We can name our quantities to make the example more realistic. We call E energy production, which permits us to produce more of G and F. Let us call G gold production and F fun production. Fun decreases growth in E and G because in fact many people do not like producing energy or mining for gold, so as soon as there is a fun event, they stop work to enjoy the fun which reduces production of E and G.

Let us assume that t=n ϵ N and that the initial conditions are $E_0 = G_0 = F_0 = 1$. Now assume that population growth would cause growth of 10 percent in each time period, but the interactions occur in the next time period. Thus $E_1 = G_1 = F_1 = 1.1$ but $E_2 = 1.21 - .055 = 1.155$ because of the fun interaction. We have $G_2 = 1.21 - .055 + .055 = 1.21$ and $F_2 = 1.21 + .055 = 1.265$. We see that the cost share c_E has dropped from 1/3 to 0.32, c_G is unchanged and c_F increases from 1/3 to .35, while $I_Y(0, 2) = 1.21$. Computing the index of each quantity separately (assuming the other quantities constant at the t_0 value, that is, assuming the index is computed as if it was computed first in [A.1.10]) we find $I_{Y_E}(0,2) \approx 1.1$, $I_{Y_G}(0,2) = 1.07$, and $I_{Y_F}(0,2) \approx 1.04$. Note that $c_{q_1}(q_2(t_0), q_3(t_0), t_1) \approx 0.366 > c_E(t_1) = 0.32$ so that $I_{c_{q_1}}(t_1, t_0) < I_{c_E}(t_1, t_0)$.

This is because E does not explain all the growth in Y. The individual scaling factors of E, G, and F are respectively .52, .35, and .19. Repeating the calculations with $E_0 = G_0/2 = F_0/2 = 1/2$, we obtain $E_1 = .55$, $G_1 = 1.1$, $F_1 = 1.1$, $E_2 = .575$, $G_2 = 1.21$, $F_2 = 1.26$. With these initial conditions, c_E decreases from .2 to .19, c_G is almost unchanged and c_F increases from .40 to .41. In this case $I_y(0,2) = 1.22$ so that a smaller initial cost share of the economic motor produces greater overall growth. From these initial conditions, the individual scaling factors of E, G, and F are .5, .42, and .28 respectively.

Remark A.2.1

Not all quantities that drag on economic growth are fun.

Notes

1 Hopkins, R. *The Transition Handbook: From Oil Dependency to Local Resilience.* Chelsea Green Publishing, 2008.
2 Hopkins, R. *The Transition Companion: Making Your Community More Resilient in Uncertain Times*, Chelsea Green Publishing, 2011.
3 Victor, P. *Managing Without Growth Slower by Design Not Disaster*, Cheltenham, UK: Edward Elgar, 2008.
4 Turchin, P., and Nefedov, S. *Secular Cycles*, Princeton, NJ, Princeton University Press, 2009.
5 Coyle, D. *GDP: A Brief But Affectionate History*, Princeton, NJ, Princeton University Press, 2014.
6 Hall, C., Balogh, S., and Murphy, D. What is the minimum EROI that a sustainable society must have? *Energies.* 2009; 2:25−47.
7 Gagnon, N., Hall, C., and Brinker, L. A preliminary investigation into the energy return on energy investment in the global oil and gas industries. *Energies.* 2009; 2:490, 503.
8 Murphy, D., and Hall, C. Energy return on investment, peak oil, and the end of economic growth. *Annals of the New York Academy of Sciences.* 2011; 1219:52−72. *Ecological Economics Reviews.*
9 Weissback, D., Ruprecht, G., Huke, A., Czerski, K., Gottlieb, S., and Hussein, A. Energy intensities, EROIs (energy returned on invested), and energy payback times of electricity generating power plants. *Science Direct.* 2013; 52:210−221.
10 Darwin, C. *The Voyage of the Beagle*, John Murray, 1845.
11 Marx, K. *Value Price and Profit*, New York International Co., 1969.
12 Mollison, B., and Holmgren, D. *Permaculture One*, Corgi, 1978.
13 Fraser, E., and Rimas, A. *Empires of Food: Feast, Famine, and the Rise and Fall of Civilizations*, Free Press, 2011.
14 Montgomery, D. *Dirt: The Erosion of Civilizations*, Berkeley, CA, University of California Press, 2007.
15 Friedrichs, J. Global energy crunch: How different parts of the world would react to peak oil scenario. *ScienceDirect, Energy Policy.* 2010; 38:4562−4569.
16 Jenkins, J. *The Humanure Handbook*, Joseph Jenkins Inc., 2005.
17 Frey, B. *Happiness: A Revolution in Economics*, Cambridge, MA, MIT Press, 2008.
18 Weimann, J., Knabe, A., and Shöb, R. *Measuring Happiness: The Economics of Well-Being*, Cambridge, MA, MIT Press, 2015.
19 Reynolds, D.B. *Scarcity and Growth Considering Oil and Energy: An Alternative Neo-Classical View*, The Edwin Mellon Press, 2002.
20 Hamilton, J. *Causes and consequences of the oil shock 2007–08.* Brookings Papers on Economic Activity, 2009.
21 Reynolds, D., and Baek, J. Much ado about Hotelling: Beware the ides of Hubbert. *ScienceDirect.* 2011: 34(1):162−170.

22 Ayres, R., and Warr, B. *The Economic Growth Engine: How Energy and Work Drive Material Prosperity*, Cheltenham, UK: Edward Elgar Publishing, 2009.

23 Kümmel, R. *The Second Law of Economics, Energy Entropy and the Origins of Wealth*, New York: Springer, 2011.

24 Giraud, G., and Kahraman, Z. *How dependent is growth from primary energy? Output energy elasticity in 50 countries*. Working Paper.

25 Illig, A., and Schindler, I. Oil Extraction and Price Dynamics. *BioPhysical Economics and Resource Quality*. 2017, 2(1), 1.

26 Schindler, I. *An empirical model for oil prices and some implications*. Blog, 2016. http://peakoilbarrel.com/empirical-model-oil-pricesimplications/.

27 Keen, S. *Debunking Economics: The Naked Emperor of the Social Sciences*, Zed Books, 2001.

28 Meadows, D. *The Limits to Growth*, Universe Books, 1974.

29 Meadows, D., Randers, J., and Meadows, D. *The Limits to Growth: The 30 Year Update*, Earthscan, 2005.

30 Bardi, U. *The Limits to Growth Revisited*, New York: Springer, 2011.

31 Lordon, F. *La Société des affects Pour un structuralisme des passions*, Seuil, 2013.

32 Lordon, F. *Conatus et institutions: pour un structuralisme énergétique*, Presses de Sciences Po, 2003.

33 Aleklett, K. *Peeking at peak oil*, New York: Springer, 2012.

34 Piketty, T. *Capital in the 21st Century* [*Capital au XXIe siècle*], Seuil, 2013.

35 Schindler, I. *Dysfunctional oil markets increase the probability of a deflationary debt spiral*. Toulouse School of Economics Debate Forum, November 2015. http://debate.tse-fr.eu/article/dysfunction-oil-markets-increasesprobability-deationary-debt-spiral.

36 Gula, A. The barrage of energy sector bankruptcies has begun. *Wall Street Daily*, April 2016. www.wallstreetdaily.com/2016/04/18/energy-sector-bankruptcies/.

37 Haggard, S., and Noland, M. *Famine in North Korea: Markets, Aid, and Reform*, Columbia, Columbia University Press, 2007.

38 Orlov, D. *Reinventing Collapse: The Soviet Example and American Prospects*, New Society Publishers, 2008.

39 Bourguignon, C. *Le sol la terre et les champs*, Sang de la Terre, 2008.

40 Paustian, K., Lehman, J., Ogle, S., Reay, D., Robertson, P., and Smith, P. Climate-smart soils. *Nature*. 2016; 532:49−52. http://dx.doi.org/10.1038/nature17174.

41 Kingsford, R.T., Watson, J.E.M., Lundquist, C.J., Ventor, O., Hughs, L., Johnston, E.L., Atherton, J., Gawel, M., Keith, D.A., Mackey, B.G., Morley, C., Possingham, H.P., Raynor, B., Recher, H.F., and Wilson, K.A. Major conservation policy issues for biodiversity in Oceania. *Conservation Biology*, 2009.

42 Schindler, J. *What is permaculture? A handful of opinions given under the shadow of environmental crises*. Master's thesis, Agrocampus Ouest, Rennes, 2011.

43 Victor, P. (2008). *Managing Without Growth Slower by Design Not Disaster*, Cheltenham, UK: Edward Elgar.

44 Holmgren, D. *The Essence of Permaculture*, 2002. Free download http://holmgren.com.au/downloads/Essence of Pc EN.pdf.

45 Holmgren, D. *Permaculture*: *Principles and Pathways Beyond Sustainability*, Hepburn, Victoria, Holmgren Design Services, 2002.

46 Mollison, B., and Holmgren, D. (1978). *Permaculture One*, Corgi.

47 Holmgren, D. (2002). *The Essence of Permaculture*. Free download http://holmgren.com.au/downloads/Essence of Pc EN.pdf.

48 Holmgren, D. (2002). *Permaculture*: *Principles and Pathways Beyond Sustainability*, Hepburn, Victoria, Holmgren Design Services.

49 Staff. *Southern California permaculture convergence website*, 2013. www.facebook.com/SoCalConvergences.

50 Hawken, P., Lovins, A., and Lovins, H. *Natural Capitalism: Creating the Next Industrial Revolution*, Little, Brown, & Company, 1999.

51 Holmgren, D. (2002). *Permaculture: Principles and Pathways Beyond Sustainability*, Hepburn, Victoria, Holmgren Design Services.

52 Diamond, J. *Collapse: How Societies Choose to Fail or Succeed*, Penguin Group USA, 2011.

53 Hopkins, R. (2008). *The Transition Handbook: From Oil Dependency to Local Resilience*, Chelsea Green Publishing.

54 Hawken, P., Lovins, A., and Lovins, H. (1999). *Natural Capitalism: Creating the Next Industrial Revolution*, Little, Brown, & Company.

55 Costanza, R., d'Arge, R., de Groot, R., Farberk, S., Grasso, M., Hannon, B., Limburg, K., Naeem, S., O'Neill, R.V., Paruelo, J., Raskin, R.G., Suttonkk, P., and van den Belt, M. The value of the world's ecosystem services and natural capital. *Nature*. 1997: 387:253,260.

56 Bourguignon, C. (2008). *Le sol la terre et les champs*, Sang de la Terre.

57 Montgomery, D. (2007). *Dirt: The Erosion of Civilizations*, Berkeley, CA, University of California Press.

58 Franceys, et al. *A guide to the development of onsite sanitation*. Technical Report, Geneva, W.H.O, 1992.

59 Homer-Dixon, T. *The Upside of Down, Catastrophe, Creativity and the Renewal of Civilization*, Random House of Canada Limited, 2006. www.theupsideofdown.com.

60 Jenkins, J. (2005). *The Humanure Handbook*, Joseph Jenkins Inc.

61 Lovins, A. *Reinventing Fire: Bold Business Solutions for the New Energy Era*, The Rocky Mountain Institute, 2011.

62 Moyer, J. *What Nobody Told Me About Small Farming: I Can't Make a Living*, Salon, 2015. www.salon.com/2015/02/10/what_nobody_told_me_about_small_farming_I_can't_make_a_living/?utm_source=

63 Laslier, J.-F., and Sanver, R. (eds.). *The Handbook on Approval Voting*, New York: Springer, 2010.

64 Brandt, F., Conitzer, V., Endriss, U., Lang, J., and Procaccia, A. (eds.). *Handbook of Computational Social Choice*, Cambridge, Cambridge University Press, 2015.

65 Gaudet, G. *Natural resource economics under the rule of Hotelling, 2007*. Presidential address delivered at the 41st annual meetings of the Canadian Economics Association.

66 Of course, for an important quantity one would expect the derivative of the cost share to be strongly negative and dominate the positive term.

67 Jevons, W.S. *The Coal Question* (2nd edition), London, Macmillan and Co, 1866.

68 Ayres, R.U., and Warr, B. Energy efficiency and economic growth: The 'Rebound Effect' as a driver. In *Energy Efficiency and Sustainable Consumption: The Rebound Effect*, Macmillan, 2009.

6 Limits to material growth and economics

Ecological conditions and values and the core components of economic theories

Roberto Burlando

1 Current crises and tenets: market fundamentalism and unsustainability

The divide on crucial environmental issues, and in particular on climate change, seems to remain large and deep among economists,[1] politicians and (possibly consequently) lay people, while natural scientists appear to share rather more convergent views.[2] Only a tiny minority of them now deny the gravity of the current situation and/or still suggest possible "escape ways" to avoid taking immediate and decisive action affecting the working of our economic and social systems. The "alternative" views and solutions proposed by this minority group, however, take an unjustified and undeserved role in the public debate and are also often instrumentally used by others, including a significant share of economists. The relevant interests at stake and the way of working of the media seem to play an important role in this. These conjectures usually take the form of various kinds of technological optimism[3] and assume that science will soon find some "simple" and resolute solution.[4] Unfortunately at the moment none of those imagined seems a viable one, at least within the time horizons required by the ecological problems we face. So, while natural sciences and technological progress are important components in any real solution we can imagine, they cannot provide any easy "technical" solution to these problems, much to the discomfort of all of us.

Any concrete solution seems, therefore, to require also fundamental changes in our societal arrangements in general and in particular some significant form of energy transition, a perspective that implies also significant and immediate costs for various industrial sectors and which is, therefore, resisted by industrialists, economists and politicians. As the "natural" scientific views have already been considered – and from various perspectives – in previous chapters of this book, this one will build on them and discuss some of the reasons for the large divergence in the opinions of economists (and, possibly, other people). It will be argued that such a divide among economists is not unique to the issue at stake here. Rather, climate change is a peculiar instance in which the still quite "separated and erroneous" (in the words of the title of the book by a well-known science philosopher)[5] and "ad hoc" nature of mainstream economics – or at least of some of its core components – can be highlighted.

As it is the case also in other disciplines, it is not easy to exactly define what constitute the mainstream (or "normal science", though this definition could also be interpreted in a different way) within economics,[6] especially as there is now an almost continuum of different approaches covering the large spectrum of economics, so that it not easy to decide where to draw the line(s). Moreover the mainstream seems to evolve (to some extent) in time, incorporating new insights and ideas. Various approaches and definitions have therefore been suggested in this respect, sometimes moving from different science philosophy perspectives. Later in this paper we will identify the assumptions that constitute, in our view, the "core components" of mainstream economics, but for now we start simply tale it to include at the micro level conceptions of economics "as the investigation of the consequences of individual striving to maximize selfish interests" (Duprè, 2001, page 3) in general and the Rational Choice Theory in specific, and – at the macro level – all theoretical constructions built on the assumptions of General Competitive Equilibrium (either as a reasonable description of the working of current economic systems or as a good instrument to make reasonable predictions and take economic policy decisions about them).[7] Extreme versions of this approach have been termed *market fundamentalism*, as they maintain that markets always work well if not perturbed from "outside" and produce an allocative configuration that is a social optimum.

Mainstream economics appears to its critics to be farther and farther away from reality,[8] up to the point to represent a form of "magical" thinking, in which some *deux ex machina* – whose existence and ways of working are assumed rather than properly scientifically explained – solves all the problems by work of magic.[9] Unfortunately this "work of magic" has not produced the so many times proudly announced greatly positive results for the world population in general, and we see the results of the deregulation and globalization[10] processes on both our natural and social environments. Nevertheless it has not been, in the last decades, a fruitless endeavour: to the contrary, it has produced a quite remarkable result: an astonishing concentration of income and wealth in the hands of very few people, both at various national and at the international levels. This however, is not the announced economic miracle or a great achievement for all: rather it looks like a conjurer's trick, realized using both power and manipulation. Certainly a good part of serious mainstream theorists did not want this (see Akerlof and Schiller, 2015) and a similar result could also have been achieved via different economic policy prescriptions, but in such a case there would be specific people and not impersonal "market forces" to be blamed for the outcomes.

Unfortunately, this "magical" attitude is one of the relevant factors preventing our societies from seriously face the threat posed by climate change. In short, we are not doing what is required[11] to avoid enormous damages and catastrophes,[12] and the pressures of business and the theorizations of many mainstream economists contribute to postpone, slow down and minimize the interventions (as they also contribute to create confusion about the issue) and to the falling short of the international agreements on the issue with respect to what would be needed.

A notable exception, within the economic analyses, in the direction of recognizing the problems posed by climate change has been the Stern Report.[13] The

Report was specifically devoted to them, did not consider and/or address any other environmental problem and explicitly focused on pro-growth solutions. Within these limits (either of analysis or of perspective) it indicated that rapid and decisive interventions against climate change (both in terms of containment and adaptation) are needed and that their cost would be a fraction of what would otherwise be the economic (and even more the social) damages produced by climate changes.[14] Though this book considers a wider set of problems and maintain that they make the further growth of material production more and more costly and damaging,[15] it is worth recognizing that the comparison of the costs of intervention vs. no intervention presented in the Report has the advantage of both simplicity and appeal, even for the growth-oriented economists and politicians. The Report should have had a significant and lasting impact, but it did not, or at least much less than it could and should have had.

An instance of its limited effect comes from the last International Climate agreement, approved by 195 States in Paris on December 2015 and operative since November 2016. Though this looks like a step forward in the right direction with respect to previous agreements, it is so mainly in theory. To the recognition of the critical situation (generalized increase in temperature due to greenhouse gases emissions) and of its origins (mainly human activities), in fact, it does not follow any immediate and concrete action. To the contrary, the introduction of new measures to reduce carbon emission is postponed to 2020, despite the declared target to de-carbonize our economies before 2050. This seems in line with the usual political approach to state significant overall targets without connecting them with operational ones, neither at single State level nor at an effective time frames.

There have been many attempts at finding explanations for the failure of politics to take actions including the role of money and of private interests in politics (Hansen, 2009) and the difficulty for politicians to take strong actions that might upset powerful lobbies and/or people and result in loosing positions. Unfortunately (as already reminded in the Introduction) the laws of physics do not take into consideration political feasibility.

1.1 Why do both business and mainstream economics downplay the relevance of these conditions?

So climate change (as other "inconvenient truths") has been and still is being denied (or at least reduced in its dimension and consequences) in various ways and for various reasons by different people. In a specific study of climate change denial, Washington and Cook (Chapter 2) list five main approaches (arguments) to denial: conspiracy theories, fake experts, impossible expectations, misrepresentations and logical fallacies, cherry picking. They also rise the, possibly more relevant, question of why too many people "let denial prosper" (Chapter 5) and consider as main reasons the fear of change, the failure in values, the fixation on economics (and, possibly, society), the ignorance of ecology (how the world really works in terms of ecosystems), the inability to understand non-linear phenomena and particularly the dynamic of exponential growth, the gambling on the future (often due to lack of understanding of probabilities), the way of working of the media (not communicating science properly – rather trying to provoke arguments and controversies in order to sell, or following pre-conceived agendas), despair (for those who understand the scale of the problem and do not see feasible solutions), apathy and confusion.[16]

Though all these reasons apply also to economists and businessman (a good number of them has had some training in economics, after all), there seems to be some specific formulations that appear more suited to the majority of their denials.

Some of them understand the reality but take a cynical and opportunistic approach in the belief/hope either to be able to find an individual (or small group) escape from the worst (and perhaps even to gain relative positions), or presuming that there is not any real way out because humankind is not ready and willing to do what is required and prefers to stay under the illusion and excite himself in the "short run".

Others maintain the idea (the discussion of which will take up the largest part of this paper) that the social and economic mechanisms that are already at work in our society will eventually react to the possible worsening of the conditions and get the system and us out of the trap. Some members of this latter group seem terribly and ideologically attached to this "magical" vision of the working of market mechanisms for political reasons,[17] while for others the question looks more complicated and involves various tenets (core ones) built in the prevailing vision of economics.

Before moving into the discussion of the "core" components of mainstream economics, some additional considerations are needed, related to the already mentioned reasons for denial. First of all, there is the fact that any serious thinking about the relation between the natural world we live in and our economic arrangements has to start with the recognition that our complex economic and social systems are subsystems of the natural one and that this is a "closed" system. As any closed system, it exchanges only energy – mainly receiving it from the sun and now trapping too much of it because of the greenhouse gases – but not matter with the rest of the universe.[18] Such recognition implies in turn the necessity to inscribe any economic (and social) analysis and development within the context and limits of the natural environment that we cannot modify at our will (we discussed this point at length in the Introduction and it will not be repeated here). The Ecological Footprint measures show that since the mid 1980s every year the world has been using (though not evenly) more than its bio capacity (about 1.6 on average) and that the "ecological overshooting" day is coming sooner and sooner each year.

A further aspect of the question is that one of the very negative consequences of CC denial is that it diverts precious and scarce (for once exactly as mainstream economics usually maintains) resources from their best and more proper use: in researches and projects – in very many disciplines as many are required to contribute to a change of the necessary dimension – and in investments aimed at "real-life" sustainability, starting with large energy transition ones. This in turn ought to include smart ways to adapt our ways of producing and consuming and to reduce the complexity of our economic and social systems in order to make them less "demanding" in terms of resources. The question of sustainability is, at the very bottom, that of what we want to sustain because it is more worth to us, as it is simply impossible to sustain everything for everyone on the planet (as many have often stressed, including J. Tainter). These simple considerations, however, open up the door to the consideration of wide and dramatic perspectives.

1.2 Complexity, economic history, scenario analyses and rents

There appears to be two main ways to reduce the complexity of our economic and social systems,[19] each passible of a number of possible further specifications and, obviously, various "middle ways" between them.[20] One is dramatic as it implies letting natural catastrophes (by themselves or with interventions facilitating the process) to drastically reduce number of people that can reach a fair amount of resources. This could take the form of either making the life of the large majority of people similar – at least in terms of consumption of natural resources – to that of centuries ago, leaving to the few others full control over the remaining stocks, or downrightly reducing the size of the human population to a fraction of its current consistency.[21] This latter option would increase the per-capita resources of the remaining ones and will allow some kind of re-start (i.e., the shifting backwards of the intercept of unsustainable exponential functions) leaving time to repeat (with possible modifications) the story humanity has already been playing for a number of decades.[22]

The opposite scenario involves fundamental changes in the ways in which we organize our production and consumption and our individual and social lives, in such a way as to – intentionally and through appropriate technological and social choices and investments – greatly reduce the average per-capita consumption of natural resources,[23] while working to substitute them in the production processes almost completely (up to their reintegration rate) as this is what is required by the physical limits to material growth. The sooner we start this process, the greater the stock of natural resources at our disposal to accomplish such "transition". Some call such a transition process "degrowth" while others term the end state aimed at a "steady state", but the work on these perspectives is still in its early stages, due also to the lack of funding. Though the debates on these themes, including the various precise meaning of such terms, are clearly of interest for our perspectives, an account of them will require at least another book (and we agreed since the Conference on the need to cover the topics currently discussed in this chapter first, while Chapters 3 and 5 provide some perspectives on those themes). Let us just say here that the steady state perspective has a long history in economics, starting at least with J. S. Mill, and has been taken up again years ago especially by one of the founding fathers of ecological economics, H. Daly. Clearly a steady state cannot be thought of as the model of a fixed system in mechanically self-reproductive equilibrium. The degrowth approach is usually associated with the name of its most popular proponent, S. Latouche, who has been able to create an active interest for this perspective but also outright rejections. It seems to us that there is currently too much confusion even on these terms and too much cheap talk, even by those who could have the instruments for proper analyses.

Certainly, what is incredibly missing is serious research money on many of the issues connected to these problems and perspectives. Our societies invest too little money in research, as compared to other services, in general and (as Emmot has emphasized with respect to the fields he knows best) waste a lot of this small amount in research that have little (if any) impact on our future but that look "harmless" from the perspective of the current state of things and economic and political climate and interests. The "transition" to a significantly different lifestyle will require – at some point – a massive effort, involving very many interrelated changes at various levels of the working of our societies, one that would involve the use of all the technological and economic instruments we have and/or could devise. It seems just obvious that such a change ought to involve (but better be preceded by) as much study, thinking and discussion as possible on its various dimensions and aspects.

Our societies have already witnessed changes of similar dimensions and scopes, such as the one brought about by the neo-liberal (though for many the term is improperly used in that respect, as we shall see soon) and ultra-conservative turn imposed by the US and UK administrations under Regan and Thatcher.[24] Though members of the younger generations possibly fail to perceive the depth of that change because they have only lived in this "new environment", those who witnessed and lived it might be able to recognise its fundamental nature, and how it affected almost everything in our lives, from work to culture and distribution of income. Another dramatic change was that brought about by the financial crisis in 2007 and 2008, followed by a harsh economic crisis. And we are at risk of another financial crisis as no serious attempts have been pursued to modify the deep conditions (financial and economic ones) that led to that one, including those related to the environmental conditions.

The main difficulty of promoting, now, a novel change of these conditions and of heading in a very different direction is that the forces that pushed for that "revolution" hold now very powerful positions[25] (more than before) and strive to keep (or, rather, further expand) them and the huge rents,[26] they perceive, that are associated to this way of working of the markets and of the overall system. They can also easily finance pseudo-scientific institutions to produce "appropriate" research (as some did with respect to a number of issues that were damaging their business, like in DDT, acid rain and tobacco cases, in addition to CC, as documented by Oreskes and Conway, 2010) and invest in the development of a fake scientific culture[27] and in various propaganda activities. At the media level, this has happened to such an extent, especially with respect to the interests of the financial institutions, that in the recent years even some top-ranking – and in many ways mainstream economists, as economic Nobel Memorial Prize winners George Akerlof and Robert Shiller[28] – felt the need to warn people against the kinds of news and economics advices suggested by financial and economic "gurus" of all sorts.

It is worth considering that the main gainers from the economics transformations of the last decades – i.e., financiarization, deregulation of the markets (a conventional term, as in reality it consisted in a huge change of rules in order to favour specific actors, as evidenced among others by D. Baker, 2016) and liberalization of international capital movements – are rent receivers (according to the traditional distinction within economics, mainstream and not). For an economist, this presents an intellectually strange side, as rents have been promoted by economic policies that were "sold" to the public as oriented to freeing the markets[29] and, in this way, increase the general welfare. However, even within the most traditional economic theory, rents are well known for being "parasitic", i.e., producing neither economic growth or development nor diffused welfare. And in the last decades we have witnessed a huge increase in rents while both profits[30] and wages have keep dramatically diminishing their worth and share. Rents are imposing a heavy burden on the rest of the economy as they subtract resources both in terms of personal income (and therefore consumption) and of productive investments. Not surprisingly the world economy stagnates.

Needless to say, the main area in which rents have been growing and subtracting income and wealth to the productive sectors of the economy – up to the point of being considered like a parasite that will eventually end up killing the host it inhabits – is finance,[31] but other services have got their share too, thanks to legislation changes.[32] This appears as the main cause of the strong process of income concentration in the hands of really few companies and people that has been documented in many recent studies[33] and that work as a suffocating constraint on any developmental perspective in these decades.

The extension of the rents-seeking activities and the attitude towards it are also, possibly, among the main reasons why suggestions[34] of strategies to combine profits with environmental concerns did not succeed but to a very limited extent, contrary to the aims and breath invoked by its proponents. They also currently appear as the main constraint on the possibility of realizing the large investments needed for a relevant energy transition.

However, very little of mainstream macroeconomics deals with these aspects, confining rent-seeking behaviour and attitudes to a "dark corner" of the discipline and to a marginal role in the current debate, while mainstream theorizing still focusses on the frictionless dynamic stochastic general equilibrium, a "Panglossian" (see Buiter, 1980) view that appears to be farther away from the reality most of us live in. Despite its formal complexity, it still depicts a fictitious world in which markets work perfectly well, quickly and – above everything – in the interests of all, so that no intervention from outside is required. There is no space for parasitic behaviour nor for inefficiencies of any sort in this "magical" world. The only problem seems to be that it must lie somewhere else, possibly just in a theoretical "parallel" world.[35]

An example of a relevant real-life feature that is never considered or even mentioned in theoretical analyses of this sort is that of tax havens. For GE theory, they are just minor (obviously dishonest) and irrelevant exceptions[36] to the working of the markets, but this is not what the studies into this topic maintain. One of them states that "*the offshore system is not just a colourful appendage at the fringes of the global economy but rather lies at its very centre*" (Shaxson, page 16). French magistrate Eva Jolie, who was the main investigative figure in the Elf-Aquitaine affair, wrote: "I realized I was no longer confronted with a marginal thing but with a system" and added "*I do not see this as a terrible, multifaceted criminality which is besieging our [onshore] fortresses. I see a respectable, established system of power that has accepted grand corruption as a natural part of its daily business"*.[37] Another key study on the issue (for the Tax Justice Network, TJN, by James Henry, a former chief economist at the McKinsey consultancy)[38] pinpointed that a global super-rich elite had at least $21 trillion (£13tn) hidden in secret tax havens by the end of 2010. Mr Henry said his $21tn is actually a conservative figure and the true scale could be $32tn (he used data from the Bank of International Settlements, International Monetary Fund, World Bank, and national governments). The TJN added that *"The lost tax revenues implied by our estimates is huge"* and *"large enough to make a significant difference to the finances of many countries"* and they maintain that, as a result, governments suffer a lack of income taxes of up to $280 billion. Moreover,

> *of the top ten players in global private banking – the business of helping the world's richest people park their wealth offshore and conceal it from the authorities and escape the rule of law – all ten (UBS, Credit Suisse, Goldman Sachs, Bank America, HSBC, Deutschebank, BNP Paribas, Wells Fargo, Morgan Stanley/SB, JP Morgan Chase) received substantial injections of government loans and capital during 2008–2012.*
>
> (Shaxson, page 13)

On the one hand, economic theories that do not consider crucial real-life features appear also unable to suggest adequate policy indications. On the other, this immediately begs the question of what other crucial aspects of current real life economy it considers as irrelevant, or at least minor, that are instead crucial for our lives.[39] This pinpoints once more the "magical" thinking of general equilibrium theorising and its distance from economic reality.

Some well-known economists (in this case the mainstream seems larger than GE-based theories) recognize the importance of institutions and of their real working. For instance, two of them maintain (in articles and in quite popular books)[40] that *"Countries differ in their economic success because of their different institutions, the rules influencing how the economy works and incentives that motivate people"* and that *"both poverty and prosperity are created by economic and political incentives, and these incentives are shaped by institutions"*. They distinguish two main types of institutions and affirm what they term a general principle: that *"inclusive economic institutions foster economic activity, productivity growth and economic prosperity, while extractive economic institutions generally fail to do so"*. *"Inclusive institutions are not just made of secure and enforced property rights for a narrow elite, but require both such rights to be available to the majority of the population"*.

Unfortunately the debates on the self-regulating attitudes of markets and the new mathematical developments of old and once "discarded" theories diverge the attention from the real problems we need to face and from the crucial point of how to design and agree upon instruments for intervention that can work properly and in the real interest of all instead of in that of a minority of powerful people – in business and in politics – that manipulate the circumstances and twist the rules in the pursuit of their personal conveniences.

In order to face the current huge challenges, therefore, economics needs a fundamental rethinking at both theoretical and applied levels, starting from the methodological and ethical dimensions in order to incorporate the thermodynamic principles and the systemic approach and to get out of the "cul de sac" in which the economists' selfish version of utilitarianism (and in particular its most recent version, rational choice theory) has placed it.

2 Rethinking economics and its core components

Needless to say, a proper work on the rethinking of economics would require at least a book,[41] therefore in what follows we will provide only hints on various crucial aspects, whose selection – however – is one of the main steps pursued in this work. An important preliminary consideration with respect to this analysis is the recognition of a large semantic problem (that seems to get progressively larger as we move further into postmodern "relativism") that risks to undermine any meaningful attempt to discuss and compare theories (and even points of view). Without any hope to fully address the problem we will at least point to some of its main dimensions, as this may also be useful as a clarification for the non-economists.

2.1 Semantic problems and real disputes

There are various dimensions of what we term here as *semantic problems*. A first one is connected to the use of terms whose meaning is often assumed as clear and possibly unique by people who, in reality, have very different conceptions of it. The specifically assumed meaning of each of these terms is not usually fully specified, as this is often supposed to be superfluous and it would take time/space and complicate the discussion, but this attitude may lead to further (and possibly unnecessary) misunderstandings. Two typical and very widely used economic terms that mean quite different things to different people are *capitalism* and *market*.

An example, relevant to the present discussion, of the lack of understanding generated by implicit assumptions about the "real" meaning of the terms is the controversy over "steady state" and "green capitalism" and the (im)possibility of any of them that took place in recent years on the Real-World Economic Review.[42] Economic historian Richard Smith started it (2010) criticizing Herman Daly – and those who adopted his "Steady State" approach (including the New Economic Foundation in London and Tim Jackson) – because in his view (following a long tradition) capitalism has an intrinsic drive and the need for growth, so that Steady State or, in his view, Green Capitalism is simply impossible ("A God that Failed" is the title of an article and then a book of his). He suggests that a kind of eco-socialism is needed if we are to avoid ecological disaster. The dispute has also involved different conceptualizations about the term *market*. In a late reply (2016) H. Daly pointed out his *"preference for the market over centralized planning as a tool for dealing with the single technical problem of allocative efficiency"*, subject to *"two major and prior macro-level constraints"*: sustainable scale and just distribution.[43] Daly clearly stated that he sees markets as useful servant rather than "bad masters"[44] and that to have them performing properly this role *"reliance on markets for allocation (now within prior ecological and distributional limits)"* must be further constrained – as it used to be in the past even within traditional microeconomics – *"by opposition to monopoly, and restriction of market allocation to rival and excludable goods"*. Daly also recognized that *"in today secularist world it is admittedly hard to envision the source for the basic moral renewal required to face growthism's threat to both sustaining and sharing the Earth's capacity to support life"* but insisted on hope. He also rejected any association of steady state economics with either capitalism or socialism, suggesting that we should rather try and avoid "past mistakes" of all sorts.

A similar discussion could be raised also with respect to the (simpler) notion of physical limits to growth, as some interpret it also as a statement that capitalism in itself is not sustainable while others already maintain that the current crises are the clear signs of the end of the capitalist era. The modest view taken here move from the recognition of the existence, in the historical as well as theoretical sense, of various types of capitalism (as pointed out by comparative economic approaches. For instance B. Amable, 2004, distinguishes five different types) of which only one (denominated by Amable as Anglo-Saxon) is based on free market and trade ideology (then become "market fundamentalism"). Certainly this model, and especially its recent financial and rentier version, is not compatible with the very concept of physical limits to growth (or Steady State, for that matter) but some of the others (especially the Rhine and the Scandinavian ones)[45] might be,[46] if incorporating the limitations and corrections suggested by Daly and others. In addition, there are many other economic models (including market socialism and decentralized solidarity-based economics) that could constitute useful references for the much needed real life experiment we have to embark in, without resorting to versions of the centrally planned approach which caused so much pain and failures (but whose methods have been praised by many mainstream economists – in a very instrumental way – when applied for years within the "capitalist" setting in the Confucian model in South East Asian countries).

A second dimension is the use of methods and concepts that are different in different theoretical frames, possibly not well known to others or erroneously attributed or not well specified. This too may induce misunderstandings, as each of us associates to them interpretations and correlations that are not generally shared.

Less difficult to recognize, in theory but perhaps more widespread in practice, is the undue and/or unqualified extension of tenets outside their historical and/or cultural context (by both supporters and critics). A relevant example here is the notion that economic growth benefits everyone, irrespectively of the relative position in the economy and society, or in the territorial area. This was, to a large extent, true in the "golden age" period of the economy in the last century (1944–1971) but it has not been so ever since[47] and certainly not in the "free-trade era" (since 1980 to currents days), in which the distribution of incomes and wealth become much more concentrated (everywhere in the world) and the social mobility much lower (at least in OECD countries).

2.2 The core components of mainstream economics

Without entering (for reasons of space constraint) a full-length methodological discussion, it is nevertheless useful to remind that the philosophy of science has produced different approaches on the meaning and ways of operating of science,[48] and that the more recent ones distinguish different dimensions characterizing a scientific paradigm.[49]

Here we propose an operational specification of this approach and consider to be core components of mainstream neo-classic economics: (i) strong and reductionist forms of individualism at both methodological and ethical levels; (ii) a mechanistic and reductionist view of human beings (at both anthropological and psychological levels); (iii) a mechanistic and reductionist view of the world we live in; (iv) a very abstract ad idealized (though presented as a "naturalistic" one) view of the ways in which real markets operate, and especially of the ways in which they operate at the macro level despite the consideration at the micro level of different market structures and results, all at odd with respect to perfect competition. These features are complemented by other, connected, quite specific assumptions about rationality, substitutability and ergodicity (Heise 2016) and are associated with a positivist deductive reductionism[50] (Lawson, 2006) focusing mainly on mathematical formalism, all of which do not connect with real life experiences.

The rest of this section is devoted to the presentation and discussion of these points and of their relevance for the lack of consideration, by many economists, of the main theme presented in this book. After few more general points, section 2.3 will concentrate on a rather technical (for the non-economists, while for many economists is will be rather too quick) discussion of the many critical assumptions that are necessary to maintain the General Equilibrium approach. This is the part that usually mostly upset the mainstream economists (even those whom I consider also friends and that are usually more open to some degree of criticism) as it points out not an alternative view but the logical limits of the construction they consider at least the best economic instrument to our disposal. The most diffused comment to this part is that, as we do not have any better theoretical tool and we all (well, almost all) know it is not perfect, it is rather tedious and excessive to pinpoint in detail its limits and shortcomings while failing to recognize its great merits. While I certainly do not deny the historical, intellectual and theoretical merits of GE theory, I can only imagine that similar – and stronger – arguments might have been used in the case of the Ptolemaic model, that was useful enough to describe planets orbits and to predict eclipses.

Section 2.4 instead is devoted to a discussion of the general methodological stance not only of economics, to the limits of mechanism, reductionism and of methodological and ethical individualism, while section 2.5 briefly discusses the clash between these stances and the classic democratic approach, i.e., Constitutions, within in the area of individual and social preferences.

The representative agent, non-satiation and instrumental rationality

In turn, the "*core components mentioned before lead to the standard assumption and usage in economics of* 'representative agent', *a supposed 'average' (therefore fictitious) actor who incorporates the only set of assumptions for the role*[51] *that are taken as 'admissible'"*. These features are usually considered to be universal traits characterizing any (instrumentally) "rational" player, while individual deviation from that norm are considered as special cases that get "washed away" when averaging behaviours.[52] Recent research in both experimental economics and micro-econometrics, however, have pointed out the fallacies of this assumption and the need to take into account, even at the macro level, the dimensions of agents' heterogeneity relevant for the problem being considered. Clearly this would downplay the pretense of universalism of simple theoretical models based on the representative agent assumption.[53]

The combination of these assumptions produces a rather peculiar world-view, that can be variously articulated – as discussions on this theme have pointed out the possibility and usefulness, in some respects, to distinguish various forms of disagreement within the mainstream – but that is both unable and unwilling to consider many aspects of the current reality, as those highlighted in the previous section.

The *mechanistic and reductionist view of the world* that still dominates our culture is the most immediately relevant and apparently easiest one to deal with, as it is simply in contrast with the laws of physics, and in particular those of thermodynamics, as we argued in the Introduction. However, their recognition would contrast both the general – mechanistic and individualistic – methodological stance of neoclassical (and in particular DSGE) economics and a strong tenet of its vision, i.e., the idea that we live in an unconstrained (but for our personal income) world, which constitute also the core of its promises and appeal. The assumption that most evidently directly contrasts the recognition of physical limits to growth is that of *non-satiation* (more is always best), on which the entire neoclassical microeconomic theory of consumption is based. If the limits are considered as purely external they could be treated as a further constraint in the optimization problem (making the approach more complex and possibly less appealing but still operating) but contrasting the non-satiation assumption may lead to the questioning also of this point, as for a good number of people satisfaction does not imply the absence of any limit, rather the opposite.[54]

The mechanistic and reductionist *view of human beings* (at both anthropological and psychological levels) have been considered in many studies[55] and here it is just worth remembering that it is an example of the disregard for studies and views in other disciplines, but for those streams that can be used to confirm the economic mainstream. This appears to be a rather common practice, that includes views form cultural anthropology and psychology (in particular the form of evolutionary psychology that fits a reductionist economic evolutionary perspective, whose limits have been discussed by Duprè, 2001).

They relate to the specific view of rationality adopted by mainstream economics, termed *instrumental rationality*. This would be perfectly acceptable if and when applied within the limits that are proper to it, which is – not surprisingly – the area of instruments. Standard mainstream economics, however, applies it beyond these limits, also to the ends[56] of human actions: an improper extension – that elicited the definition of "rational fools" used by A. Sen, 1977, to epitomize this perspective – that transforms a reasonable instrument into an unreasonable general principle. Again, this goes hand-in-hand with the individualistic and reductionist perspectives on both methodology and ethics, making up a rather complex and problematic interlocking.

To be fair, one has to recognize that a similar perspective is to be found also in other disciplines pursuing the same trajectory, as pointed out by M. Benasayag (2016, pag.15, my translation from the Italian text):

> *Molecular biology and the so called 'neurosciences' present themselves as if they would move from a position that is 'almost' without any hypotheses. The question would simply be that of empirically studying what exists in the way it does. [. . .] the current dominating tendency in research in this area pretend in this way to be operating without models and any 'a priori', but this is just an illusion and a dangerous one given the fact that it is impossible to work without any hypothesis [. . .] in reality the models that today pretend to be neutral – because they are simply quantitative ones – eclipse or ignore the research starting hypothesis.*[57]

The other two core components of mainstream economics, i.e., the ideological view of the working of the market and the peculiar ethical stance, will be considered in more detail in what follows.

2.3   Mainstream economics as "magical" thinking: markets and the orthodox economist's trinity[58] (prices, property rights and rates of substitution)

Another crucial dimension for the ecological concerns is the interpretation of the role and functioning of the main (if not – as in some versions – unique) instrument conceived by mainstream economics, the *markets*. As already pointed out, while it is clear that real life markets are a fact and an essential tool of economic interactions, their role and their working are among the most debated topics within economics.

General equilibrium approach simply assumes that markets work perfectly on their own leading to a unique and stable intertemporal equilibrium which provides the best allocation of resources (given their initial distribution), and therefore it is best to let them work without interferences.[59] This is the real "magical" (though declined in a very mechanistic way) core of the theory, evidenced by the fact that any theoretical demonstration of the existence, uniqueness and stability of General Equilibrium rests on a number of very demanding assumptions, including perfect competition (see note 30) and market completeness, in addition to methodological and ethical individualism and other peripheral (but no more realistic) technical ones.[60] As they are clearly contradicted by everyday experiences and theoretical reflections, in order to maintain this point various further assumptions have to be made. In the critics' opinion, these evidence the unrealism of the pretense but they are instead taken for granted by those committed to the paradigm.

Most neoclassical economists prefer to simply adopt this complex association of hypotheses at the macro level, while at the micro one many of them are concerned with the working of various market forms, i.e., markets characterized by various forms of "imperfect" competition, in which at least some firms have some kind of market power. As this might sound like a more realistic description and explanation of the world we live in, the *methodology of positive economics* (instrumentalism) maintains that descriptive and explanatory capabilities are irrelevant, as much as it is the realism of assumptions. The additional assumptions "may save" the theoretical construct (there are many doubts and discussions about this point) but at the cost of making it even more distant and irrelevant for real life, and definitely more magical.

The crucial magical assumptions are aimed at and supposed to be exempt from the need to have respectively perfect competition and market completeness. The first one, therefore, maintains that there is no need for a market to be really competitive to get the best allocative results from it: it is sufficient that such a market is "contestable", i.e., that there is the possibility that some other firm may enter it.[61] To many it seems like pretending that a fictitious player, never actually entering the play, might make a real game more competitive: though it is possible to imagine that in some (extreme) cases he could, these seems to require the other players to estimate as high the probability of him actually entering the game and certainly this is not normally the case.

The *perfect competition* hypothesis performs two crucial operations within neoclassical economics and its policy implications. On the one side, it provides the only possible (though not necessary to everyone's liking) ethical justification for a "technical" market distribution of income[62] and, on the other, contributes to the related idea that[63] a system of decentralized markets can produce by its own an allocative configuration that is a social optimum[64] (though not necessary a palatable one, as we shall see).

To reach the social optimal configuration, however, perfect competition is a necessary but non-sufficient condition: there must be also *market completeness*, which is usually meant to imply lack of externalities, of goods that are not private in an economic sense (i.e., no public and/or common), lack of transaction costs and asymmetric information.

These conditions appear to be as "magical" as the previous ones. *Externalities*, in particular, are to be found everywhere around us and – though climate change is its single biggest case – each of us experiments various forms of it in everyday life, so that they cannot be denied. Therefore another "magical" assumption is needed to "protect" (by word of magic, like a spell) the market efficiency hypothesis. Such an assumption goes under the name of *Coase theorem* and states that if it were possible to have a complete distribution of property rights, covering all the aspects of our lives such that all externalities could and had to be counted and paid by the producer to the ones who unwillingly get them, markets could properly and efficiently allocate such property rights and each person could be compensated for the damage received, while the producers would see their costs increased by that amount and consequently reduce the level of production.

Some have interpreted the Coase theorem as the possibility that attributions of property rights can enlarge the dimensions of the proper working of the markets to areas characterized by externalities, but others have interpreted the very same theorem as an evidence of the unrealistic conditions under which this could happen. Certainly, if we are to make the theorem working, albeit only approximately, in real life we would need to develop the property rights much further than they are now, even in countries like the US, and until we have done that (as unlikely as it appears to many, including this author) we should not assume that it can provide a rapid solution, to the contrary.

As to asymmetric information it should be sufficient to remember that it was a theoretical breakthrough of some decades ago, whose consideration led to the development of the concepts of "moral hazard" and "adverse selection" to explain further market failures – for which the various suggested solutions have proved to be of some use but certainly not definitive ones. In addition, one can also consider the further reflections on these arguments that have been put forward by two of the economists that won the Nobel Memorial Prize for that innovative development, G. Akerlof and J. Stiglitz (see note 29).

The *rates of substitution* should, in principle, be a rather applied and technical question, whether they are marginal rates of substitution for the consumers or technical ones (rates of substitution between two factors of production) within the production functions, or those of transformation between different goods. In reality, many of them are rather theoretical and not observable, but as the mathematical logic of the models (their internal consistency) requires them to satisfy equilibrium requirements (usually equality between two of them or between those of two different individuals or firms), the neoclassical theory simply assumes they are. Even when this implies assuming rather demanding conditions on the technologies in order to allow for the perfect substitutability between factors in the production of a good (if they were not the production functions could present discontinuities and therefore could not insure differentiability and optimality everywhere). As they are taken to guarantee such perfect substitutability, why should other rates of substitution present dissimilar features? In specific circumstances a lesser degree can be the case, but in general they have to exhibit such convenient feature, and this is also the case of the rate of substitution between natural capital and manmade (mainly industrial) one. The default theoretical assumption now is that this rate of substitution is between 0 (non-substitution at all) and 1 (perfect substitution), but in practice it is usually assumed to be closer to 1 than to zero.

Relative prices (the ratio of the prices of two different goods or inputs) are considered the single most relevant economic variable and adjustment tool within the neoclassical perspective, and almost nobody denies their relevance. However, there is strong disagreement on the extent of their working and capability to lead to a real general equilibrium. The dominating part of the so-called "neoclassical synthesis" school (and in particular that following the lead of Modigliani, who paved the way for the more recent so called "neo-Keynesian" version of General equilibrium approach) downplayed the limits on the working of such adjustment tool as theorized by J.M. Keynes, presenting it as just the tenet that in the short run many economies exhibit fixed or slow adjusting prices. However, this is really no more than a caricature of what the great British economist was focusing on, and an easy and cheap way to restore the confidence on the working of this mechanism. The real point is whether price flexibility is sufficient to lead not to some adjustment but to General Equilibrium (GE). This is a much more complex task, one for which even a useful instrument might not suffice. To solve the coordination (of individual decisions and actions by those participating to the economy) problem L. Walras imagined an "ideal" (i.e., ingenuous but totally fictitious – or "magical") working of the market mechanism, based on the famous figure of the "(walrasian) auctioneer". This is supposed to tentatively announce on each specific market a price, register the quantities of the specific good demanded and offered at that price and adjust it until the two result equal. Only after such and equilibrium price had been fixed the transactions start and they have to be realized only at that price in order to reach the GE.[65] An additional constraint is that a GE has to be a simultaneous equilibrium on all markets. Recent formulations in terms of intertemporal equilibrium perspective require specific conditions to make it possible to decide in the present the best (equilibrium) course of actions for the entire future. Such time paths are uniquely determined and may be altered only in face of changes in some exogenous variables, which modify the optimization conditions.

Contrary to this approach Keynes, and then Hicks, maintained the idea that *money* is used also as a store of value and that "liquidity preference" is the choice to do so in order to take time and defer decisions in circumstances of proper uncertainty.[66] Keynes also evidenced that the walrasian construction could work only in an exchange (or in barter) economy but not in a production one, as production takes time and implies that producers have to formulate expectations on the future level of the demand (and therefore on the relative price) of their produce. This raised the further question of the way to formulate *expectations*, which has not found as yet a proper solution. In order to "save" once more the GE approach, however, the mainstream has adopted an extreme view of the expectation formation mechanism, called "rational expectations". This basically assumes that the individuals use the "true" data generating process of that variable – which is obviously incorporated in the mainstream model – to make prediction, irrespective of the facts that there might not be a general agreement on which such "true" process is and that expectations could be part of it.

It is worth emphasizing that in market forms that are different from perfect competition prices are not assumed to work in the same "optimal" way and be unique for each product in a given moment of time, even if they are a crucial variable in firms and consumers decisions. Market experiments seem to confirm the peculiarity of perfectly competitive settings, but they look like the only places in which the strict rules of such market structure are really operating.

According to most more "proper" Keynesian economists one of the more important (if not the most important, Patinkin – 1976, page 106 termed it the "apex") insights of Keynes's General Theory (developed in its Chapter 19th) is the suggestion that "*a decentralised market economy might lack the required equilibrating forces to ensure its intertemporal stability at full employment*". And this is not due to wage rigidities and/or sluggish price adjustments, but to the very fact that "*there may be no equilibrium market forces to rely on*". Others (Leijonhufvud, 1968) recognized this point pinpointing that "*the actual information mechanism composed of existing markets lacks certain 'circuits'*" (Leijonhufvud, 1968, page 280), one of which is the forward markets for a wide range of commodities.

Cui prodest?

These considerations lead to asking a very old (a sort of methodological one) question: *Cui Prodest*? Who has an interest in the "proper" and stable working of the markets and of the economy and society and who, instead, has an interest in generating cycles of crises and interventions, knowing to have much to gain from both? Crises and adjustments are either heavy prices to pay or great occasions for conspicuous earnings (either or both in monetary terms or in power) for those who follow rent-seeking strategies, as they can take advantage of their position in both the economic (including abusing of their market power) and the political[67] arenas.

The dissolution of the "naturalistic" illusion about the optimal allocative configuration guaranteed by the markets, however, take it down with it also the pretense of complete self-sufficiency, autonomy and independence associated with the neoclassical GE theoretical construction, opening ample spaces for the recognition of the relevance of reflections on economics and economic behaviours from other disciplines.

There is not enough space here to deal with all the relevant interactions, but two dimensions appear crucial for our purposes: those from the philosophy of science and methodology questioning the reductionist view associated with methodological individualism and those from moral philosophy, which present both an irreducible plurality of visions[68] and plenty of reserves about the selfish utilitarian view adopted by mainstream economics that is considered peculiar when not downright untenable, even by various utilitarian moral philosophers.[69]

2.4 The methodological stance: mechanism, methodological individualism and reductivism vs. systemic approach

The theoretical construction of mainstream neoclassical and GE economics is based on Newtonian physics (mechanics) – like the sciences of the eighteenth and nineteenth centuries. It has evolved its mathematical formulation to include dynamic optimization, but this has not changed its fundamental view and perspective. The point of interest here is that the Newtonian approach is still valid and useful within the limits of mechanics, but since Newton (1642–1727) many significant discoveries have been made (like electricity, magnetism, thermodynamics and many others in various natural sciences) that depict the world, even the physical one, in a much more complex way. Newtonian physics see the world as a machine that can be analyzed studying its single smaller components, *"the material particles, the forces between them, and the fundamental laws of motion"* that *"were considered fixed laws according to which material objects moved"* (Capra and Luisi, 2014, p. 29) generating a rigorous determinism (as for Newton all was created by God in the beginning). Despite its huge success and enormous contribution to the advancement of science, the Newtonian theory proved insufficient to explain many real-life phenomena and moving from its achievements new areas of inquiry were created, opening up our understanding. Some of these developments maintained the same Cartesian reductionist approach (which is the fundamental trait on which Newton's mechanics was built) in their attempt to explain all aspects and properties of the world by reducing them to "the physical and chemical interactions of their smallest constituents" (Capra and Luisi, 2014, p. 36). Other ones led, instead, to the recognition that while the structures of any system are made of parts and can be reduced to their smallest components, molecules in the case of living organisms, *"this does not imply that their proper-ties can be explained in terms of molecules alone"*, because *"the essential proper-ties of a living system are emergent properties"* that *"arise from specific pattern of organization – that is, from configurations of ordered relationships among the parts"* (Capra and Luisi, 2014, p. 35).

At the methodological level, the strong individualism that is proper of neoclas-sical economics opposes not only holism but also the systemic approach, and imply the reduction of the working of any system at that of its single smallest components, denying any relevance to the "emerging properties" that character-ize the specific forms of interaction among them that emerged during the forma-tion and evolution of the system. This assumption is functional to the pretense of the theory to provide a universal and timeless account of the behaviour of both individuals and economic systems (firms, markets, etc.) but proves a crucial step in making its application appropriate only in the extreme cases corresponding to that atomistic view. These imply the lack of any meaningful personal contact and relationship – as results in experimental economics and other experimental social sciences have shown – and with respect to market forms are to be found only in the case of perfect competition (and possibly monopoly).

It seems interesting to compare this stance of mainstream economics with that taken within a recent debate in analytical sociology (also called social mechanism perspective or sociology of causal processes, one that ought to interest also the economists), that dwells on these issues in its questioning the positivist concept of explanation and the instrumentalist identification of prediction as the only aim of science. Within such a perspective, the positivist concept of explanation has been criticized[70] for a number of reasons and in particular for: (a) its being a vision of science as an empirical analysis of functional relationships among vari-ables, without any attempt to search for (rather incorporating an outright refusal to search for) the causes (or, as the analytical sociologists call them, the genera-tive mechanisms) of the social phenomena; (b) its tenet that the main aim of sci-ence is prediction – as this is what allow reformatory actions – and therefore that explanation has to be discarded as a scientific goal; (c) the tendency to explain everything in terms of laws or regularities (nomological ones); (d) the absence of any explicit reference to non-observable processes and dimensions (like beliefs, desires, reasons, intentions, etc.). To these positivist assumptions analytical soci-ology opposes the centrality attributed to the explanation and, in it, to causa-tion, in terms of the identification of the "generative process" (this is why this approach is also called social mechanism perspective). Even more, after having distinguished between two traditions of causal analysis within sociology – that of causal effects and that of causal processes – most authors within this recent tradition opt for the analysis of causal processes. For them, the scope of a theory is the identification of the causal process(es) or mechanism(s) that produce the (empirically observed) relationship between dependent and independent vari-ables. In this perspective, theoretical models are a crucial component and they are interpreted as "realistic abstractions", stemming from a preliminary descrip-tive exercise and meant to provide a stylized representation of the "generative forces of the phenomenon being studied" (Barbera, 2006, 32) and, in this way, a satisfactory explanation of the same. In opposition to other sociological currents (and especially social theory) here theoretical models are not merely narratives, as they have to identify a causal mechanism that can be applied to other phenomena besides the one from which it has been identified. On the other hand, they are not seen (and in this respect the comparison with neoclassical economics is explicitly made) as having a claim to universality; the most ambitious step in this direction is just the preference for abstract conditions of validity of parameters specifications over the concrete space-time conditions, as this increases the transferability of the argument and thus the generality of the model.[71]

In such a perspective, the link between individual (micro) processes and aggregate (macro) ones plays a crucial role and certainly cannot be taken as given via a simple and mechanical additive or aggregative approach. The perspective adopted by these authors is definitely more complex and it implies the explicit consideration of the *"relevant relational structures in which the real-life individuals are rooted"* (Coleman). As R. Boudon points out, there are numerous entities that exist in our world, like churches, political institutions, birth rates, nations, climate data, cities, traditions and so forth, including individuals. It seems quite difficult to distinguish these different types of entities according to their degree of reality (if this expression means anything). And it seems even more difficult to distinguish them according to a causal or temporal perspective. Such a foundation has given way to a further inquiry into the relationship between methodological individualism and system theory. In the debate on this aspect, many authors have been trying to accommodate the two perspectives by proposing revised (i.e., non reductionist) versions of the former.[72] Among the various proposals it is worth mentioning at least the following: "structural individualism", "individuolism" or "individualistic holism", "methodological localism", "systemism" (Bunge, 2000) and "weak methodological individualism" (Udehn, 2001).

A crucial feature of contemporary methodological individualism is that in it the explanation requires also the consideration of entities and activities characterized by non-individualistic properties, particularly relational ones (see Hedström). According to its champions, the cost of missing them out is the well-known reductionist fallacy. Such problem is inherent in the assumption of individualistic atomism, which still characterize most economic theorizing.

On the one hand, the distance with respect to holism is large and clear, as the recognition of the role of relational properties does not imply attributing them any autonomous and independent power (with respect to individual choices and actions). On the other hand, despite such recognition, the intentional action paradigm maintains an aspect of methodological individualism that leads its advocates to still define themselves as methodological individualists. (Other authors criticize either the distinction they make or, more often, the fact that it is used to maintain such a self-definition while in their view it does belong to a different approach). This point might be quite complex and would require greater attention and deeper consideration than is proper and possible here, but we will at least try to give a flavour of the points in discussion. Although the relational properties are considered a crucial feature of systemic interactions, and therefore the "social" structure is recognized as playing a causal role, there is also the acknowledgment that in order to manifest themselves the effects of these entities necessitate of individual choices and actions. In other terms, the choices and actions are individual ones, but the same choices and actions in different structural contexts will produce different consequences, effects. Therefore, in the paradigm terminology, "*the social structure is not appropriate to illustrate and understand the generative causation processes but it is nevertheless causally effective*" (Lewis). A proper explanation (of a process) needs to take into account both its generative causations and its causally relevant conditions, but the two have to be considered separately and their difference clearly recognized. The crucial aspect seems to be whether it is still possible to consider choices and actions as properly "individual" ones when the fundamental role of the contexts in influencing them has been recognized (this is the main reason for the various definitions and terms used to specify various approaches to the "new" methodological individualism). In biology, for instance, in the last decades the notion of "emerging properties", i.e., properties that belong to a certain state (or level) of a system, has become quite popular. The working of one of such systems cannot be reduced to that of its components because these "properties" do not belong to them but are a generated by their interaction in certain (more or less specific) conditions. Also in such a "classical" systemic approach the role of individuals (i.e., single component of any given system) is considered crucial and it is possible (perhaps in principle more than when facing a real phenomenon) to distinguish both the characteristics of different individuals and how they are influenced by the actual ways in which the interactions happen.

To complete the picture, we need to also consider the other dimensions of methodological individualism and the main differences that are acknowledged by the authors in the intentional action paradigm with respect to the standard approach within economics, i.e., the rational choice one.

The two further components of "old" methodological individualism that are recognized and shared by the "new" versions are understand-ability and reason-ableness. The first one concerns the possibility of making sense of each action (therefore ruling out outliers due to madness and the like, that could be relevant only in some very specific case and not in general), while the second adds the specification that each action has to be considered as caused by individual reasons. It is in the specification of the nature of these individual reasons, however, that the two brands of methodological individualism depart. The differences between the two approaches, in fact, concern consequentialism, egoism and maximization. These cornerstones of the old version (and *a fortiori* of mainstream economics) are simply rejected by the new one. They might be listed among the many possible different specifications of individual attitudes and choices but certainly are not considered as universal characteristics.

At the methodological level, the relationship between individualism and systemic approaches is still highly debated, but there is a growing recognition of the role of "emerging properties", features that cannot be attributed to any of the single components of any system but that nevertheless characterize it in a very relevant way. However, mainstream economics so far has been moving in the opposite direction, strengthening the grasp on individualism, after the focus on macroeconomics and its relative independence from microeconomics brought about by Keynes. The debate in the 1970s on microfoundations of macroeconomics based on explicit individual maximization saw few opponents, who pointed to the need, rather, of macrofoundations of microeconomics, evidencing the constraints that the contexts (including rules, laws, habits, social norms) were posing to individual choices. And it did so despite some recognition of problems of aggregation and evidence of irreducible agents heterogeneity in various dimensions.

2.5 Ethics, constitutions and social preferences

The other crucial dimension in rethinking economics is the ethical one. Mainstream economics is built on an apparently unquestionable selfish utilitarian perspective, in which egoistic individual choices are supposed to lead to the general welfare via their composition through the market mechanisms (the invisible hand), whose limits we have already discussed. The individualistic and selfish approach of mainstream economics is criticized also by various utilitarian moral philosophers, who point out that classic utilitarianism (since its founder, J. Bentham, not to mention J. S. Mill) was fundamentally universalistic and that a proper moral philosophy cannot leave this aspect out, even if it can imagine other mechanisms to work in this direction as the interpersonal and social dimensions have to be directly part of the ethical concern.

Other ethical approaches, in particular the ethics of virtues and the deontological school in their various declinations, recognize explicitly this "human" dimension as the core of any proper ethical reflection (Kant posed it as "the foundation" of any possible ethical thinking in his "Critique of Applied Reason" and this constituted the cornerstone of J. Rawls's reflections).

One somehow peculiar aspect of neoclassical economics is that its hard methodological individualism, resulting in an equally hard scientific reductivism, is associated with a reductive view of individuals, human beings and of their differences. While on the one side this shows a continuity in reductionism, so a coherence within the approach; on the other, it appears to be in sharp contrast with the proclaimed attention to the individuals, who are reduced to their role of consumers. Not surprisingly, A. Sen has accused[73] the mainstream economic approach to be strongly paternalistic and to deny at the root what should be the real aim of any proper democratic construction: real individual freedom, which implies to consider not what any theory or elite considers best for the others but what each of us does for him/herself as an individual and a member of a community.

This kind of reductionism is what make of us individuals that may have some more money but at the cost of a shorter or worse off life because of "externalities" associated with the production that provides this additional cash. As an example, according to the latest data, about 500,000 Europeans die every year because of air pollution,[74] and kids growing in big cities have on average 26 percent more probabilities of be affected by respiratory problems. But we are not really given to choose between some more income associated with higher risks to our health or less of both, our only possibility being again an individual one of leaving cities and most polluted areas; but this usually imply a much higher cost than renouncing to that small additional income and for many is not altogether a viable option. This is a very strong reduction of individual freedom, but it is usually framed as a fact of life because the predominant view takes for granted that this is just an individual choice between money and other concerns, thus assuming money or utility as universal unit of measure for anything despite the fact that it is not for very many people.

To properly consider this point implies in turn considering the real differences across individual (and possibly those in their capabilities). As there seems no point in denying that some people exhibit individualistic and selfish attitudes and behaviours, the same can be said with respect to the evidence that others behave in a fundamentally different way whenever this is possible, i.e., depending on the possibilities that the rules of the specific game allow.

Both real life and experiments in various social dilemmas have established this fact, and the opinion is now relatively common that as the situations move away from the rules imposing the atomistic attitude of perfect competition, it becomes increasingly common to see behaviours that are at odds with the simplistic self-ish utility maximization. In the context of the public good game, for instance, it is common to observe that the clear majority of players (on average all over the world, though with significant local differences) tend to be either reciproca-tors or (to a lesser extent) cooperative and/or altruistic, even when they clearly understand the rules and the monetary incentive structure of the game. Similar distinctions can be seen in other economic games exhibiting the social dilemma conditions, like the ultimatum game, etc.

All in all, it seems clear that there are relevant differences among people whose nature is much deeper than that about preferences with respect to bundle of goods. Nor is it acceptable any more to assume that preferences are the solely product of individual nature as if the cultural and social context would not matter and the media had not the influence on people for which advertisements and marketing have been developed and receive huge amounts of money.

So either one is ready to endorse the idea that the majority of people are "irratio-nal" and keep being so despite learning and experiences or there is evidence that individuals are different in various crucial dimensions and that the assumptions of selfishness and instrumental rationality largely over represent a significant but still largely minoritarian fraction of people. In addition, the standard notion of "instrumental rationality" appears as just one of the possible notions of rational-ity and a particularly narrow one, being built on specific and rather questionable views of human nature and moral philosophy.[75]

Leaving aside the anthropological aspect[76] (as it would require books in its own right) let us turn a bit more on the ethical one.

The standard mainstream approach to social choice and welfare treat them only in terms of the sum of individual preferences, but this presents enormous problems (and not just of aggregation) as individuals in isolation might (and often do) take for granted what is already there, even when these are among the most important aspects of their lives. On the opposite, direct approaches to social preferences are not only the possible result of theocracies or tyrannies, as they are often presented, they can also be the result of proper Constitutional processes that have produced charts and codes that are the main reference for democracies. Without them there will not be Constitutional democracies.

In these years the limits – in terms of guarantees of the health and rights of all citizens – that Constitutions pose to the expansion of business at any price are being perceived by the more powerful economic players as a problem and we are witnessing the beginning of the clash between two conceptions of life and democracy, as testified by the now infamous indication within the report of a multinational bank (Barr and Mackie, 2013) about the need to reform the Constitutions of some European countries, as they are seem as protecting too much labour and citizen rights and therefore constraining the possibilities of lucrative business (being framed in terms of economic growth). Something similar is happening with the prospect of international commercial treatises assuming a predominant role with respect to the Constitutions of the participating States.[77]

The reference to Constitutions (and in specific to the US one and to their "Founding Fathers") and to the public debate as a necessary component of the formation of social preferences is a fundamental aspect of the reflections of (already quoted) contemporary philosopher M. Nussbaum and economist A. Sen. Nussbaum in particular reminds to us the lesson of Aristotle (who maintained that desires and preferences are not to be denied but also not to be taken as wise and proper guide for action) and proposes a principles-based approach, that appears as an extension on this level of the capability approach and a generalization (via the general principle, of liberal political tradition, of consensus by intersection) the centrality of Constitutions.[78]

Notes

1 Various chapters of this book and the literature mentioned in them provide examples of this, but see also in specific Oreskes and Conway, Chapter 6, and the Foreword and Introduction of Brown and Timmerman. Also, the business world is divided, and Bill Gates has expressed serious concerns about the need to produce much more clean energy (at the beginning of 2016, in the annual letter he wrote with his wife as part of the activities of their Foundation).

2 Some of the difficulties in reaching further convergence, that are considered by various authors (the already-mentioned Oreskes and Conway, and Washington and Cook, 2011), however seem to have more to do with ideology and private interests than with science itself.

3 For a specific discussion of this topic see the chapter by Tainter and colleagues in this book and its references.

4 In the end, most of them seem to reduce to the development of nanotechnologies (requiring a fraction of materials and energy currently used in production), the colonizing of other planets (a solution that up to now only worked in fiction and movies. A variant of this suggestion is that some other space inhabitants will come and rescue us, but of recent this appears less popular), or the discovery of ways to get to "parallel universes" where these limits are not binding. Within the technological stream a more robust approach has been proposed by David and van Zon, 2014.

5 Hausmann, 1992, highlights the distance between economics and other sciences and some of the problems with the methodology of mainstream economics.

6 For instance, Heise, 2016, writes that "neoclassical orthodoxy still remains the 'normal science' standard procedure and provides the foundation for economic education" (page 1).

7 On this point, see Buiter, 2009.
8 A proper treatment of the many dimensions on which neoclassical economics (as the founding view of current mainstream) needs discussing would require at least a book. Certainly, one aspect on which it is not lacking (to the contrary it can be considered a noteworthy achievement) is internal consistency and rigorous mathematical formulation. Unfortunately, the same cannot be said about external relevance, or correspondence.
9 In recent years, a number of books have pinpointed the similarity of neoliberal economics and particularly market fundamentalism to religious beliefs (Stockhouse and Nelson, 2001); here we consider another aspect, its resemblance with magic. Though fundamentalism is to be found in both religion and science, and is equally despicable, it is not a necessary trait of any of the two. In addition, a significant part of theology has to do with proper metaphysical questions – that are outside the domain of science – while this is not (or at least should not be) the case for economics. The continuous use of assumptions that do not find correspondence in reality (so much that the methodology of positive economics has to rely on the rather "magical" instrumentalist postulate of the "irrelevance of the assumptions") puts this kind of economics on the same level of its assumptions, i.e., that of a sort of magical thinking.
10 References about it are really numerous (and coming from different theoretical perspectives), so here we just point out that in the last decades many works of Nobel Memorial Prize winners J. Stiglitz and A. Sen provide good arguments and discussions, as does a recent book by M. Hudson (2015).
11 A similar opinion has been recently expressed with respect to another, related, aspect of the current situation – the population dynamic – by S. Emmot (2013). His conclusion is that we are "done" precisely because we do not do what is required, even if we know what is needed and could do it.
12 So much so that, according to some leading scientist, we are already gone too far beyond earth carrying capacity limits and all we can do now is to try and limit the size of the disasters coming onto us.
13 See Stern, 2007a.
14 There were some discussions about the Report findings and it was attacked for the use of a very low discount rate (though higher than the current one) in the estimate of the current value of future damages (the reply was the in tragic choices as the ones considered that was the only appropriate way) but mainly it was put on a side, while Stern was given significant research money to continue investigating the issues. For a discussion of the problem of "tragic choices" see Dasgupta, 2008.
15 Both in terms of the various dimensions to be considered in the analysis and in that of the limits of any standard economic cost-benefit analysis, due to its "reductionist" nature.
16 We refer the reader to the book for a more detailed discussion of the various forms and for additional ones.
17 For they seem to apply the arguments advanced by Oreskes and Conway with respect to the bunch of aerialists within the natural sciences, i.e., a form of out-dated (as being grown in the Cold War years and remained unchanged) anti-communism that ideologically identify market fundamentalism with individual freedom. They seem to maintain that similar concerns and views motivated also economists T. Schelling and W. Nordhaus in their role within the 1980 US National Academy of Science Report on climate change.
18 One of the dreams of some scientists is that of being able to get rid nuclear waste sending it to burn against the sun, but nothing of the kind seems feasible in any sufficiently short term.
19 An appeal for the simplification of the legal system and a return to simplicity has been proposed years ago by a leading US academic authority in the field (Epstein, 1994). Though we share the concerns that motivated those reflections and the recognition of the need to simplify our ways of life, the approach and the suggestions presented there

seems based on another version of the same "magic" approach to economics that we criticize here. In particular, we do not see how those suggestions would induce any serious action to prevent climate change. Rather, we fear they could pave the way to moves directed toward the first of the scenarios discussed in the next lines.

20 The scenario analysis has been practiced in various periods and with various different starting hypotheses. The Global Scenario Group has proposed another (somehow similar) perspective in which the two main possible scenarios (the third, the prosecution of the current worlds, has almost no chances to be a real option for us) are either catastrophic or require fundamental changes. See Raskin et al., 1998.

21 One of the first descriptions of such a scenario is included in Susan George, 2000.

22 This is the way in which I read some analyses, like those suggested by D. Lane and associates.

23 Simple examples are drastic reduction in the use of fossil fuels in production and consumption, for instance, via investments in public/common transports to reduce individual ones and developing alternative sources of energy for transportation.

24 At the time, many institutional arrangements were out-dated as they were designed for a different world, one facing the task of post-war reconstruction in many parts of the world (and especially Europe) and characterized by fixed exchange rates and a stable international institutional context, provided by the Bretton Woods agreements. The "new" came after a decade of instability (unilateral denunciation of fixed exchange rates by President Nixon, oil crises, stagflation and beginning of the financiarization process) and the keywords of the new institutional and social design were *deregulation* and *globalization*, which included international capital mobility and favoured financial speculation. See Burlando, 2011.

25 For years, anyone suggesting that (obviously) strong economic powers had plenty of reasons to try and reach various forms of business agreements and even to influence political decision making and agreements was treated either as an insane lunatic (though there are also people of that sort) or a traitor of his/her country or culture (see Korten,1995; George, 2000; Lasch, 1995, among the others). Now even liberal political theorists from respected universities highlight the uneven political influence of the wealthy that threatens the basis of liberal democracy (see Martin Gilens and Benjamin I. Page, 2014) and "un-ideological" network analysis shows that the level of connections among the economic powers are tighter than most imagined, making a sort of top influence group (Vitali, Glattfelder, and Battiston, 2011). Such a powerful alliance could exert a tremendous force in any direction, and the problem lies both in what it does consider its best interest and in the lack of any proper anti-trust policies, that used to be an essential component of the economic vision of the "old" monetarists like M. Friedman.

26 The term is used in the classical economic meaning, and in particular it refers to positional rents, assured by legal arrangements and market power, often obtained and maintained via legal arrangements.

27 The suggestions in this direction go even beyond what reported and documented by Oreskes and Conway, and involve various types of shifting of research agendas, up to the financing of conservative think tanks that have been used instrumentally on various occasions, including in the denial of climate change. Even the funding of research at universities (both private and public, during certain administrations) has been questioned in this respect.

28 See Akerlof and Shiller, 2014. Already in the book web page they warn us that: "*As long as there is profit to be made, sellers will systematically exploit our psychological weaknesses and our ignorance through manipulation and deception. Rather than being essentially benign and always creating the greater good, markets are inherently filled with tricks and traps and will 'phish' us as 'phools'*", but also that "*Our political system is distorted by money*" and that "*Drug companies ingeniously market pharmaceuticals that do us little good, and sometimes are downright dangerous*". Many others have strongly criticized the turns within the economy and economics of the last

decades. Among the better known (and relatively less far from orthodox economic theory) there are J. Stiglitz, and J. Galbright.

29 For the non-economists, it is worth remembering that the term *free markets* has a double and rather opposite meaning. In economic theory, it properly refers to the strict conditions assuring perfect competition (many firms, all small with respect to the size of the market they operate in, perfect information, homogeneous products, freedom of market entry and exit at very small cost) while in common usage it often means simply the lack of any regulation, which often allows the stronger player to dominate the market if not to takeover its real rivals. Such a condition has even been epitomized in the say "free wolves in free hen-roosts".

30 The evidence of slow (or no) growth and reduction in profits has been generating discussions about a possible "secular stagnation", which however (but perhaps not surprisingly) only hinted at this points in some of the contributions. See Teulings and Baldwin, 2014.

31 See Michel Hudson, 2015. In the opinion of many critics, finance has stopped being a useful servant of the real economy to become progressively more and more speculative and autonomous, turning the real economic sectors its own servants.

32 In particular those related to the extension of intellectual property rights channelled in the Us by the Bayh-Dole Act in 1980 – thus creating legal monopolies – and extended at the international level by the WTO in 1994 (with the so called Trips Agreements). This is just the opposite of what a proper liberal economic policy is expected to do and it is also in contrast with the strong anti-monopoly attitude of old breed monetarists like M. Friedman.

33 See OECD, 2007; Picketty, 2014; Milanovic, 2016.

34 As those suggested by Hawken, Lovins and Lovins in "Natural Capitalism", 1999.

35 At least a good number of game theorists clearly recognize to be interested only in abstract modelling and not to care about the relationship between their models and everyday worldly reality.

36 "*Because of tax havens, we have ended up with one set of rules for the rich and powerful and another set of rules and laws for the rest of us – and this applies to citizens of rich and poor countries alike*". And "*This book will show that the offshore system is the secret underpinning for the 'political and financial power of Wall Street today'*" – Shaxson, 2011: 12. "*The U.S. government needs foreign funds to flow in, and it attracts them by offering tax-free treatment and secrecy. This is offshore business, Spencer explained, and it had become central to the U.S. government's global strategies for financing its deficits*". "*Offshore connects the criminal underworld with financial elites and binds them together with multinational corporations and the diplomatic and intelligence establishments. Offshore drives conflict, shapes our perceptions, creates financial instability, and delivers staggering rewards to 'les grands', the people who matter. Offshore is how the world of power now works*" – Shaxson, page 13.

37 Eva Joly, Notre affaire à tous, quoted in Shaxson (page 171, footnote 10).

38 James S. Henry, The Price of Offshore Revisited, 2012.

39 Clearly offshore money increases the total amount of parasitic rents – and the level of inequality at the world level – thus subtracting huge resources that could be used to fight climate change. This is precisely the theme of a second TJN report by Shaxson, Christensen, Mathison (Inequality: You Don't Know the half of It), 2012.

40 Acemoglu and Robinson, 2012a and 2006.

41 And quite a good number have been published recently that address various aspects of the task; the titles of some of them are included in the references, but there are too many worth using than it is possible to deal with in a paper.

42 Daly, 2016; Smith, 2010, 2011, 2016; NEF, 2010; Jackson, 2009.

43 Daly, 2016.

44 For the non-economists, this means he does not take on any strong notion of market efficiency and/or assumptions about their self-regulating nature. They are, rather, simply assumed to be a useful instrument, that (as any instrument) has proper and

improper use. In general, assuming that they work well for any type of goods and in any situation leads to improper usage and significant problems (see Anderson).

45 Though both of them appear currently being substituted even in their motherland by the free trade model. See *Wolfgang Streeck, 2012*.

46 In addition, capitalism has historically proven capable of transforming itself much more than it has been credited by its critics and could do it again. Rather than a terminological or philosophical question, the real problem seems to be the turn that the world will take and the scenarios already discussed.

47 According to many also not, in general, before that period, but a proper consideration of this tenet – or of its opposite – would need discussions of specific times and locations.

48 For presentations of such large discussion we refer to Guala, 2006 and to Caldwell, 1982.

49 One way, resting on the approach proposed by I. Lakatos, of dealing with them is to consider three main areas: ontological (heuristic), epistemological and methodological and the components in each of them. Though this is a heuristically useful distinction, we are convinced that reality is not so clear-cut as some representations of this distinction would like to maintain and that these dimensions intersect and interact in various ways, as do the positive and normative ones.

50 When not associated to old instrumentalism, due to the influence of Milton Friedman. This methodological approach – named by its proponent (Friedman, 1953) the methodology of positive economics – is rather disregarded now within the philosophy of science but it is nevertheless still relatively popular among economists. It is rather peculiar in that it maintains that a theory scope should only be that of forecasting the future values of the variables it concentrates on and that both the description of the phenomena and their explanation are of no interest. For this reason it maintains that the assumptions on which a theory is based are irrelevant and can be plainly unrealistic (see Friedman, 1953; Guala, 2006). The lack of attention to explanation has led to terming this approach as «the *monetarist black box*». One of its better known and more relevant criticism has been suggested by the leading theorist of the «second generation» monetarists, R. Lucas, who in his criticisms evidenced the need to distinguish, within economic models, what is invariant and what can change as a result of changes in policy regimes or in exogenous conditions (see Lucas, 1976; Guala, 2006: 81–82).

51 These considerations will be expanded in a next section – dealing with methodological individualism – when the evidence of agents' heterogeneity will be discussed.

52 Recently, however, even within the mainstream, analyses have been produced that refuse this assumption and require the consideration of a certain degree of heterogeneity on specific dimensions.

53 This appears to be one of the instances of application of an old joke about economic approaches stating that the neoclassical one aims at being "perfectly and mathematically wrong about reality" while the keynesian one attempts to be "rather imprecise but more or less right".

54 Without it, it would be impossible to depict the solution of the consumer maximization problem as that of choosing the highest indifference curve attainable with someone's budget constraint and the entire theoretical construction of the "family" of indifference curves non crossing each other would be at risk, as its construction requires that, ceteris paribus, more of one good in each of them increases total utility. Even the most modern versions of this theory, and first of all the rational choice theory, are been built on these bases, and they appear as relevant components of the general theoretical construction. Of course, it would be possible to reframe everything in terms of satisficing instead of maximizing behaviour, but this option has been proposed already in the past (most notably by H. Simon) and the facto rejected.

55 Too many to mention, but the already quoted Duprè contains a good selection of relevant references.

56 See also SP Hargreaves Heap, 1989, 1992.

57 It is not a case that various economists have been attracted by these conceptions and that "neuroeconomics" is a relatively popular sub-discipline within economics.

58 This specific term was used by a mainstream economist (of the neo-Keynesian version of General Equilibrium theory) in his talk at the Conference from which this book originates.

59 However, the late M. Friedman explained his perspective in this way: "Speaking for myself, I do not believe that I have more faith in the equilibrating tendencies of market forces than most Keynesians, but I have far less faith than most economists, whether Keynesians or monetarists, in the ability of government to offset market failure without making matters worse. (Friedman's interview in Snowdon and Vane, 1999: 138).

60 It is not easy to think that all this theoretical and mathematical work has been an important step in the mapping of the chart of real economics, but that at the end of the day it is just an invention, a fantasy. A comparison with the semi-scientific (as it proved useful to predict eclipses and various phenomena) complexity and beauty of Ptolemaic conception has helped this author to come to terms with this recognition.

61 See Baumol, Panzar, and Willig, 1982. The same Baumol who introduced the idea, however, wrote (1982: 2) that perfectly contestable markets do not populate the real world and that the concept does not serve in first place to describe reality but acts as a theoretical reference point.

62 Perfect competition is needed in order to guarantee that the system is characterized by constant returns, which in turn is needed to guarantee that the market distribution, i.e., that at the marginal productivity of each factor of production produces an optimal allocation of resources. By the way, this does also imply that in the long run there should not be any extra-profits and the level of "normal" profits should be comparable with that of other sources of income.

63 See N. Acocella, 2007, chapter 6 (especially pages 145–147).

64 An "optimum" in a very specific, allocative, meaning: even if it existed it would be basically made of more consumer goods (as they would cost less because perfect competition is the only market form that could lead to reach the minimum of average cost curve), and irrespective of their distribution across the population. Not many (besides among economists and businessman) would agree that this qualifies as a proper vision leading to a good life (more on this point in the following). For one, Amartya Sen noticed that Sen (1970, see also Sen 1977) it is possible for a society to be at the same time in a (allocative) Pareto optimum and (ethically and socially) perfectly disgusting.

65 Up to now, this appears to be the only "mundane" explanation (rather than simply an ideological assumption) for the so called "invisible hand" suggested by Adam Smith. Many other interpretations have been suggested, moving from the fact that Smith was a Presbyterian pastor and moral philosopher before turning to the study of economics. One such interpretation is that the "invisible hand" would be God's (see Evensky), as hypothesised by Smith about planets' orbits.

66 Traditionally, since I. Fisher, in economics uncertainty had been distinguished from risk, as only in the second case it is possible to define a distribution probability of possible future events. The semantic slip mentioned before has implied instead even in later technical language the se of "uncertainty" to characterize situation that should be classified as risky.

67 As in the case of Genovesi (and many other authors), contemporary conditions tend to influence theoretical visions, so any reference to current economic reality at the world level and to political ones, especially at Italian one, are likely not to be accidental.

68 There are three main "schools" within it, two of which clearly reject the strict consequentialism of utilitarianism. A good number of utilitarian moral philosophers, however, strongly reject and define unfounded and unpalatable the selfish approach of the version adopted by mainstream economics, which goes against the original universalistic formulation by J. Bentham, J. S. Mill and others.

69 See Peter Singer, 1993, but also the writings of G. Pontara.

70 See Cherkaoui, 2000: 131–134; Barbera, 2006: 33. The order in which these critiques are presented here, however, is different.

71 Undoubtedly, economists will easily recognize the similarity with methodological discussions within their own subject and in particular the dispute over M. Friedman's once popular "methodology of positive economics".

72 It may be worth it to remind the reader that many other authors, both philosophers and methodologists but also sociologists belonging to different schools, maintain that a proper systemic approach is alternative to both holism and methodological individualism. This is certainly the opinion of scholars like Bunge, A. Caillé (of this author see in particular, the third paradigm) and others (including the author of this paper). For many of them, it is nevertheless interesting to follow this debate and look into the analyses the "dissection" of M.I. lead to.

73 In many of his works but in particular in "Liberta individuale come impegno sociale" (of which I have not found an English version).

74 40,000 in UK, of which 10.000 in London.

75 See SP Hargreaves Heap, 1989 and SP Hargreaves Heap et al., 1992

76 But for some references like Grasselli, 2007, and the entire psychoanalytic (and group analytic in particular) literature.

77 Interesting enough, this turn was detected already in the 1990s by a US historian, C. Lash, who analyzed this trend (in his "The Revolt of the Elites and the Betrayal of Democracy") but also the associated development of narcissistic tendencies in both US culture and society (soon to be exported).

78 Ayres, R., and Warr, B. (2006). REXS: A forecasting model for assessing the impact of natural resource consumption and technological change on resource consumption. *Structural Change and Economic Dynamics*.

Bibliography

Acemoglu, D., and Robinson, J.A. (2006). *Economic Origins of Dictatorship and Democracy*, Cambridge, Cambridge University Press.

Acemoglu, D., and Robinson, J.A. (2012a). Why nations fail. *The Montréal Review*.

Acemoglu, D., and Robinson, J.A. (2012b). *Why Nations Fail: The Origins of Power, Prosperity, and Poverty*, Crown.

Acocella, N. (2007). *Economia del benessere*. La logica della politica economica, Roma, Carocci.

Akerlof, G., and Shiller, R. (2015). *Phishing for Phools: The Economics of Manipulation and Deception*, Princeton, NJ, Princeton University Press.

Amable, B. (2004). *Les cinq capitalismes – Diversité des systèmes économiques et sociaux dans la mondialisation*, Paris, Seuil.

Anderson, E. (1990). The ethical limitations of the market. *Economics and Philosophy*, 6.

Anderson, E. (1993). *Value in Ethics and Economics*, Cambridge, MA, Harvard University Press.

Aristotele (1993). *Politica*, Bari, Laterza.

Aristotle (1976). *The Nicomachean Ethics*, London, Penguin Books.

Arnsperger, C., and Van Parijs, P. (2003 [ed. or. 2000]). *Quanta disuguaglianza possiamo accettare?* Bologna, Il Mulino.

Arthur, W.B. (2013). *Complexity economics: A different framework for economic thought*. Santa Fe Institute Working Paper No. 2013-04-012

Backhouse, R. (2004). A suggestion for clarifying the study of dissent in economics. *Journal of the History of Economic Thought*, 26(2), 261–271.

Baker, D. (2016). *Rigged. How Globalization and the Rules of the Modern Economy Were Structured to Make the Rich Richer*, Washington, DC, Center for Economic and Policy Research.

Barbera, F. (2006). A star is borne? The Authors, Principles and Objectives of Analytical Sociology, *Revista de Sociologia*, 80, 31–50.

Barbera, F., and Negri, N. (2008). *Mercati, reti sociali, istituzioni: Una mappa per la sociologia economica contemporanea*, Bologna, Il Mulino.

Bardi, U. (2003). *La fine del petrolio*, Roma, Ed. Riuniti.

Barr, M., and Mackie, D. (2013). The Euro area adjustment: About halfway there. *JP Morgan Europe Economic Research*, 28 maggio. www.jpmorganmarkets.com

Bauman, Z. (2008). *Does Ethics Have a Chance in a World of Consumers?* Cambridge, MA, Harvard University Press.

Baumol, W.J. (1982). Contestable markets: An uprising in the theory of industrial structure. *American Economic Review*, 72.

Baumol, W.J., Panzar, J.C., and Willig, R.D. (1982). *Contestable Markets and the Theory of Industry Structure*, New York, Harcourt Brace Jovanovich.

Becker, G. (1976). *The Economic Approach to Human Behaviour*, Chicago, Chicago University Press.

Benasayag, M. (2016). *Il cervello aumentato, l'uomo diminuito*, Trento, Erickson.

Bensusan-Butt, D.M. (1978). *On Economic Man: An Essay on the Elements of Economic Theory*, Canberra, Australian National University.

Boland, L.A. (1982). *The Foundations of Economic Method*, London, Allen & Unwin.

Bonaiuti, M. (ed.) (2005). *Obiettivo decrescita*, Bologna, EMI.

Booth, W.J. (1994). On the idea of the moral economy. *American Political Science Review*, 88, 3.

Borghesi, S., and Vercelli, A. (2006). *La sostenibilità dello sviluppo globale*, Roma, Carocci.

Broome, J. (1999). *Ethics Out of Economics*, Cambridge, Cambridge University Press.

Bruni, L., and Porta, P.L. (2004). *Felicità ed economia*, Milano, Guerini.

Bruni, L., and Zamagni, S. (2004). *Economia civile*, Bologna, Il Mulino.

Buiter, W.H. (1980). The macroeconomics of Dr. Pangloss: A critical survey of the new classical macroeconomics. *Economic Journal*, March, 34–50.

Buiter, W.H. (2009). The unfortunate uselessness of most 'state of the art' academic monetary economics. *VoxEU*, 6 March 2009. http://willembuiter.com/unfortunate.pdf

Bunge, M. (2000). Systemism: An alternative to individualism and holism. *Journal of Socio-Economics*, 29.

Burlando, R. (1998). Biens collectifs et économie expérimentale. In C. Roland-Lévy and P. Adair (eds.), *Psychologie Economique: Théories et Applications*, Paris, Economica.

Burlando, R. (2001). Values, ethics and ecology in economics. *World Futures*, 56, 1st special issue on "Values, Ethics and Economics".

Burlando, R. (2004). Ethics and economics: Towards a solidarity-based economy. *Council of Europe, Trends in Social Cohesion*, (12), 35–47.

Burlando, R. (2008). Bio-economics, energy and development patterns: Pre-announced crises vs structural adjustments. In G. Grimaldi (ed.), *Political Ecology and Federalism: A Multidisciplinary Approach. Towards a New Globalisation?* Milano, Giuffrè.

Burlando, R. (2011a). *Core components of opposite views: Methodology and ethics within economics*. Paper presented at the conference "Market and Happiness", Milano, Bicocca, June.

Burlando, R. (2011b). Le crisi attuali ed i ritardi teorici dell'economia. Una prospettiva economica civile e Gandhiana. In P. Della Posta (a cura di), *Crisi economica e crisi delle teorie economiche*, Napoli, Liguori, 179–203.

Burlando, R. (2014a). Etica ed economia in sanità. In Alastra V (a cura di), *Etica e salute*, Milano, Eriksson, 135–162. ISBN: 978-88-590-0624-4

Burlando, R. (2014b). Scienze umane ed economia: una riflessione epistemologica. In *Potere e Limiti, Quaderni di Gruppoanalisi*, n. 18, Torino, Ananke, 77–98.

Burlando, R. (2016). *Etica ed Economia*, Teoria, ...

Burlando, R., and Guala, F. (2005). Heterogeneous agents in public goods experiments. *Experimental Economics*, 8, 35–54.

Burlando, R., and Hey, J. (1997). Do Anglo-Saxons free-ride more? *Journal of Public Economics*, 64(1), 41–60.

Caillè, A. (1991). *Critica della ragione utilitaristica*, Torino, Bollati Boringhieri.

Caillè, A. (1998). *Il terzo paradigma*, Torino, Bollati Boringhieri.

Caldwell, B.J. (1982). *Beyond Positivism: Economic Methodology in the Twentieth Century*, London, Allen & Unwin.

Caporael, L., et al. (1989). Selfishness examined: Cooperation in the absence of egoistic incentives. *Behavior and Brain Sciences*, 12, 683–739.

Capra, F. (1996). *The Web of Life*, New York, Doubleday-Anchor.

Capra, F., and Luisi, P. (2014). *The System View of Life: A Unified Vision*, Cambridge, Cambridge University Press.

Capra, F., and Pauli, G. (1995). *Steering Business Toward Sustainability*, Tokyo, The United Nations University.

Carabelli, A., and De Vecchi, N. (2000). Individuals, public institutions and knowledge: Hayek and Keynes. In P.L. Porta, R. Scazzieri and A. Skinner (eds.), *Division of Labour and Institutions*, Aldeershot, Elgar.

Cassidy, J. (2010). *How Markets Fail: The Logic of Economic Calamities*, New York, Farrar, Straus and Giroux.

Chakravartty, A. (2016) Scientific realism. In *The Stanford Encyclopaedia of Philosophy* (Winter 2016 edition). https://plato.stanford.edu/archives/win2016/entries/scientific-realism.

Cherkaoui, M. (2000). *La stratégie de mécanismes générateurs comme logique del'explication.* In: Bacheler, J. (ed.). L'acteur et ses raisons. Mélanges pour RaymondBoudon. Paris: Puf, 131–151.

CMESPS (2008) *Report of the Commission on the Measurement of Economic Performance and Social Progress*, Paris, www.stiglitz-sen-fitoussi.fr

Colander, D. (2005). The making of an economist redux. *Journal of Economic Perspectives*, 19(1).

Combs, A. (1995). *Cooperation*, Philadelphia, PA, Gordon and Breach.

Cremaschi, S. (2005). *L'etica del novecento*, Roma, Carocci.

Da Re, A. (2004). Figure dell'etica. In C. Vigna (a cura di), *Introduzione all'etica*, Milano, Vita e Pensiero.

Daly, H.E. (1992). *Steady-State Economics* (2nd edition), London, Earthscan.

Daly, H.E. (1994). Farewell lecture to the Wold Bank. In J. Cavanagh, D. Wysham and M. Arruda (eds.), *Beyond Bretton Woods*, London, Pluto Press.

Daly, H.E. (1996). *Beyond Growth*, Boston, MA, Beacon Press.

Daly, H.E. (2016). Growthism: A cold war leftover. *Real-World Economic Review*, 77, 26–29.

Daly, H.E., and Cobb, J.B. Jr. (1989). *For the Common Good*, Boston, MA, Beacon Press.

Damasio, A.R. (1994). *Descartes' Error: Emotion, Reason and the Human Brain*, New York, Putnam.

Dasgupta, P. (2005). What do economists analyze and why: Values or facts? *Economics and Philosophy*, 22, 221–278.

Dasgupta, P. (2008). Discounting climate change. *Journal of Risk and Uncertainty*.

David, P., and van Zon, A. (2014). *Designing an optimal 'Tech Fix' path to global climate stability: Integrated dynamic requirements analysis for the 'Tech Fix'*. SIEPR DP n.13–39, Stanford Institute for Economic Policy Research.

De Vroey, M. (2009). On the right side for the wrong reasons: Friedman on the Marshall-Walras divide. In U. Mäki (ed.), *The Methodology of Positive Economics, Reflections of the Milton Friedman Legacy*, Cambridge, Cambridge University Press.

Diamond, J. (2005). *Collasso: Come le società scelgono di vivere o morire*, Torino, Einaudi.

Diwan, R. (2001). Relational wealth and the quality of life. *Journal of Socio-Economics*, 29, 4.

Dryzek, J. (1989). La razionalità ecologica. *Ancona: Otium*. doi: 10.1007/s11166-008-9049-6

Duprè, J. (2001). *Human Nature and the Limits of Science*, Oxford, Clarendon.

Duprè, J. (2007). Fact and value. In H. Kincaid, J. Duprè and A. Wylie (eds.), *Value-Free Science? Ideals and Illusions*, New York, Oxford University Press, 27–42.

Easterlin, R. (1974). Does economic growth improve the human lot? Some empirical evidence. In David and Reder (eds.), *Nations and Households in Economic Growth: Essays in Honour of Moses Abramowitz*, New York, Academic Press.

Easterlin, R. (1995). Will raising the income of all increase the happiness of all? *Journal of Economic Behaviour and Organization*, 27, 35–48.

Emmot, S. (2013). *Ten Billion*, London, D Godwin Ass.

Epstein, R.A. (1994). *Simple Rules for a Complex World*, Cambridge, Harvard UP.

Evensky, J. (1993). Retrospectives – ethics and the invisible hand. *Journal of Economic Perspectives*, 7, 2.

Fehr, E., and Gächter, S. (2000). Cooperation and punishment in public goods experiments. *American Economic Review*, 90, 980–994.

Fligstein, N. (2001). *The Architecture of Markets: An Economic Sociology of Twenty-First-Century Capitalist Societies*, Princeton, NJ, Princeton University Press.

Frey, B. (1953). *Essays in Positive Economics*, Chicago, University of Chicago Press.

Frey, B. (1997). *Not Just for the Money*, Cheltenham, Elgar.

Friedman, M. (1953). *Essays in Positive Economics*, Chicago, University of Chicago Press.

Friedman, M., and Friedman, R. (1990). *Free to Choose: A Personal Statement*, San Diego, CA, Harvest.

Galbright, J. (2014). *The End of Normal*, New York, Simon & Schuster.

Gallino, L. (2011). *Finanzcapitalismo: La civiltà del denaro in crisi*, Torino, Einaudi.

Gallino, L. (2013). *Il colpo di Stato di banche e governi: L'attacco alla democrazia in Europa*, Torino, Einaudi.

George, S. (2000). *Il rapporto Lugano*, Trieste, Asterios.

Gilens, M., and Page, B.I. (2014). Testing theories of American politics: Elites, interest groups, and average citizens. *Perspectives on Politics*, 12(3).

Global Scenario Group. *Great Transition*. www.gsg.org

Grasselli, P. (a cura di) (2007). *Economia e concezione dell'uomo*, Milano, Angeli.

Guala, F. (2006). *Filosofia dell'economia: Modelli, causalità, previsione*, Bologna, Il Mulino.

Hahn, F. (1985). *Equilibrium and Macroeconomics*, Cambridge, MA, MIT Press.

Hahn, F.H. (1977). Keynesian economics and general equilibrium theory: Reflections on some current debates. In G.C. Harcourt (ed.), *The Microeconomic Foundations of Macroeconomics*, London, Macmillan.

Hamilton, C. (2010) *Requiem for a Species: Why We Resist the Truth About climate change*, Sydney, Allen and Unwin.

Hansen, J. (2009). *Storms of My Grandchildren: The Truth about the Coming Climate Catastrophe and Our Last Chance to Save Humanity*, London, Bloomsbury.

Hausmann, D. (1992). *The Inexact and Separate Science of Economics*, Cambridge, Cambridge University Press.

Hawken, P., Lovins, A., and Lovins, L.H. (1999). *Natural Capitalism*, Little, Brown & Co.

Heise, A., (2016). Whither economic complexity? A new heterodoxeconomic paradigm or just another variation within the mainstream?, ISSN 1868-4947/58, *Discussion Papers*, Hamburg.

Henry, J.S. (2012). *The Price of Offshore Revisited*, Tax Justice Network.

Hodgson, G.M. (1986). Behind methodological individualism. *Cambridge Journal of Economics*, 10, 211–224.

Hodgson, G.M. (1987). Economics and system theory. *Journal of Economic Studies*, 14, 4.

Hodgson, G.M. (1992). *Economics and Evolution: Bringing Back Life Into Economics*, Cambridge, Polity Press.

Hudson, M. (2015). *Killing the Host: How Financial Parasites and Debt Bondage Destroy the Global Economy*. Petrolia, California, CounterPunch Books.

IPCC WG (2007). *Climate change*, 3 vol. (the Physical Sciences Basis, Impacts and Adaptation, Mitigation of climate change), Cambridge, Cambridge University Press.

Jackson, T. (2009). *Prosperity Without Growth*, London, Earthscan.

Keynes, J.M. (1971–89). *The Collected Writings of John Maynard Keynes*, 30 vols., London, Macmillan for the Royal Economic Society.

King, D.A. (2004). The science of climate change: Adapt, mitigate or ignore? *Science*, 303.

Kirman, A. (1989). The intrinsic limits of modern economic theory: The emperor has no clothes. *The Economic Journal*, 99.

Korten, D.C. (1995). *When Corporations Rule the World*, West Hartford, Kumarian Press.

Krugman, P. (1999). *The Return of Depression Economics*, London, Penguin.

Kuhn, T. (1962). *The Structure of Scientific Revolutions*, Chicago, Chicago University Press.

Laidler, D. (2010). Lucas, Keynes, and the crisis. *Journal of the History of Economic Thought*, 32(1), 39–62.

Lasch, C. (1979). *The Culture of Narcissism*, New York, Norton.

Lasch, C. (1984). *The Minimal Self*, New York, Norton.

Lasch, C. (1995). *The Revolt of the Elites and the Betrayal of Democracy*, New York, Norton.

Laszlo, E. (1972). *The System View of the World*, Oxford, Blackwell.

Laszlo, E. (1991). *The Age of Bifurcation*, Philadelphia, PA, Gordon and Breach.

Laszlo, E. (1997). *Third Millennium: The Challenge and the Vision*, London, Gaia Books.

Latouche, S. (2004). *Decolonizzare l'immaginario*, Bologna, EMI.

Lawson, T. (1997). *Economics & Reality*, London, Routledge.

Lawson, T. (2006). The nature of heterodox economics. *Cambridge Journal of Economics*, 30(4), 483–507.

Lea, S.E.G. (1994). Rationality: The formalist view. In H. Brandstatter and W. Guth (eds.), *Essays in Economic Psychology*, Berlin, Springer-Verlag.

Leijonhufvud, A. (1968). *On Keynesian Economics and the Economics of Keynes*, Oxford, Oxford University Press.

Lovelock, J. (1988). *The Ages of Gaia*, Oxford, Oxford University Press.

Lucas, R. (1976). Econometric policy evaluation: A critique. In K. Brunner and A. Meltzer (eds.), *The Phillips Curve and Labor Market*, Amsterdam, North Holland.

MacFadyen, A.J., and MacFadyen, H.W. (1986). *Economic Psychology: Intersections in Theory and Method*, Amsterdam, North Holland.

McCloskey, D.N. (1986). *The Rhetoric of Economics*, Brighton, Wheatsheaf.

Meadows, D.H., Meadows, D.L., and Randers, J. (2006). *I nuovi limiti dello sviluppo*, Milano, Mondadori.

Meadows, D.H., Meadows, D.L., Randers, J., and Behrens, W. (1972). *The Limits to Growth*, New York, Universe.

Milanovic, B. (2016). *Global Inequality: A New Approach for the Age of Globalization*, Cambridge, MA, Belknap.

Mini, P. (1974). *Philosophy and Economics*, Gainesville, FL, University of Florida Press.

Nadeau, R.L. (2006). *The Environmental Endgame: Mainstream Economics, Ecological Disaster, and Human Survival*, New Brunswick, NJ, Rutgers University Press.

Nelson, R.H., and Stackhouse, M.L. (2001). *Economics as Religion: From Samuelson to Chicago and Beyond*, Penn. State University Press.

New Economic Foundation (2010). *Growth Isn't Possible*, London, NEF.

Nordhaus, W. (2007). Critical assumptions in the stern review on climate change. *Science*, 317.

Nussbaum, M.C. (2003a). Capabilities as fundamental entitlements. *Feminist Economics*, 9, 33–59.

Nussbaum, M.C. (2003b). *Capacità personale e democrazia sociale*, Reggio Emilia, Diabasis.

Nussbaum, M.C. (2007). *Who is the happy warrior? Philosophy poses questions to psychology*. mimeo.

Nussbaum, M.C. (2012). *Creare capacità*, Bologna, Il Mulino.

O'Brien, J.C. (1981). The role of economics and ethics in civilisation and progress. *International Journal of Social Economics*, 8, 4.

OECD (2007). *Growing Unequal? Income Distribution and Poverty in OECD Countries*, OECD publishing. ISBN: 9789264044180

Oreskes, N., and Conway, E.M. (2010). *Merchants of Doubts: How a Handful of Scientists Obscured the Truth on Issues From Tobacco Smoke to Global Warming*, New York, Bloomsbury.

Ormerod, P. (1994). *The Death of Economics*, London, Faber & Faber.

Osberg, L., and Sharpe, A. (2003). *Human well-being and economic well-being: What values are implicit in current indices?* CSLS Research Report 4, Ottawa.

Ostrom, E. (2005). *Understanding Institutional Diversity*, Princeton, NJ, Princeton University Press.

Ostrom, E. (2009). *A polycentric approach for coping with climate change*. World Bank background paper to the 2010 World Development Report.

Parfit, D. (1984). *Reasons and Persons*, Oxford, Oxford University Press.

Patinkin, D. (1976). *Keynes' Monetary Thought: A Study of Its Development*, Durham, NC, Duke University Press.

Perkins, J. (2005). *Confessioni di un sicario dell'economia*, Roma, Minimumfax.

Picketty, T. (2014). *Capital in the Twenty-First Century*, Princeton, NJ, Harvard University Press.

Prigogine, I. (1997). *La fine delle certezze*, Torino, Bollati Boringhieri.

Prigogine, I., and Stengers, I. (1989). *Tra il tempo e l'eternità*, Torino, Bollati Boringhieri.

Raskin, P., et al. (1998). *Bending the curve: Toward global sustainability*. PoleStar report n. 8, Global Scenario Group, Stockholm Environmental Institute.

Rawls, J. (1971). *A Theory of Justice*, Cambridge, MA, Harvard University Press.

Rawls, J. (1986). *Political Liberalism*, New York, Columbia University Press.

Rivot, S. (2013). Gentlemen prefer liquidity: Evidence from Keynes. *The Journal of History of Economic Thought*, 35(3), 397–422.

Sacco, P.L., and Zamagni, S. (a cura di) (2002). *Complessità relazionale e comportamento economico*, Bologna, Il Mulino.

Sandel, M. (2010). *Justice*, London, Penguin.

Sandel, M. (2013). *What Money Can't Buy: The Moral Limits of Markets*, London, Penguin.

Scaperlanda, A. (1993). Christian values and economic ethics. *International Journal of Social Economics*, 20(10), 4–12.

Schor, J.B. (2005). Prices and quantities: Unsustainable consumption and the global economy. *Ecological Economics*, 55(3), 309–320.

Schumacher, E.F. (1977). *A Guide for the Perplex*, London, Abacus.

Schumacher, E.F. (1975). *Small Is Beautiful*, New York, Harper & Row.

Sen, A. (1970). *Collective Choice and Social Welfare*, London, Oliver & Boyd.

Sen, A. (1977). Rational fools: A critique of the behavioural foundations of economic theory. *Philosophy and Public Affairs*, 6.

Sen, A. (1987). *On Ethics and Economics*, Oxford, Blackwell.

Sen, A. (1997). *La libertà individuale come impegno sociale*, Bari, Laterza.

Sen, A. (2000). *Lo sviluppo è libertà*, Milano, Mondadori.

Sen, A. (2009). *The Idea of Justice*, London, Penguin.

Sertorio, L. (2005). *Vivere in nicchia, pensare globale*, Torino, Bollati Boringhieri.

Sertorio, L. (2008). *La transizione da energia fossile a solare*. mimeo.

Shaxson, N. (2011). *Treasure Islands: Uncovering the Damage of Offshore Banking and Tax Havens*, New York, Palgrave Macmillan.

Singer, P. (1993). *How Are We to Live?* Oxford, Oxford University Press.

Smith, P., and Bond, M. (1993). *Social Psychology Across Cultures*, Hemel Hempstead, Harvester Wheatsheaf.

Smith, R. (2010). Beyond growth or beyond capitalism? *Real-World Economic Review*, 53, 28–42.

Smith, R. (2011). Green capitalism: The god that failed. *Real-World Economic Review*, 56, 112–144.

Smith, R. (2016). *Green Capitalism: The God That Failed*, London, WEA/College.

Smith, R., Neil, W., and Zimmerman, K. (2016). Capitalism, corporations and ecological crisis: A dialogue concerning green capitalism. *Real-World Economics Review*, 76, 136–145.

Snowdon, B., and Vane, H.R. (1999). *Conversations With Leading Economists, Interpreting Modern Macroeconomics*, Cheltenham, Edward Elgar.

SP Hargreaves Heap (1989). *Rationality in Economics*, Oxford, Blackwell.

SP Hargreaves Heap, et al. (1992). *The Theory of Choice*, Oxford, Blackwell.

Stern, N. (2007). *Stern Review on the Economics of climate change*, Cambridge, HM Treasury and Cambridge UP.

Stern, N., and Taylor, C. (2007). Climate change: Risk, ethics and the stern review. *Science*, 317.

Stiglitz, J. (2001). *In un mondo imperfetto*, Roma, Donzelli.

Stiglitz, J. (2002a). *Globalization and Its Discontents*, New York, Norton.

Stiglitz, J. (2002b). *Making Globalization Work*, New York, Norton.

Streeck, W. (2012). On re-forming capitalism. *The Montréal Review*.

Tainter, J.A. (1988). *The Collapse of Complex Societies*, Cambridge, Cambridge University Press.

Teulings, C., and Baldwin, R. (2014). *Secular Stagnation: Facts, Causes, and Cures*, London, CEPR, VoxEU.org eBook.

Udehn, L. (2001). *Methodological Individualism: Background, History and Meaning*, London, Routledge.

Udehn, L. (2002). The changing face of methodological individualism. *Annual Review of Sociology*, Vol. 28, 479–507.

UNDP (2008). *Human Development Report 2007/2008: Fighting climate change: Human Solidarity in a Divided World*, UNDP.

UNFCC, United Nations Framework convention on climate change. http://unfcc.int. resource/convkp.html

Vitali, S., Glattfelder, J.B., and Battiston, S. (2011). The network of global corporate control. *PLoS ONE*, 6(10), e25995. doi:10.1371

Walker, G., and King, D. (2008). *The Hot Topic: What We Can Do About Global Warming*, New York, Bloomsbury.

Washington, H., and Cook, J. (2011). *Climate change Denial: Heads in the Sand*, Abingdon, Earthscan.

Webley, P., Burlando, R., and Lea, S.E.G. (2001). Quali mercati per la psicologia economica? In S. Zappalà and S. Polo (eds.), *Prospettive di psicologia economica*, Milano, Guerini.

Webley, P., et al. (2002). *The Economic Psychology of Everyday Life*, London, Psychology Press.

Wiles, P., and Routh, E. (1984). *Economics in Disarray*, Oxford, Blackwell.

World Commission on Environment and Development (1987). *Our Common Future*, Oxford, Oxford University Press.

Zamagni, S. (2002). L'economia delle relazioni umane: verso il superamento dell'individualismo assiologico. In *Sacco e Zamagni*, op.cit.

Zwiers, F.W., and Weaver, A.J. (2000). The causes of 20th- century warming. *Science*, 290.

Conclusions

Throughout this book, we have presented a concatenated series of arguments on the sustainability – actually the unsustainability – of mankind's present way of life. In the various chapters, we have considered the unavoidable depletion of non-renewable resources; the present trends of climate, which will last for decades irrespective of our immediate actions; the progressive drift out of control of a growing complexity system; the ongoing diminishing return from technological improvements; the need and difficulty to find a reasonable non-reductionist (unlike the GDP) way to measure the performance of an economy; finally some of the main limits of current mainstream economics that prevent it from properly addressing the issues previously discussed and to constructively interact with the other sciences to find and put in place appropriate measures.

Is there any conclusion that we can draw from the above review? We think that the answer is at the same time trivial and puzzling.

The apparently trivial point is that the arguments we have recalled and illustrated clearly show that the present trend of global human activities, if unchanged, is heading toward disaster. The collapse would affect a large part of humanity and of the living beings, and a further decline in well-being would involve everybody, even though somebody would certainly gain additional power over the others (the rest of us).

A close rational examination of facts tells us that we must introduce important changes in the way we use natural resources and manage the exchange relations among us, if we wish to avoid the above-mentioned "disaster". We can still succeed to a significant extent, even though the endeavour is not easy at this date. As we already said in the introduction, there are no miraculous recipes and, first of all, we cannot hope to be as rapid as it would be necessary; we know where we should go, but the details of the journey have to be found out day by day, provided we really decide to go in the right direction. We know that for such a journey, we cannot rely simply and only on the functioning of markets (especially when unregulated) but also know that the current way the political process works, both in various countries and at the international level, is not very reliable. This is certainly a very important area for both economists and political theorists to work on, considering the ways in which the various institutions (markets and states) can be led to work properly and in the interest of all in reality, as opposed to in theory or in some form of "magical" thinking.

As to the puzzling part of the conclusion, the fact that human activities and economic systems are unavoidably subject to material constraints has been known for a very long time. In recent decades, the debate has come out of restricted academic circles to be brought to the public awareness, and it is then that various forms of denial have been activated and manifested.[1] We are not referring here to the very important scientific attitude of prudence and healthy scepticism, rather to the rejection of the rational implications of the existence of physical limits to the growth of material production. The initial naïve economic attitude relied on the assumption of natural resources being "practically" infinite; but this is not the case, as it becomes more and more evident approaching these material limits. From that naïve attitude, part of economics shifted then to another type of pretended infinity: that of the surrogates. Use wood, then coal, then oil, then gas, then nuclear, then sun (why not?), then. . . , then. . . . Rationally, we know that the series cannot be infinite, even without calling in the laws of thermodynamics, but who cares? This attitude, nicknamed "technological optimism", is either a faith (something like the "cargo cult" in the Pacific) or the expression of a radical pessimism about the capacity of humans of using their own intelligence for changing their way of life instead of pursuing irrational technological miracles.

Facing the first evidence of a global change (the case of climate change) induced by human behaviours, the various forms of uneasiness towards our responsibility converged into an attitude of shear denial. However, facts and data have progressively scaled down denial from an initial aggressive mood to the current rear-guard manifestations. Yet, refusal of scientific evidence appears to be an underground river, sporadically coming to light and then plunging out of sight for a while. Using a metaphor, we have shifted from Dr. Jekyll's thoughtful analyses to Mr. Hyde's selfish arrogance. Reason has to face a stubborn rejection of any suggestion of the need for substantial changes in our business-as-usual trend.

Evidence gathered in different scientific fields tells us that the main pillar of unsustainability is the continuous growth of exploitation and manipulation of matter: if we wish to make our system sustainable (i.e., "indefinitely" lasting), we have first to stabilize matter and energy fluxes. However, looking around to economic, business and political circles, we find a continuous hysterical use of the word *growth*, invoked, longed, advocated, even predicted . . . economists around the world even continue to organize conferences on "sustainable growth" insensitive to, but sometimes even blissfully unaware or arrogantly ignorant of, the contradiction in terms! As many have already noticed, this recalls the behaviour of a drug addict craving for his dose: you may warn him about the need to get rid of his addiction, but he will go on shouting to get his daily intake, irrespective of the consequences.

The above-mentioned unscientific approach has further ideological components (as already highlighted by many and also in the last contribution in this book) making up a complex erroneous story (and, obviously, serving clear though narrow interests). In this blind perspective, the engines relied upon for pushing the mythological and salvific "growth" are *competition* and *technological improvements*. So here it comes another "sacred" concept and another dogma: the only way out of the current "crisis" is "competition". We all must enhance locally our capability to "compete". Rationally it is easily seen that in a competition there are losers and winners and, obviously, for each winner there are many losers, so that this cannot be a recipe that works for all. As many have argued, within an evolutionary perspective competition might have a positive role in a kind of "frontier" environment, with plenty of empty space to colonize, but in conditions of relative congestion, like the ones humanity is now facing, collaboration appears both globally more profitable than competition and certainly needed to avoid great damages. Furthermore, when material constraints on growth exist, competition leads to increasing differences in the access to wealth, therefore inequality will be growing (again a trend proved by facts). In turn, rising inequalities go hand-in-hand with migrations and, at the global scale, mass migrations and conflict, at both social and interstate levels. The evidence of a trend of increasing income and wealth inequalities during the last four decades has been confirmed by many different analyses (OECD and Picketty,[2] to cite only the better known). The consequences of such trend are under our eyes and have also been discussed by many in various circumstances, but yet there is no sign of a change in the direction.

Once more the foundation of the still dominant way of thinking is a dogma and a form of radical pessimism: humans are irredeemably egoist and cannot curb their own egoism, even when their reason tells them that cooperation would be more profitable. Assuming this as an indisputable axiom – despite the many controversies (considered in the last chapter of this book) – leads to a cynical attitude and to the practical suppression of the future: what matters is now, while the future will be someone else's worry.

There is by now a long list of formulations of this "program", from the literary Oratius's "carpe diem" (seize the day) to the ironic Groucho Marx's "why should I care for posterity? Posterity has ever done something for me?", to the regal Louis 15th "après nous le déluge". However, the implementation of this "program" is especially visible in the policy-making in the advanced countries during the last decades. Most often the farthest time horizon is the next elections and the impelling exigency is to capture (in *competition* with others) an immediate consensus. The looked for consensus is usually based on emotional short-term moods and fears, often also manipulated in various ways, rather than on informed reasoning. The problem is that the future is more and more impending (among the side effects of growth there is a continuous shortening of times) and any further delay does increase the difficulties and costs of the interventions.

So what? May we "conclude"? We stick to the idea that the majority of us (i.e., the non-addicted), once we have really understood and learned something, can conform our actions to what has been learned and understood, despite the fact that old views and current interests (usually of a powerful small minority) keep trying to make us do otherwise.

If so, it is important to go on diffusing rational information about facts and physical constraints and stimulating the public rational debate about the strategies to be adopted in order to comply with natural constraints that no exorcism can remove. We may also call in proper emotional reactions – of preoccupation, indignation and will to act. Of course, producing the needed changes is not simply a matter of individual understanding, since mankind altogether is a very complex, highly non-linear, system and the dynamics of an entire society is not simply a rescaling of the individual one. Furthermore, as it cannot be denied that we are endowed with reason, at the same time we must recognize that irrational, short time drives are present in our nature too and are very strong. Nevertheless, we still believe that understanding and reason will lead our will in the right direction, though probably in times longer than what would be safe. Meanwhile, nature goes on its way, perfectly insensible to our feelings, thoughts and theories, but not to our actions.

> ***Quos vult iupiter perdere, dementat prius***

Notes

1   Again we refer to Oreskes and Conway, 2012.
2   OCED, 2017; Picketty, 2014.

References

OECD (2007). *Growing Unequal? Income Distribution and Poverty in OECD Countries*, Paris, OECD, ISBN: 9789264044180 (print)

Oreskes, N., and Conway, E.M. (2012). Merchants of doubt. In *How a Handful of Scientists Obscured the Truth on Issues From Tobacco Smoke to Global Warming*, New York, Bloomsbury Press.

Picketty, T. (2014). *Capital in the Twenty-First Century*, Princeton, NJ, Harvard University Press.

Index

For Product Safety Concerns and Information please contact our EU
representative GPSR@taylorandfrancis.com
Taylor & Francis Verlag GmbH, Kaufingerstraße 24, 80331 München, Germany